NATURE-ORIENTED
ACTIVITIES

A Leader's Guide

NATURE-ORIENTED ACTIVITIES

A Leader's Guide

Betty van der Smissen, Re.D.

Oswald H Goering, Re.D

Judy K. Brookhiser, Re.D.

Cover and Book design: Michael Warrell
Editorial services: Margaret Haywood
Composition and Illustration: Cenveo Indianapolis

Front cover photo credits: (left to right)
Ben Deering, Catalina Island Camps, Howlands Landing, CA;
Camp Voyageur, Ely, MN;
Girl Scouts Connecticut Trails Council, Camp Laurel, Lebanon, CT;
stock photo

American Camp Association
5000 State Road 67 North
Martinsville, Indiana 46151-7902
765-342-8456
800-428-2267 (CAMP)
www.ACAcamps.org

ISBN 0-87603-192-0

A CIP catalog record for this book can be obtained
from the Library of Congress.

CONTENTS

FOREWORD

A Leader's Guide: Nature-Oriented Activities, is a timely book that describes many purposeful activities out-of-doors. The authors suggest a wide variety of approaches in getting acquainted and working with the natural world. The book is an outgrowth of the extensive experiences of the authors as leaders of youth and adults, as teachers, and as observers of nature programs in many communities.

We in American are living in an increasingly urbanized culture. In spite of this situation (and also because of it), interest in the out-of-doors and in all forms of outdoor recreation has been intensified. Public and private agencies serving youth and adults are becoming more aware of their opportunities to educate people to enjoy and appreciate their natural environment. Schools, by stepping up certain science courses and other outdoor-related programs, are contributing in an important way to the knowledge and understanding of the out-of-doors. The land-holding and recreation-related agencies of the government, which have a special responsibility for helping people learn how to use and enjoy their natural environment, are expanding their education programs in this area.

Lack of trained leadership for good outdoor programs has been a major roadblock for public and private agencies. This book is an outstanding source of information for both professional and volunteer leaders. Directions for carrying out many projects are given in detail, making the book a practical aid even to users who may not have technical backgrounds.

The authors realize that it is not enough merely to suggest outdoor activities. Our natural lands today receive such heavy usage that they will be destroyed unless American citizens become concerned about the underlying principles of conservation and pattern their behavior accordingly. The suggestions in this book should lead to usage that will contribute greatly toward the conservation of outdoor America.

Reynold E. Carson
Professor of Recreation and Park Administration, Indiana University
ACA National President, 1949–1950 (1901–1997)

This is the original Foreword taken from the first edition published in 1965. The authors chose to use this original stating, "These words apply as much now if not more!"

ABOUT THE AUTHORS

Betty van der Smissen holds a Doctorate in Recreation from Indiana University and a Juris Doctor Degree from the University of Kansas. She has been a member of the Bar of Kansas since 1952. Betty's extensive legal training has focused on legal issues and risk management in outdoor programs, but her heart has forever remained true to her roots in camping. She has served at the national level with NRPA (National Recreation and Park Association), ACA (American Camp Association), AEE (Association for Experiential Education), AAHPERD (American Alliance for Health, Physical Education, Recreation and Dance), Girl Scouts of America, YMCA, National Safety Council, National Council on Accreditation (academic) and a myriad of others. Her work with ACA alone, has spanned fifty years and included serving as: president of the association in the 1980's, the national trainer of trainers for the ACA OLS and camp-craft programs, and research chair. From program director at the Ohio District YMCA through distinguished faculty and administrative leadership positions at universities including professor and chair of the Department of Park and Recreation Resources at Michigan State University and her current work developing a doctoral program at the Univeristy of Northern Iowa, Betty has cut a broad swath through the recreation and camp communities. Stressing commitment to quality, responsibility, and training, she feels that young people today more than ever need the committed service of well trained leaders. Ever reluctant to share an unparalleled and exemplary record of awards, honors, degrees, and service, she states simply, "I am imminently qualified to write this book. Not only have I taught camping, environmental education, and nature-related programs, but have direct experience as a counselor, program leader, and administrator of nature programs."

Oswald H. Goering holds a Doctorate in Recreation and has served as Professor of Outdoor Teacher Education, O.T.E. Faculty Chair for Northern Illinois University; Dean of Men and Associate Professor of Recreation, Director of Kauffman Museum, and Director of Peace Lecture Series for Bethel College. In his long distinguished career he has made a difference in the lives of children and adults in Puerto Rico, Paraguay, Poland, Germany, Austria, Denmark, Mexico, Italy, Greece, and Ukraine, through his work in the field of recreation, as an award winning Rotarian and a member of the International Task Force to Alleviate Poverty and Hunger. His professional career has been highlighted by many publications and awards including, Perspective in Adult Basic Education for Administrators, Northern Illinois University, 1972, Perspectives in Outdoor Education, W.C. Brown Co., 1972,

Household Word Award from State of Kansas, Citation for Meritorious Service Award from the Rotary Foundation, and the Outstanding Alumnus Award, Bethel College, `Ozzie,' as he is known by his friends, has followed his humanitarian and educational work around the world. He deftly adds his extensive knowledge of environmental education to this title. When ask about touring to help with the book's publicity, he first reminded me of his age, 81, then said "I am a little restricted in my activities, but we were in Ukraine in May taking part in a ceremony giving dairy cows to poor farmers."

Judy K. Brookhiser holds a Doctorate in Recreation and currently works as Assistant Dean, College of Health Sciences & Human Services, Murray State University. From her adventures as a Peace Corps volunteer in Gambia, Africa, Judy, through her work as a teacher in public schools and Penn State University, Indiana University, and Murray State has influenced learners, children, and adults in the camp field. Judy's 35 year experience in camps (nonprofit and private) has reaped many camp specific achievements. Just a few of these are, enthusiastic camper at age seven, camp director of Camp Lookout in Iowa, Camp Elliott in PA and Camp Tapawingo in IL; program leader and developer of Native Youth Training Program in native American villages throughout Alaska; worked with ACA to help develop a scoring system for camp accreditation standards; has earned the Distinguished Service Award from two ACA sections; and developed and directed Camp G.U.T.S. (Gearing Up for Success). Judy has presented workshops in Belize, participated in Murray State University exchange programs with China and South Korea, and taught graduate classes at the Panamerican Institute for Physical Education, in Maracaibo, Venezuela that resulted in students directing a summer camp in the Andes. In 2004 she returned to South Korea to deliver the keynote address to the South Korean Institute for Forest Recreation, a group that has focused primarily on facilities and desires to emphasize programming in natural areas. Eleven years directing a camp that served children and adults with disabilities and a long stretch of work with the Institute for the Study of Developmental Disabilities and the Center for Autism at Indiana University has given her particular insight into creating adaptable materials and programs. Judy puts her special needs, international lens on this manuscript in an impressive manner. .

PREFACE

HOW TO USE THIS BOOK

This Guide is for leaders (and parents and individuals) who wish to use outdoor/nature-oriented activities in their programs or daily lives or with their families. It includes:

- *How-to-do-it* activities
- Ideas to stimulate new or to modify nature-oriented programs and activities
- Resources for additional information on the various nature topics

These programs, activities, and ideas can be used by both the experienced and the inexperienced leader for all persons, regardless of age, race, ability, in varied settings of camps, clubs, families, playgrounds, and so on. Also, this Guide can be used by the leader who is looking for an activity for a specific program, ideas for program planning, or resources to provide additional background on a specific outdoor/nature topic.

The Guide encompasses broadly the outdoor/nature-oriented field; that is, it relates directly to learning about nature and its interrelationships. This includes using natural materials in creative learning programs and activities, discovering how nature interrelates in the natural environment and the impact of human beings, and developing an appreciation for nature and the out-of-doors.

Terminology about the out-of-doors has changed over the decades. Words like *conservation, ecology, environment,* and *ecosystems* overlap, diverge, and mesh together, depending on the context. The term *nature* has fallen in and out of popularity, often being supplanted by *environment.* However, *nature-oriented* embodies the entire focus of this Guide and it is used purposefully. Here we explore how the natural world has been used for subsistence, for art, and for various activities of daily life. We want to help people learn about, appreciate, and enjoy the natural world. Before the industrial revolution, before the technological evolutions, people lived simply off the land, knowing that their continued existence depended upon protecting the environment. Our continued existence depends upon protecting the environment, but most of us are far detached from realizing the ultimate impact on the environment of what we do in our daily lives. Thus, an effort has been made to emphasize the importance of environmentally sound practices and safety for the participants.

Chapter 1 provides basic information, program development, and community resources to establish and develop nature-oriented programs. Section A includes the what, why, and who of nature-oriented programs and the characteristics of these programs. An important aspect of this section addresses inclusion of persons with varying needs and abilities. Section B focuses on program organization, including how programs may be structured, type of leadership needed, and risk management. The final section reviews community resources and organizations to help the leader.

The next four chapters are how-to-do **crafts (Chapter 2)** and **games (Chapter 3)**, and **outdoor living skills** (Chapters 4 and 5). Each gives some specific activities with detailed instructions and references for additional activities. Chapter 2 includes crafts from trees, other plant materials, and nonplant materials, as well as reproductions and preservation. There are five types of games in Chapter 3—map and compass, campcraft, hiking and trailing, searching and seeking, and quiet games. Chapter 4, "Outdoor Living Skills" gives suggestions and resources related to campsites/gear/shelter; firecraft; ropecraft; and toolcraft. Chapter 5 focuses on outdoor cooking with menus and recipes for different styles of fire places.

Chapters 6: "Projects and Hobbies" and **Chapter 7: "Adventure Outing Sports"** can serve the leader well as a resource for programming ideas. Chapter 6 is especially rich in activity suggestions related to animals, birds, insects, plants, rocks and minerals, astronomy, weather/atmosphere, water/streams/ponds, nature photography, creative expression, and historical-cultural activities. Resources and ideas for eleven ever-popular adventure/outing sports are given in Chapter 7 initiative/challenge activities; bicycling; canoeing/kayaking/ river running; field archery; casting and fishing; firearms safety and hunting; navigating in the outdoors; cross-country skiing and snowshoeing; and spelunking (cave exploring). Because of the instructional nature of these activities, detailed "how-to" information is not included; however, excellent resources provide this information.

Chapter 8: "Program Themes" looks at a variety of programming ideas for nighttime and winter activities, campfire programs, and Native American-oriented activities. The nature trails and related activities section is especially good for community-service projects. The final section of the chapter is Classic Nature-Oriented Readings and includes selected books on pioneers and champions of conservation and environmental appreciation and protection.

Resources

An important aspect of this Guide is *resources*, both general and specific. . Since one book cannot cover the scope of how-to for every activity or category of nature-oriented programs, these resources provide additional information. The resources include books and internet sites.

Books. There is an extremely large number of books relating to nature and the out-of-doors. Many of those, especially for children, have a very appealing appearance, but often fall short in areas of sound environmental practices and basic knowledge about nature. Most all of the books listed have been reviewed to make sure they fit with the topics and emphases valued in this Guide. Brief annotations are provided for some of the resources. Some older, out-of-print references have been purposely included because they contain excellent information not found in the current literature. Frequently these out-of-print resources can be found in public/school libraries or on the internet.

Internet. The resources and information available on the Internet is ever expanding. A few sites have been suggested and although we have tried to select sites from well-established organizations or agencies (nonprofit, private, and governmental) that are likely to remain over time, there are always changes. Suggestions have been provided for search words that have been used with some success when looking for information about specific topics. Of course, everyone, persons of all ages, abilities, backgrounds, and interests, are encouraged to go outside and be immersed in nature, to experience directly the environment. The Internet should be used only to get additional information regarding the natural environment and possible activities and projects.

Keep Up-to-Date. New resources (books, videos, and Internet sites) can be found in periodicals and publication catalogs. Nature/interpretive centers, children's museums, conventions and workshops, outdoor-related organization periodicals, Sunday newspaper book sections, and bookstores are also good places to check out the latest resources. County extension agents frequently have a variety of helpful resources, including pamphlets, software, and booklets. Caution: be sure to check that crafts, games, and other activities are *nature-oriented*; too many suggestions in popular resources misuse nature's materials or do not involve environmental education.

ACKNOWLEDGMENTS

The authors acknowledge with appreciation the contribution of the following people who reviewed the manuscript and provided expertise, insight, and recommendations, especially in the respective areas indicated, although most gave general suggestions, too.: Dr. Sheryl Jo Stephan, Eastern Kentucky University, environmental education and camping;   Dr. Jean Kinnear, Northern Michigan University, interpretive services and boating;   Dr. Gail VanderStoep, Michigan State University, interpretive services;   Dr. Kathy Scholl, University of Northern Iowa, soil impact exercises;   Dr. Susan Gavron, Bowling Green State University; and the late Dr. Phyllis Ford, camping.

1

DEVELOPING A PROGRAM

Every child should have mud pies, grasshoppers, water bugs, tadpoles, frogs, mud turtles, elderberries, wild strawberries, acorns, chestnuts, trees to climb, brooks to wade in, water lilies, woodchucks, bats, bees, butterflies, various animals to pet, hay fields, pine cones, rocks to roll, sand, snakes, huckleberries, and hornets, and any child who has been deprived of these has been deprived of the best part of his education.
—LUTHER BURBANK

This chapter includes some of the basics for developing nature-oriented programs. Section A: The What and Why of Nature-Oriented Activities; Section B: Program Organization; and Section C: Community Resources.

SECTION A

THE WHAT AND WHY OF NATURE-ORIENTED ACTIVITIES

WHAT ARE NATURE-ORIENTED ACTIVITIES?

Nature-oriented activities include those outdoor experiences related to using, understanding, and appreciating the natural environment and those indoor activities related to using natural materials, maintaining the natural integrity of those materials, and understanding and appreciating the out-of-doors.

Three interrelated areas of activity are:

1. *Knowledge* involves an understanding of the materials, processes, and relationships among the various natural science fields dealing with rocks and soils, plants, animals, and water and also the impact of people on their environment.

2. *Appreciation* involves aesthetics and discernment. It includes beauty of form, design, and color and an appreciation of literature, our cultural heritage as related to the natural environment, and the importance of our natural environment to individuals and society.

3. *Action skills* involve the use of hands and body in crafts, games, sports, and hobbies.

WHY NATURE-ORIENTED ACTIVITIES?

Nature-oriented activities contribute to the protection and enhancement of the environment in which we live and enrich the personal quality of life of individuals.

People are a strange paradox! Three centuries ago our American ancestors' very existence depended upon their mastery of the outdoors. The heritage of the pioneers was rooted in the soil and there was abundance for all. But, as the explorers and the early settlers pushed westward, they also exploited the wide-open spaces and the natural resources until today, with an ever-increasing population, the need for conservation of these spaces and resources is critical.

Participation in outdoor recreation—boating, camping, fishing, pleasure driving, outdoor sports, and picnicking—is extensive and thus has an impact on the environment. Strangely, people do not seem to realize that their continued enjoyment of nature-oriented and outdoor recreation activities depends upon their attitudes and conduct while they are in the natural environment and the manner in which they use and protect it.

CHELEY COLORADO CAMPS, CHELEY, CO.

Furthermore, there appears to be inadequate understanding of the problems of, as well as appreciation for, the world in which we live. Environmental concerns apply not only to America, but to the entire world, with its ever-increasing population and resultant poverty and hunger, the threatened depletion of natural resources worldwide, increased demand for energy and water, and especially, the decline in environmental quality.

Nature-oriented programs play a vital role in today's world because they can:

- increase understanding and appreciation of natural history and of the heritage of the American people;

- develop skill and interest in activities that use the natural environment for lifelong personal recreational pursuits and pleasure;

- promote perceptions resulting in appreciation of the beauty and serenity of the natural world and an awareness of the infinite variety in the world;

- stimulate a desire to gain greater knowledge and understanding of the processes of growth and development of the natural world and its interrelatedness and interdependence;

- make people aware of their dependence upon natural resources and their responsibility for conserving them; and

- recognize the worldwide communal need for quality environment to enhance the lives of all people.

While the foregoing are indeed true of the activities of nature-oriented programs, perhaps the greatest value of such activities lies in their development of the person and the enhancement of an individual's quality of life. The following are examples of these attributes:

- The *exhilaration* that comes from outdoor activities, such as white water canoeing, mountain climbing, and backpacking, that give a "natural high" in peak performances and experiences;

- The *healthy lifestyle* that is facilitated through exercise in the out-of-doors and dietary understandings related to plants and animals;

- The *caring* that is integral to gardening and plant care and to pets, wherein a relationship is established with living, responding plants and animals;

- The *self-expression* in which one can freely engage in the creative arts;

- The *personal gratification* that comes with accomplishment, whether it is learning about the intricacies of nature, the mastering of an outdoor skill, or the completion of a project;

Such attributes are important to all age levels, from preschoolers to the older adults and from the most physically and mentally gifted person to the individual who faces physical or mental challenges. These attributes are also vital in all settings, be it in the home; in a rural or urban environment; or in a hospital, a residential living environment, or a nursing home.

WHO SHOULD SPONSOR
NATURE-ORIENTED PROGRAMS?

All organizations and agencies with an interest in and concern for the natural environment and people's relationship to it should actively sponsor nature-oriented activities and programs. Also, those organizations and agencies that are seeking to enable individuals to gain greater self-fulfillment through activity will find the outdoors an enriching environment. Nature activities are a modality, a programming vehicle that can greatly enhance effectiveness in working with people by providing powerful settings for teaching and a variety of human development activities. Thus, there are two dimensions to consider when asked: "Who should sponsor programs?". . . those organizations that promote programs using nature-oriented activities as part of environmental education and those that use activities as a modality.

Not-for-profit youth agencies, such as Boy Scouts, Girl Scouts, Camp Fire, Boys and Girls Clubs, and 4-H Clubs, have excellent opportunities to provide participants with nature-oriented programs through their structured programs of merit and proficiency badges, through their summer camps and year-round outing programs, and through their activities of community service and in group meetings.

Religious organizations of all doctrines and structures can make use of nature-oriented programs in their religious instruction and social activities through summer camp programs, tripping and the outing sports, and weekend "retreats," as well as nature-oriented activities at informal meetings, church school, and other services in various contexts and for different ages.

Other organizations that focus upon *enhancement of the individual* can use nature-oriented programs and individual activities. For instance, schools and organizations concerned with social deviance and behavior management may offer adventure/challenge programs of extensive durations, such as a year or six months, or short-term experiences. Senior citizen centers and clubs, as well as preschool day centers, can integrate with their activities a nature-oriented program that focuses upon the care and accountability for living plants and animals, as well as individual activities, including day trips to various community nature-related resources.

Schools, both through curriculum experiences and through extracurricular activities, are increasingly using the natural environment as an integral aspect of the education process, as well as taking advantage of the interpretive services provided by public agencies for both learning and behavior management. Schools, in the broadest sense, include home schooling and day care centers. Schools with children and adults with disabilities may share meaningful, integrated peer experiences in the out-of-doors.

Private organizations, such as sportsmen's clubs, garden clubs, Audubon Society chapters, and special interest clubs, actively promote nature-oriented activities not only for their own members but also for the citizenry of the community.

Private resorts and campgrounds, to enhance visitor services for both children and adults, are adding to their recreational opportunities unguided and guided trails, special nature crafts and hobby opportunities, tripping and outings, and educational displays and videos.

Museums are of many types such as scientific, industrial, and historical. In the nature area, museums have generally been dedicated to the preservation and display of nonliving materials illustrating natural and human history. However, the museum curator is not merely a custodian of treasures of civilization, but a creative educator. Rather than simply housing a collection of specimens, artifacts, and curios in an austere and formal display, the modern museum makes history come alive by telling a story in an attractive manner, frequently with action displays, living history reenactments, and objects that viewers can touch. Many museums have extensive programs for children, youth, and adults of all backgrounds and abilities.

Children's museums and science centers usually touch on a variety of fields of interest to young people in addition to natural science. Their displays are presentations that tell stories about life processes and natural history. The emphasis in the past usually has been on the preservation of nonliving materials. The children's museums have become highly interactive and have taken on many of the functions of the interpretive nature-center, gathering into one building activities such as hobby clubs, classes, workshop space, library, lectures, and demonstrations, as well as the usual displays and exhibits. The emphasis is on activities for youth. Although a nature center may have a "museum" area, most frequently a children's museum is a separate structure located in a population center without an adjacent natural area. This limits the capacity for outdoor programs of the kind a true nature center has.

Public recreation and park systems often have diverse and abundant natural resources. In response to the public's interest in outdoor recreation and the vital concern necessary for the conservation of the natural environment, many public recreation and park systems are developing extensive nature-oriented programs. While emphasis has been primarily upon interpretive services, other types such as clubs, instructional activities and special events are sometimes part of park programs.

Internet sites abound that deal with all aspects of the natural environment. They are sponsored by long-established and respected agencies and organizations, as well as entrepreneurs, hobbyists, and individuals with a specific interest or experience. Various sites attract both those with intensive interest and extensive experiences to those who are new to any nature-oriented activity. Innumerable chat rooms exist on the Internet for persons interested in nearly anything related to nature or outdoor activities. For example, the *Family of Nature* site (http://familyofnature.com/index.htm) has a chat room for butterflies and a chat room for birds. These chat rooms function very similarly to clubs and can involve people from around the world. In addition, various forms of topical communication areas have developed on the Internet and will continue to evolve at remarkable rates. For example, BLOGS (short for Weblogs) are areas where people give their opinions on various topics.

WHO WILL ENJOY NATURE-ORIENTED ACTIVITIES?

The out-of-doors has a lure for everyone, regardless of ability or mobility, although the way in which each person responds may be different. Programs of nature-oriented activities are for the:

- *generalist* who just likes the out-of-doors and all it activities;
- *concerned citizen* who seeks greater global environmental quality;
- *intellectual person* who studies the ecology of the environment and ecosystems;
- *senior citizen* who appreciates and enjoys the out-of-doors;
- *person with a disability* who wants to experience the outdoors just like everyone else;
- *outdoor person* who seeks rugged outdoor living, fishing, and hunting;
- *inquisitive person* who finds the wonders of nature fascinating;
- *creative person* who excels in the arts of painting, sketching, crafts, poetry, and music;
- *physically skilled person* who is exhilarated by skiing, skating, boating, and horseback riding;
- *traveler and observer* who enjoys museums, zoos, formal gardens, and historical sites;
- *daring adventurer* who engages in tripping, spelunking, and mountaineering;
- *armchair nature lover* who relaxes with literature and nature videos, and Internet websites and chat rooms;
- *beautiful-day person* who loves to drive through the park, attend a band concert on the green, or walk in the woods; and
- *hobbyist* who intensely pursues bird watching, photography, or gardening.

INCLUDING PERSONS WITH SPECIAL NEEDS

While the orientation of this guide is inclusive for people with differing abilities, there is a need to identify and highlight nature-oriented programming for individuals with special needs. Throughout this guide the reader will not find specific activities for any one group, because *all activities can be used with diverse groups and with all age levels.* There are not different activities for those with special needs. The activities are the same; however, sometimes adaptations need to be made to fit the specific needs of the individual.

While acknowledging that there are sometimes "extra" needs for people with differing abilities, it is not their differences, but their similarities that should be emphasized. People with special needs, whether they be children with developmental disabilities, senior citizens with mobility impairments, or individuals with sensory impairments (e.g. hearing, sight), are essentially human beings with the same needs and interests as all of us. What changes is how the activity is presented or adapted to include individuals with special needs. The basis or underlying nature of the activity should not be lost because of adaptation. Both persons without disabilities and those with disabilities should expect to gain the same benefits from the nature-oriented experience.

Informed Leadership Required

People with differing abilities have a right to access the outdoors and nature-oriented activities. Leaders' perceptions of a disability, age, or heritage as a limiting factor or increasing liability should not be a barrier to participation. Neither should a leader with limited experience working with persons with special needs believe that separate is equal or better. Therefore, it is the leader's responsibility to be informed about basic elements of human behavior and development from childhood through old age, as well as the cultural ramifications (such as the separation of males and females in some cultures or religions) of using the outdoors.

There are many resources available for leaders who are not knowledgeable about working with persons with varying abilities. There are numerous books on general therapeutic recreation and adapted physical education that provide the basic understandings and information. They include information on causes (etiology) of disabilities, the impact of disabilities on mobility and motor output, and teaching/leadership adaptations that have proven successful. Leaders may also wish to visit programs that exclusively serve persons with disabilities to observe specific adaptations and needs. In addition, there are sport-specific or activity-specific books that focus on general and specific disabilities. The Internet also is a powerful resource for many advocacy groups that provide detailed information and oftentimes suggest adaptations and additional resources relating to nearly all disabilities.

The most important awareness that leaders can have is that persons with disabilities are *people first*, with the same interests, aspirations, and dreams as everyone else. Their disability, whether it is mobility, sensory, or mental, does not describe who they are at heart. This same focus must be applied to persons who have different cultures or belief systems. Everyone must be respected for who they are, separate from any stereotypes or labeling. It is this humanistic attitude that the leader must pass on to all participants so that people with differences can be genuinely integrated into the group and the nature-oriented experience will be successful for all.

Fostering Inclusiveness

Inclusion does not just happen. In order for inclusion to be successful, several things must occur. For example, if leaders have little or no experience working with people of varying abilities, they must be trained to do this. Placing children or adults with differing abilities into the natural environment with untrained or unsensitized leaders is a prescription for failure. Training is the most basic element for facilitating a successful experience for all... the leaders and the group.

A second basic element of inclusiveness is working with those who do not have disabilities to be accepting and welcoming of those who do. Leaders must not only model appropriate behaviors, but also pave the way for understanding and acceptance by helping to education the nondisabled peers about specific conditions. It is often helpful to have a parent or caretaker of a person with a disability visit the group prior to the arrival of the person with the disability or to have the parent or caretaker come with the person the first time. Again, these strategies will be determined by the needs of the individual and the characteristics of the group.

Following are a few general suggestions that leaders can use to foster successful integration:

- Assess participants for skills and ability related to the activity.
- Adapt the activity without losing the essence of the experience.
- Be prepared to allow more time to complete an activity.
- When necessary, change the surface on which the activity occurs.
- Shorten or lengthen the distance of the activity.

The successful inclusion of people with different abilities largely depends on the ability of the leader. A leader must have the support (training, resources, facilities, etc.) for inclusion, as well as the knowledge and desire to attend to the unique psychological and social needs of people with and without disabilities. In short, we are essentially more alike than different, regardless of appearance. Those who work best with persons with disabilities are those who work best with people in general.

 Books on Including Persons with Special Needs in Nature-Oriented Programs

See master publicatons list for cities of Publishers.

Block, M.E. (1994). *A Teacher's Guide to Including Students with Disabilities in Regular Physical Education.* Paul H. Brooks: Baltimore, MD.

Brennan, Steve, et al. (2003). *Including Youth with Disabilities in Outdoor Programs: Best Practices, Outcomes, and Resources.* Sagamore Publishing:

Champaign, IL. Focuses on inclusive outdoor programming for youth, including benefits of inclusion in traditional outdoor programs and practical information on best practices and ways to evaluate outcomes.

Dattilo, John. (2002). *Inclusive Leisure Services*. 2nd ed. Venture Publishing: State College, PA. Provides well-developed process for including persons with disabilities in integrated programs.

Ellmo, Wendy and Jill Graser. (1995). *Adapted Adventure Activities: A rehabilitation model for adventure programming and group initiatives*. Kendall/Hunt: Dubuque, IA. (A Project Adventure publication.) Written for professionals working in rehabilitation.

Kreider, Betsy. (2002). *Growing with Care: Using Greenery, Gardens and Nature with Aging and Special Populations*. Venture Publishing: State College, PA. Covers gardening with persons with special needs.

Johnson, A.M. (2001). *High Adventure Outdoor Recreation: The Right to Risk*. In G. Doll-Tepper, M. Kroner & W. Sonnenschein (Eds.). New Horizons in Sport for Athletes with a Disability. Proceedings of the International Vista 99 Conference (pp. 617-618). Meyer & Meyer Sport: United Kingdom.

Smith, R.W.; D.R. Austin; D.W.Kennedy. (2001). *Inclusive and Special Recreation*. 4th ed. McGraw-Hill: Boston.

WHAT ARE THE ADVANTAGES OF NATURE-ORIENTED ACTIVITIES?

As a program area, nature-oriented activities offer many advantages:

- *Low in Cost.* In many areas nature's treasures are still abundant and free to all. The nature-oriented program can be one of the least expensive program areas.

- *Year-Round.* Interests aroused in the summertime can be carried throughout the year, for nature is ever-changing with the seasons. "Every season has a reason."

- *Pleasurable.* Nature experiences are pleasurable in themselves for they provide exercise, relaxation, or escape from urban environment and daily stress.

- *Ever-changing.* Nature is life itself, and therefore ever-unfolding. One never learns everything about nature; interest can endure for a lifetime.

- *Adaptable/Varied.* The tremendous variety of activities available makes nature adaptable to various age and ability groups and special interests. Furthermore, many community resources are available to be used.

- *Easily Integrated.* Because of their variety and adaptability, nature activities can be integrated easily with such program areas as drama, music, arts, and crafts.

In addition, programming with nature-oriented activities accomplishes the following eight unique or special values:

1. *Promotes Environmental Quality.* Quality of life is entwined with the quality of environment in which one lives. Nature activities not only can develop citizen concern for environmental quality, but also stimulate action to enhance the quality of the environment.

2. *Teaches Conservation.* Conservation of natural resources is of prime importance today. Nature activities can teach the reason for conservation and provide suggestions on how best to conserve resources.

3. *Stimulates Learning.* Projects help people acquire knowledge without their realizing they are learning. Such projects and activities may also stimulate them to learn more about the world in which they live, to appreciate how nature influences design, to develop interest in indigenous people, and to study the history of crafts.

4. *Encourages Appreciation.* People acquire love of the out-of-doors, respect for growing things, and appreciation for the way the beautiful things of nature enrich life.

5. *Offers Satisfactions* While interacting in the natural elements, individuals may learn to appreciate the basic things of life, which are beautiful in their simplicity. Nature crafts offer opportunity for expression of creativity, ingenuity, and originality-an unexcelled field for self-expression.

6. *Provides for Adventure.* People, children in particular, have a basic need and craving for adventure that is both physically challenging and intellectually stimulating.

7. *Enhances Ecological Understanding.* Knowing something about the interrelationships and interdependence of the ecosystem elements, including the impact of human beings, is the foundation for action to sustain environmental quality nationally and worldwide.

8. *Encourages Citizen Action.* Through a greater understanding of the interrelationships within the natural environment and the impact people (society) have, citizens may be inspired to take actions related to the environment, such as recycling, not taking artifacts, not disturbing plants and animals in parks and preserves, and conserving energy.

CHARACTERISTICS OF NATURE-ORIENTED PROGRAM RESOURCES

There are five unique characteristics of nature that enhance its use in programming. They are: (1)The common; (2) real objects; (3) action; (4) timeliness; and (5) stimulant

The Common

"We are surrounded, but we know not."

Because people have not really trained all of their senses to function effectively, particularly the powers of detailed observation, there are many so-called commonplace nature objects which are in reality storehouses of fascinating program materials. A person need not seek out the strange or import the exotic. Gaining new insight into everyday surroundings is one of the primary functions of nature programs. These programs should focus upon activities that reveal such basic principles of the natural environment as balance of nature, growth, and development.

Real Objects

"One frog in the pond is worth five in formaldehyde."

Natural objects in their natural setting are the best approaches to program content—nothing can ever take the place of firsthand experiences with a real nature object. Here focus in the beginning must be on the specific, not the general. A person does not learn about all animals at once, but begins by learning about a particular type of animal or an aspect of animal life.

Action

"Only I can discover."

The program must be based on doing things rather than on hearing about them. People's interest is sustained only when they make discoveries themselves; their curiosity and initiative are whetted only when they may explore new vistas.

Timeliness

"Here today, gone tomorrow."

Ever-changing, ever-changing, ever-changing—that's the prime characteristic of the natural environment. Therefore, it behooves every program planner to take advantage of the season at hand, shifts in weather, and "the teachable moment" when something outside the aim of the specific activity arises.

Stimulant

"Ignorance is not bliss."

What individuals have not experienced and do not know, they will not try without encouragement. A prime function of a nature-oriented program is to introduce the various activities and inform the potential participants of those in their special interest area. Certain program content must be selected for its contribution to this informative and interpretive role. Without exposure to opportunities, individuals may be oblivious to the joys of the outdoors.

SECTION B
PROGRAM ORGANIZATION

Program organization is addressed by structural organization of programs, identifying the leadership required, and risk management.

STRUCTURAL ORGANIZATION OF PROGRAMS

A wide variety of nature-oriented activities may be utilized in programming and thus can be organized in many ways. However, there are basically four types of structure: (1) individual activities selected for the program; (2) instructional activities (classes, workshops, Internet courses, study groups, etc.); (3) clubs (hobby and special interest clubs); and (4) special events and festivals.

Individual Activities Selected for the Program

Many nature-oriented activities fit very well into an ongoing program of a Scout troop, playground, day camp, senior center program, and so on. In such, the nature aspects may be planned as individual activities or a part of a day or evening program, an outing, or as concentrated studies for a short time.

An Example: Nature on the Playgrounds. May it be said first that there are no specific so-called playground nature activities. Most of the nature-oriented activities presented in this guide may be used in the playground program—adaptations come from the environment, the playground participants, and the other community offerings.

Nature-oriented activities should be a part of the program throughout the total summer, and year-round if playgrounds are open all year. To have a "nature week" is definitely limiting to the program; if such a week is to be designated, it should be for the purpose of highlighting, as a climax to the total nature-oriented program. For simple ideas that any inexperienced playground leader can manage with an in-service training program, refer to the activities in the various sections of this guide.

Instructional Activities

Instructional activities may include classes, workshops, study groups, and Internet courses. Untold possibilities exist for extending our knowledge and understanding of the natural environment and for teaching skills through instructional programs.

Internet Offerings. There are a wide variety of classes that involve environmental sciences and nature-related topics on the Internet. For example, WorldWideLearn, an online directory of courses, lists a number of classes available under Environmental Sciences. (http://www.worldwidelearn.com/environment.htm)

Study Groups. Study groups are very similar to hobby and special interest clubs but focus upon study of a nature area rather than projects or activities. Most frequently these groups will "instruct themselves" through shared leadership and will use expert consultants only occasionally. These organizations sustain unity over a considerable period.

Classes. Many individuals like to have some instruction and formal study in a particular subject but are not sufficiently interested to join a study group that meets regularly over the entire season or year and in which one must participate in leadership. For these people, a real service can be rendered through short courses. Frequently, class sessions are held weekly over a six- or eight-week period. The instructor is a specialist in the area and course content is formalized, although there is seldom much, if any, "homework." Examples of such topics of instruction are: family camping techniques, mountaineering techniques, lapidary, firearms safety, nature photography, nature crafts, and backpacking.

Workshops. Workshops are sessions covering a single evening, one day, or a weekend. Workshops may utilize the same topics that are presented through classes; however, the material needs to be limited to either a general overview or an in-depth study of one small facet of the topic.

Clubs

Often a community has a number of special interest clubs ("rock hounds," bird watchers, and archery, for example) that are a familiar way of offering a nature program. Anyone interested, regardless of age, may attend and participate. These clubs may be organized as autonomies or independent clubs, but also may be affiliated with local or national organizations. For example, a field archery club may affiliate with the National Field Archery Association; a hostelling club with the American Youth Hostels; and a family camping club with the Family Campers and RVers, (formerly the National Campers and Hikers Association). Many club groups are sponsored by public recreation departments, voluntary agencies, churches, civic groups, libraries, and museums.

Another type of special interest club is limited to a certain age group, usually youth. These clubs may be interested in nature in general-Junior Naturalists-or in a specific aspect of nature or outing activities-Junior Bird Watchers. They also may be associated with such national programs as the Junior Audubon Club, the Junior Air Rifle Club, the NRA Junior Rifle Club, and 4-H Club. Most national groups give organizational help; however, affiliation with a national organization certainly is not necessary. Many club groups are sponsored by public recreation departments, voluntary agencies, churches, civic groups, libraries, and museums. There are also specialized experiences available for those with differing abilities.

Special Events and Festivals

Special events and festivals are single occurrence activities, many lasting more than one day. Some of these may even become traditional and be held each year, They serve three purposes: (1) to give individuals an opportunity to demonstrate their hobbies and activities to the public; (2) to stimulate interest among people who are not presently participating, and (3) to provide an opportunity for persons who are interested in occasional participation but feel they do not have the time or interest to participate regularly in a club or other activity. Examples of some special events are science fairs, illustrated lectures, hobby shows, wildlife art shows, and tournaments (e.g., casting, skeet shooting).

Outings may be for an entire day or part of a day and may be conducted as part of another program or as a special event complete within itself. An outing usually is composed of several activities but with one central feature.

WHAT LEADERSHIP IS REQUIRED?

Ideally the nature-oriented program is under the direction and supervision of competent and well-trained professional staff. Very few organizations, however, employ full-time naturalists or environmental interpreters to conduct their programs unless they maintain a full-scale nature center complete with interpretive services. In carrying out programs, most organizations rely heavily upon part-time and volunteer leadership.

Two types of leadership are of great importance to the success of any nature-oriented program, regardless of whether the leadership is volunteer or professional. Both the *organizing leader* and the *knowledge leader*, each serving special functions, are essential to the operation of a successful program. The primary task of the organizing leader is to determine interests, assess resources, stimulate participation, and develop organizational structure. The primary function of the knowledgeable leader is to bring to the nature-oriented program authenticity and accuracy in the basic understanding of nature. The organizing leader and the knowledge leader may be embodied in one person, as certainly is true of professional interpretive personnel. If an organizational leader lacks nature knowledge, the nature-oriented programs can still be offered-team up!

The Organizing Leader

Contrary to popular belief, the organizing leader need not be an expert on nature to spearhead the development of a nature-oriented program or to organize nature-oriented activities. The primary task of the organizing leader is to determine interests, assess resources, stimulate participation, and develop organizational structure. The organizing nature leader should have these characteristics:

- *Genuine enthusiasm* for the outdoors that will inspire others to enjoy it also

- *General knowledge* of the outdoors with the ability to use resources for increasing knowledge. The nature leader who is organizing the program or who conducts general activities on an elementary basis does not need to be an expert, nor even to know all the answers to questions raised by participants. The leader must not be afraid to say, "I do not know," but must be willing to work with the group in finding answers to their questions. There should be no hesitancy in calling upon experts to assist in the program.

- *Curiosity and awareness.* The leader need not be creative, but must try to be discerning and perceptive in the study of nature.

- *Ability to converse easily with people* and to have a genuine liking for them.

- *Concern for a quality environment.*

Often this organizing leader is a professional person responsible for developing programs-the recreation leader of the municipal recreation department, a Y youth worker, a Boys' Club leader. Or, this leader may be serving in a volunteer capacity with a responsibility for nature-oriented programs, for instance, a Scout troop leader.

The organizing leader may conduct some general nature-oriented activities, but, for the most effective program, this leader must make use of the knowledge leader. *Too frequently this is where many nature programs fail.* The activities are too shallow in basic natural science knowledge and many activities are without substance. Only when a knowledgeable leader is used will a program really stimulate a deeper inquiry into the natural sciences and give the greatest satisfaction.

The Knowledge Leader

The primary function of the knowledge leader is to bring to the nature-oriented program authenticity and accuracy in the basic understanding of nature. It is not necessary that a person knowledgeable about nature serve on a full-time basis. Many capable people in the community are not available for full-time service, but are willing to serve on a part-time basis. For example:

- Hobbyists, members of specialized clubs or individuals
- Camp leaders and individuals who have grown up enjoying the outdoors
- Teachers in the natural science fields
- Professional people in fields related to natural science-taxidermists, horticulturalists, gardeners, geologists
- Local and state government employees-natural resource/conservation personnel, extension service agents and soil conversation personnel
- Federal government employees-Departments of Agriculture and Interior, Army Corps of Engineers, U.S. Forest Service, National Parks Service, Bureau of Land Management, and so on
- Persons who may not hold professional positions, but majored in the sciences in college or have taken up the natural environment (or some aspect of it) as a serious hobby

Judy Brookhiser, Great Smokey Mountains, Clingmans Dome, NC

These knowledgeable experts, working cooperatively with the organizing leader, will enable the development of an effective and dynamic nature-oriented program in the community. They can be asked to accompany and serve as the resource leader on a hike, conduct a field trip, present a special program in their area of interest, lead an interested group of adults or youngsters, assist in laying out a nature trail, instruct a class for interested people, or train others to lead elementary nature activities. Many retirees and older citizens are exceptionally effective with children, making intergenerational experiences quite enriching.

Many people are willing to give their time generously for single activities and short-term projects; however, a person asked to assume leadership of a class that involves special preparation over a long period should be offered remuneration or honorarium of appreciation.

Education and Training Programs

Training programs for adult and junior leaders are becoming increasingly important. Training programs are directed toward leadership—schoolteachers who want to include some environmental education in their curriculum, scout leaders who seek ideas for nature-oriented activities for their troop members, and camp staff who desire basic campcraft and counseling skills along with some understanding of the natural environment.

Special instruction resulting in certification by national or state organizations may also be offered. Some examples are: outdoor living skills by the American Camp Association; instructor training programs of the National Rifle Association, National Association of Casting and Angling Clubs, and National Field Archery Association; and hunter safety and home firearms safety courses sponsored by the National Rifle Association, frequently in cooperation with state conservation commissions. Leadership training programs may take the form of a one-day clinic, an institute, a workshop, or even an extended formal course with methods and materials.

RISK MANAGEMENT CONSIDERATIONS (NATURE-ORIENTED)

One of the concerns of individual leaders and their organizations is perceived legal liability that comes from potential injury to participants engaging in nature-oriented activities, especially adventure/challenge activities. It is not possible to assure that no injuries will occur; risk of injury is inevitable with active participants regardless of the activity. However, risk management can provide practices that minimize such risks. You need not fear legal liability if you understand the basic concepts of risk management. All agencies should have a risk management plan with procedures and all leaders, including volunteers, should be oriented as to their involvement and responsibilities.

There are many different types of risk that an agency must plan to manage; however, the focus here is upon the leader's role in managing risks when engaged in nature-oriented activities. There are five guiding principles for managing risk in nature-oriented activities.

1. Appropriate leadership. The activity should be conducted by the appropriate leadership (see section on types of leadership), who understand the participants, the activity, and its inherent risks and the safety practices needed to reduce or minimize injury risks. This includes proper supervision and understanding of environmental conditions.

2. Agreement to participate form. The organization sponsoring the activity should have a completed agreement to participate form for each participant. This form should include (a) the nature of the activity in which the individual will participate, including potential injury; (b) the expectations of the participant in terms of skill level, if any; physical conditioning, as appropriate; and behavior expectations, and (c) any equipment or clothing required. It also should indicate any disabilities or health concerns that the leader should be aware of because participation may be affected, such as seizures, diabetes, recent illness that may limit stamina, etc.

    A participant, including minors, assumes the inherent risks of an activity, that is, those risks of injury that are a part of the activity. However, in order to assume such risks, the participant must be knowledgeable about the activity and that is why the participant must understand the requirements of safe conduct of the activity. It is the responsibility of the leader to help the participant, both minors and adults, understand the activity requirements and to give appropriate warnings of possible injury risks.

    If the participant is a minor, this form should include a parental permission for the child to participate and a list of contact persons and telephone numbers to contact in case of emergency. The form also should have parental permission for the leader to render emergency care to the child, including information regarding participant's health insurance.

    The leader should have a copy of this form, but the privacy of the individual participant's personal information must be protected. The form may be for a program as a whole, that is, for the year, or it may be for an individual activity. The participant, regardless of age, signs, as well as the parents, if participant is a minor.

    Although no one is protected from negligence or wrongful conduct, an agreement to participate has been effectively used to limit liability or share responsibility with the participant...even minors. Note that an Agreement to Participate Form is not a waiver. Liability waivers and indemnification forms are valid in most states for adults and in a few states for minors if properly written. [See Cotten & Cotten: Waivers and Releases of Liability. (2004)] Consult an attorney before attempting to develop and use any such agreement.

3. First aid/CPR training. Every group engaged in activity should have someone with first aid and CPR skills.

4. An emergency plan. The leader should know the agency's emergency plan. Be prepared! An emergency plan should include procedures not only for physical injuries that might occur but also procedures in case of fire and natural disasters (tornadoes, hurricanes, strong winds, floods, lightning, etc). There also should be procedures for lost children, runaways, and kidnapping (includes the "right" parent picking up a child).

5. Accident reporting. It is very important that every agency have a good accident reporting form that includes (a) identification information: activity/event date and time, person in charge, person injured with permanent address and telephone number, witnesses with addresses, participant's insurance; (b) specific location where injury occurred; (c) factual description of what happened . . . action of the injured –not opinion or what the leader thinks caused the injury; (d) what the injured could have done to prevent or reduce the severity of the injury (important related to participant's assumption of risk and reduction of any award in comparative fault states, which most states have); (e) the sequence of activity; (f) aid procedures; and (g) disposition, including medical diagnosis and amount of time before returned to activity

   The form should be completed promptly by the leader, if the leader witnessed the injury, or, if the leader did not witness the injury, by someone who was present. The form should be filed with the agency and retained for the period of time specified by state law for statute of limitations. Be careful of "hear-say"!

   Most agencies have liability insurance coverage for its leadership, including volunteers, or they provide liability indemnification. Further, the Federal Volunteer Protection Act provides for immunity for ordinary negligence to qualified volunteer leaders in public and nonprofit agencies, and many states have a similar immunity law for nonprofit agency volunteers. "Qualified" means holds the appropriate credential, where there is one; for example, if life guarding, one should hold a valid life saving certificate.

To learn a little more about risk management related to outdoor activities, see:

Standards Programs:

   Accreditation Standards for Camp Programs and Services. Martinsville, IN: American Camp Association. See latest edition. The American Camp Association (ACA) also has additional risk management materials.

   Manual of Accreditation Standards for Adventure Programs. Boulder, CO: Association for Experiential Education. See latest edition. AEE also has additional materials on risk management.

Releases and Waivers:

Cotten, Doyice J., and Mary B. Cotten. *Waivers and Releases of Liability.* 2004, 4th ed. Sport Risk Consulting, 403 Brannen. Dr., Statesboro, GA 30458.

Risk Management:

Safety-wise. Girl Scouts of the USA. Especially for the individual leader.

Priest, Simon, and Michael Gast. *Effective Leadership in Adventure Programming.* Champaign, IL: Human Kinetics, 1997. Chapter 10. Risk Management.

van der Smissen, Betty, and Charles "Reb" Gregg. "Chapter 39. Legal Liability and Risk Management" in Miles, John C., and Simon Priest (editors). *Adventure Programming.* State College, PA: Venture Publishing, 1999.

Head, George L., and Melanie L. Herman. *Enlightened Risk Taking, A Guide to Strategic Risk Management for Nonprofits.* 2002. Washington, DC: Nonprofit Risk Management Center.

Herman, Melanie L., and Barbara B. Oliver. *Vital Signs, Anticipating, Preventing and Surviving a Crisis in a Nonprofit.* 2001.

Washington, DC: Nonprofit Risk Management Center. The Center has additional risk management materials: check website — www.nonprofitrisk.org

SECTION C
COMMUNITY RESOURCES

Before an overall program of nature-oriented activities for the community can be developed, program developers must be knowledgeable regarding the many nature-oriented services available in the community. A community survey must be taken that asks three basic questions:

1. What nature-oriented activities are currently being conducted in the community for various age and ability groups?

    •   What are schools doing in their science classes and in extracurricular activities? Do they have an environmental education program?

    •   Are voluntary agencies involved in nature-oriented programming?

    •   What are nature centers, arboretums, gardens, libraries, museums, zoos, nurseries, greenhouses, and so on, doing in the way of community programs?

    •   Which community clubs and organizations are active in nature-oriented programs and activities?

2. What is needed in the community to have a well-balanced and complete nature-oriented program?

    •   Determine which population groups are not receiving an opportunity to participate.

    •   Determine which facets of the nature-oriented program areas are not being provided.

3. What resources are available for meeting recognized needs?
   - What natural and human resources in the community are available for developing nature-oriented program areas to meet specific needs?
   - Is the agency that you represent the best one for carrying out a specific type of nature-oriented program?
   - What are the opportunities for developing partnerships and cooperative agreements?

TYPES OF COMMUNITY RESOURCES

There are many community resources for the leader, including:: (1) natural areas to which field trips can be made; (2) organizations that offer nature-oriented programs to groups; (3) nature-related businesses; and (4) people with an interest in the environment and with either general knowledge regarding the outdoors or knowledge in a specific aspect of the outdoors.

Natural Areas

The out-of-doors, and its vast storehouse of native materials, is not far away. You need only to step outside the door to find yourself in nature and at a place where you can begin outdoor activities. Different areas that contribute to nature programs and serve as resources and places to go on field trips can be found in every community. A number of such places are described in this section. Take time to look around in your community for areas that can be used for nature activities. Make a few inquiries. You will be amazed at the many opportunities waiting for you and others who are interested in nature. What community does not have a park, forest area, or stream nearby? Vacant lots, gardens, and other natural areas are just around the corner waiting to be explored. Most of the natural areas that you will want to visit are free. If private property is to be visited, proper arrangements should be made including securing permission and letting the owner know your plans ahead of time.

Wildlife Preserves and Bird Sanctuaries. Many communities are near areas set aside as wildlife preserves. An effort is made to provide the type of habitat that will attract and hold wildlife. Hunting is not permitted in these areas and animals show less fear than they do in other settings. Therefore, it becomes an excellent place to observe wildlife in its natural environment. Many communities and organizations maintain their own bird sanctuaries and feeding stations.

Farms. For many urban children, few experiences are as thrilling as spending time on a farm exploring. Most farms have a variety of intriguing areas that offer opportunities for nature study. On the farm children can have firsthand experiences with domesticated animals and learn about their living habits as well as how they are cared for.

Some farms have small wooded areas where visitors can become familiar with the woodland plants and life. Prairie flowers and animal life abound in pastures. Some farms have a pond, stream, or lake where you can try your hand at fishing or studying water life.

Carefully choose the farm to visit to be sure it contains the kinds of things that will help you achieve your objectives. If the farmer is enthusiastic, likes people, and has the knack for creating interest, a great deal can be added to your group's trip to the farm. Some farms are highly specialized in such areas as poultry or dairying, and you may be disappointed if you expect to find other types of animals or activities. However, visits to specialized "farms" can be very educational and interesting. Some farms specialize exclusively in vegetables or even a specific vegetable (pumpkins, watermelon, tomatoes, etc.); other farms specialize in more unusual animals or products such as minks, hamsters, guinea pigs, bees, domesticated rabbits, or an endless variety of other specialties.

Parks. Parks vary greatly in purpose, size, and content, but almost every community has a park of one type or another. It may be the small neighborhood park which consists primarily of a playground for the children; or it may be a large city park complete with playgrounds, picnic areas, nature trails, and zoos.

Outside the city one may find county, state, or national parks, some of which may contain thousands of acres of natural area. Many of these parks provide the opportunity to study unique geological formations, plant and animal life, and natural history. They also provide opportunities for individuals/groups to engage in conservation service activities

Many of the larger parks and cities have interpretive services. (See Chapter VII, Section 8) Parks and other small park-like spaces in urban environments should not be overlooked for nature activities—from individual aesthetic enjoyment, bird walks, and care of plants to day camping and field plot studies.

Forest and Woodlands. Forests provide opportunities to conduct explorations as well as to carry on individual study in nature-related areas. Forests usually permit harvest of lumber, hunting, grazing, and other multiple uses that are not commonly permitted in parks. Forests tend to be larger in size and not as highly developed as parks, but often contain picnic areas and campgrounds. In the ecosystem, forests serve the crucial function of water conservation; therefore, they commonly have streams and lakes.

Forests are maintained by many different groups including government agencies, nonprofit organizations, and private ownership. Many state and federal government agencies manage woodlands, including the U.S. Forest Service, the National Park Service, the Bureau of Land Management, and the Corps of Engineers, and many others. Local, county, and regional parks also manage extensive acres of woodlands. Some of the larger metropolitan, county, and regional parks have areas of natural woods that can be easily utilized and are usually accessible.

Occasionally, forests are owned and maintained by community groups. Usually they are located on marginal land that was available at low cost. Woodlands may also be maintained by conservation districts to protect watersheds, and "natural areas" may be preserved by the Nature Conservancy and other private nonprofit groups dedicated to preserving the environment. These lands are usually available for educational and recreational activities.

Civic leaders, who understand the importance of forests in ecosystems, as well as their recreation benefits, are setting aside areas known as forest preserves located near heavily populated areas. Woodlands adequate for many nature activities are also owned by individual farmers and "second home" developments.

Gardens and Arboreta. Gardens vary in size. Some small private gardens are kept indoors, while some cities have botanical and flower gardens that cover many acres and contain a great variety of plants. Arboretums, under both private and public auspices, are found in many communities and provide a wide diversity of trees, shrubs, and other plants.

Many cities have flower gardens and arboretums which are open to the public where not only native plants and flowers can be seen but also plants and flowers from all over the world. In almost every community there are private flower gardens available for viewing. Some cities prepare maps for walking or driving tours to see these during the flowering period of plants, such as roses or azaleas. Also, festivals may be organized around plants (gardens), such as tulip festivals, cherry blossom time in Washington, D.C., and azalea festivals.

Historical/Cultural Resources. In 1996, the United States celebrated its Bicentennial recognizing the country's founding in 1976. This commemoration spanned a host of events focused on colonial history and highlighted the importance of cultural and historical interpretation as a vital part of understanding the environment. In early 2000, the nation commemorated the Lewis and Clark "Voyage of Discovery," commissioned by President Thomas Jefferson to explore the newly acquired Louisiana Purchase in hopes of finding a river route up the Missouri River to the Pacific Coast. The trip, from St. Louis to the Pacific Ocean off the coast of Washington State, lasted from 1804 through 1806 and was one of the most adventurous and daring journeys into often pristine lands. The Lewis and Clark Expedition were the first to encounter many groups of Native Americans where they lived and discovered many plants and animals that were unknown to their Eastern counterparts. The celebration of this milestone in American history resulted in numerous commemorative events and reenactments between 2004 and 2006 from Washington, D.C., to -Washington state. Traveling museums, exhibits, and first-person interpretive programs crossed the country. All of these activities rekindled interest in daily life in the early days of the country that was so closely intertwined with nature.

There are a continuing parade of states and cities that celebrate their past heritage through centennials and sesquicentennials, festivals, and oftentimes annual picnics and events. All of these events continue to emphasize the importance of understanding and valuing our historical heritage and resources.

Some parks, school environmental education programs, and historical societies have established "living crafts" or "pioneer crafts" centers, as well as special events such as medieval fairs and Civil War reenactments. In these centers individuals may practice the various skills that pioneers used in their daily lives. Visits to these centers and actual participation in their crafts provide excellent opportunities for nature activities for people of all ages. Village people specializing in the rural craft arts are also a fine community resource.

Further, most communities have areas and structures of historical significance that may be used to interpret their culture of times past. The local historical society and library is usually most willing to provide both personnel and literature resources. An increasing number of archeological "digs" have also been taking place and you may be fortunate to have one in your community or within easy field trip distance. A nearby college anthropology/archeology department may be able to help you in this type of activity. (See Historical-Cultural Activities in Chapter 6 .)

Rock Quarries. Working with rocks and minerals is a hobby that is developing an ever-growing number of enthusiastic supporters. Interests include rock and fossil collections, rock polishing, and gem making. Rock quarries are excellent hunting grounds for specimens. Permission should be obtained before entering, and safety precautions must be observed if you are taking a group of children to a quarry on a field trip. Sand pits also make interesting field trips. (See Chapter 6, Section E for rocks and minerals activities.)

Water Areas and Wetlands. Water areas and wetlands should not be overlooked in searching the community for areas in which to conduct your nature program. Usually the land bordering rivers, streams, and lakes is not suitable for farming. When these lands are not within the limits of a park or forest, they may provide you with an area undisturbed by people. Frequently, these will contain backwater, lagoons, bogs, and swamps which attract numerous species of animal life. The place of wetlands is being recognized today as an important part of our natural resources. They provide a home and food for many birds and animals and have a valuable contribution to make to our eco-system.

In addition to these areas (usually on private property), do not overlook public properties owned by the Corps of Engineers and other federal government agencies, as well as those owned by state agencies. Fish hatcheries are especially good educational field trips. And don't forget local water supply reservoir areas. (See Chapter 6, Section 8: Water, Streams, and Ponds)

Organizations that Offer Nature-Oriented Services

There are community resources dedicated to teaching about environmental quality. A few of these include the local public health departments (water quality), soil natural resource/conservation services, and county extension offices. These usually have printed materials, as well as personnel to assist.

There are facilities in communities that offer services to groups, in addition to serving the general public. These include museums, observatories, aquariums, zoos, and interpretive centers. These facilities have a staff, provide instructional activities and programs, and may host conventions and meetings.

Museums. Museums of some type can be found in almost every city. Most of these contain materials that help to interpret natural history and can be used to illustrate relationships. Museums are excellent places to obtain help in identifying materials gathered on field trips or to find detailed information concerning things you may have merely glimpsed while out in the field. Many museums have displays using native mounted animals and birds in simulated natural habitats which may be inspected from close range. They also contain rock and mineral collections that can be helpful in identifying rocks.

Many museums endeavor to make their program truly come alive and have interpretive naturalists on their staffs to help visitors. Museums often will send out specimens for nature centers to use. Some museums have workshops and offer courses related to nature study. See comments regarding museums and children's museums in previous section on "Who Should Sponsor Programs?" Do not overlook collections of many fields of natural science (e.g., rocks and minerals, insects, and plants), which may be maintained for instructional purposes by science departments in local colleges and universities.

Observatories and Planetariums. For individuals who are interested in exploring the heavens, a trip to the observatory and the planetarium is a must. An observatory is a dome-shaped building usually set on a high hill away from city lights. It contains such equipment as telescopes for the purpose of observing and studying heavenly bodies. The planetarium, on the other hand, usually has a dome-shaped ceiling that is used as a screen on which are shown pictures of stars and planets as they are seen in the sky. While the program emphasis at the observatory is often primarily on research, the program at the planetarium is educational. The planetarium staff will hold regularly scheduled lectures for visitors and classes for those who are interested in astronomy or in the making of telescopes. Many of them have workshops equipped to grind lenses. They also have many displays and exhibits.

While planetariums typically are found in larger cities, many smaller communities and some schools have observatories. Frequently the observatory is connected with a college and used in its astronomy department. (See Chapter 6, Section F: Astronomy.)

Aquariums. There has been a proliferation of aquariums at the end of the twentieth century, continuing into the twenty-first century. At one time, most all of the aquariums were located near oceans or other large bodies of water; now there are many that are quite distant from any sizable body of water. In addition to aquariums that interpret ocean ecology, there are now aquariums that focus on fresh water ecosystems.

In addition to exhibits that often include hands-on and interactive displays, aquariums typically have seminars and instructional opportunities. Group discounts and guided tours are usually available. Aquariums do an excellent job of helping the public to understand the critical importance of wetland, river, and ocean ecosystems.

Zoos. Children enjoy visits to the zoo. Here they have the opportunity to observe animals at close range where they can study in detail their shapes, colors, and movement. In modern zoos the animals are kept in natural areas simulating their native habitat. Many zoos now have children's areas with domesticated and baby animals that children are permitted to pet. Just as museums have extended their educational services, so have zoos, with many conducting special events, offering classes and workshops, and preparing exhibits which tell "a story" and interpret better the concerns regarding animals in the world.

Interpretive Centers. Interpretive centers have a long history as leaders in the environmental instruction, awareness, and appreciation movement. From the early days when many centers displayed specimens in jars and stuffed animals, these centers have evolved to focus on interpreting the natural environment in more and more meaningful ways to the general public and community groups and organizations.

Interpretive centers generally seek to inspire all citizens to be environmentally aware and responsible. Numerous programs range from discovery of the interrelationships of living things in the local environment to seminars and classes on recycling, composting, and making butterfly gardens. Interpretive centers are sponsored by both private and public agencies. (See Chapter VII, Section 8: Interpretive Services.)

Nature-Related Businesses

There are several nature-related businesses that usually are very willing to help with nature-oriented programs.

Greenhouses basically are indoor gardens, and the owners usually are happy to help people start their own gardens by providing them with seeds and plants. Why not take your group to visit a greenhouse and have the people there explain their program? Elevated plant boxes, commonly found in greenhouses, are especially effective for person using wheelchairs or those who have difficulty bending and stooping. However, there may be difficulties with maneuvering in small aisles, so the facility should be scouted prior to taking a group.

Commercial nurseries, as well as state nurseries, are excellent resources. These can be used to discuss home landscaping and the growth of woody plants, including Christmas trees.

Outdoor equipment stores often offer a wealth of services, some gratis and others with fees attached. These services include advice and consultation, workshops and courses, and trips and expeditions.

People with Interest in and Knowledge about the Environment

Don't forget to include local personnel in your inventory of resources. Every community has people who have become specialists in certain areas of nature study through participation in lifelong hobbies and interests. These people almost always are willing to share their enthusiasm and knowledge with anyone who shows interest. Frequently these people can be used effectively in leadership roles for programs, giving demonstrations or presenting a specific point of view. Many of these people have valuable and interesting collections and are eager to help others start collections of their own. They may serve as sponsors for youth hobby clubs. (See Knowledge Leader Section B in this chapter.) For example, gardening clubs are very active in many areas and the Master Gardener program is a nation-wide training system with organizations at the county level.

ORGANIZATIONS TO HELP YOU PLAN

Throughout this guide are many resources specific to the activities being discussed, including both literature and organizations websites. However, some organizations encompass many areas of nature-oriented activities and can be of considerable help to you not only in overall planning but also in keeping you informed of happenings in the environmental education and outdoor recreation fields. An organization you may wish to join is the National Audubon Society (http://www.audubon.org/) 700 Broadway, New York, NY 10003, Phone: (212) 979-3000, Fax: (212) 979-3188.

Its annual membership fee is reasonable and includes a subscription to its monthly magazine, *Audubon*. Other services include: Audubon camps in summer, usually for two weeks, as training sessions for teachers, youth leaders, and other interested adults; Audubon junior clubs; publications, such as nature bulletins and charts; photo and film services; Audubon centers, sanctuaries, wildlife research, and nature centers; wildlife tours; and consultative services. Many other organizations (most of which are cited in this manual under the appropriate activity) are excellent resources.

Environmental Organizations

American Forests, PO BOX 2000 | Washington, DC 20013
http://www.americanforests.org/

American Forest Foundation, 1111 19th Street, Suite 780, NW, Washington, DC 20036
http://www.affoundation.org/

American Nature Study Society, c/o Pocono Environmental Education Center, RR 2, Box 1010, Dinghams Ferry, PA 18328 http://www.nature-study.org/

Conservation International, 1919 M Street, NW Suite 600, Washington, DC 20036
http://www.conservation.org/xp/CIWEB/home

Environmental Defense Fund, 257 Park Avenue South, New York, NY 10010
http://www.environmentaldefense.org/home.cfm

Leave No Trace Center for Outdoor Ethics, P.O. Box 997, Boulder, CO 80306
http://www.lnt.org/index.php

National Wildlife Federation, 11100 Wildlife Center Drive, Reston, VA 20190-5362
http://www.nwf.org/

The Nature Conservancy, 4245 North Fairfax Drive, Suite 100, Arlington, VA 22203-1606
http://nature.org/

The Wildlife Conservation Society, 2300 Southern Boulevard, Bronx, New York 10460
http://www.bronxzoo.com/
(of course there are 100s of major museums and zoos)

Sierra Club, 85 Second Street, 2nd Floor, San Francisco, CA 94105
http://www.sierraclub.org/

See also the annual edition of *Conservation Directory*, published by the National Wildlife Federation. Extensive listings of organizations and agencies with addresses, officials, et al. (citation under General Nature Books)

Professional Organizations

American Camp Association, 5000 State Road 67 North, Bradford Woods, Martinsville, IN 46151-7902.
http://www.acacamps.org/
(focuses on organized camping, both day and resident camps.)

Association for Experiential Education, 2305 Canyon Boulevard, Suite #100, Boulder, CO 80302-5651
http://www.aee.org/

Canadian Camping Association, Box 74030, Edmonton, AB · T5K 2S7
http://www.kidscamps.com/canadian-camping/

National Association of Environmental Professionals, P.O. Box 2086, Bowie, MD 20718
http://www.naep.org/

National Association for Interpretation, P.O. Box 2246, Fort Collins, CO 80522
http://www.interpnet.com/interpnet/about.htm

National Marine Educators' Association, P.O. Box 1470, Ocean Springs, MS. 39566-1470
http://www.marine-ed.org/

North American Association for Environmental Education, 410 Tarvin Road, Rock Spring, GA 30739
http://naaee.org/

Government Agencies

Bureau of Land Management, Learning Landscapes, U.S. Department of Interior.
http://www.blm.gov/education/

County Extension Offices. Most counties have an office operated by the U.S. Department of Agriculture and the state land grant university. Many excellent booklets, services (such as garden plot analysis, soil testing, etc), and personnel are often available and most willing to assist in program development. The Cooperative State Research, Education and Extension Service (CSREES), an agency in the Department of Agriculture, provides a list of state administrators with telephone numbers, e-mail and fax numbers. These contacts can identify local agencies and provide overview of services available.
http://www.csrees.usda.gov/qlinks/ extension/state_directory.html

Forest Service (U.S. Department of Agriculture), P.O. Box 96090, Washington, D.C., 20090-6090
http://www.fs.fed.us/

National Park Service, 1849 C Street NW, Washington, DC 20240
http://www.nps.gov/

Soil Conservation Districts (Local districts can be located using the National Association of Conservation Districts site:
http://www.nacdnet.org/)

U.S. Geological Survey.
http://www.usgs.gov/

Youth Groups

Boy Scouts of America, National Council, P.O. Box 152079, Irving, Texas 75015-2079
http://www.scouting.org/

Camp Fire USA, 4601 Madison Avenue, Kansas City, MO 64112 (national office)
http://www.campfire.org/start.asp

Girl Scouts of the U.S.A., 420 Fifth Avenue New York, NY 10018-2798
http://www.girlscouts.org/

4-H and local County Extension Office, 4-H in the USA, 1400 Independence Ave. SW, Washington DC 20250-2225
http://www.4h-usa.org/

YMCA, 1701 K Street, NW, Suite 903, Washington, DC 20006 (many summer camps and year round camp facilities across the country)
http://www.ymca.net/index.jsp

Activity Specific Organizations

American Hiking Society, 1422 Fenwick Lane, Silver Spring MD 20910
http://www.americanhiking.org/index.html

Garden Clubs of America, 598 Madison Avenue, New York, NY 10022
http://www.gcamerica.org/ (could not confirm this address from website)

Izaak Walton League of America, 707 Conservation Lane, Gaithersburg, MD 20878
http://www.iwla.org/ (fishing)

National Audubon Society, 700 Broadway, New York, NY 10003
http://www.audubon.org/ (Birds)

National Field Archery Association, 31407 Outer I-10, Redlands, California 92373
http://www.nfaa-archery.org/

National Rifle Association of America, 11250 Waples Mill Road, Fairfax, Virginia 22030
http://www.nra.org/

National Speleological Society, Inc., 2813 Cave Avenue, Huntsville, AL 35810
http://www.caves.org/

North American Nature Photography Association, 10200 West 44th Avenue, Suite 304, Wheat Ridge, CO 80033-2840
http://www.nanpa.org/about.html

PERIODICALS

There are many specific topic periodicals. The following periodicals are of a general nature and include publications of some organizations listed in preceding section.

American Forests
Audubon
Backpacker
Camping Magazine
Christian Camping
The Conservationist (NY)
Current, J of Marine Education
EEK: Environmental Education for Kids Interactive Magazine, Wisconsin
    Department of Natural Resources.
       http://www.dnr.state.wi.us/org/caer/ce/eek/
Extensive Service Review
Journal of Environmental Education
Journal of Experiential Education (AEE)
National Geographic
National Geographic World
National Parks & Conservation Magazine
National Wildlife
Natural History Magazine
Nature Study (ANSA)
Outdoor America
Outside
Ranger Rick
Soil Conservation
Wilderness

GENERAL RESOURCES

Selected resources have been provided following certain sections; however, the following list includes general nature resources. These resources have ideas and projects relating to all of the sections in this chapter.

Copies of most all of the books cited have been reviewed, as have all of the Internet sites recommended. Brief annotations are provided for some of the resources.

Some references that are older and out of print have been purposely included when they provide excellent information. Frequently these resources can be found in public/school libraries or on the Internet. County extension agents frequently have a variety of helpful resources including pamphlets, software, and booklets.

The resources and information available on the Internet is ever expanding. A few sites have been suggested and although we have tried to select sites from well-established organizations or agencies (public, private, and governmental) that are likely to remain over time, there are always changes. We have provided suggestions for search words that we have used with some success when looking for information about specific topics.

Lists of ever-evolving, new materials can be found in periodicals and publication catalogs. Nature centers, conventions and workshops, and bookstores are also good places to check out the latest resources. Caution: be sure to check that crafts, games, and other activities are *nature-oriented*; too many suggestions in popular resources misuse nature materials or do not involve environmental education.

 General Nature Books and Periodicals

See master publicatons list for cities of Publishers.

Albert, Toni. (1998). *A Kid's Winter EcoJournal: With nature activities for exploring the season.* Trickle Creek Books: Mechanicsburg, PA. Provides writing pages where kids can keep a journal or write expressively. Includes short stories about nature and is chock-full of activities for kids in winter.

Albert, Toni. (1997). *A Kid's Spring EcoJournal: With nature activities for exploring the season.* Trickle Creek Books: Mechanicsburg, PA. Provides writing pages where kids can keep a journal or write expressively. Includes short stories about nature and is chock-full of activities for kids in the spring.

Albert, Toni. (1998). *A Kid's Summer EcoJournal: With nature activities for exploring the season.* Trickle Creek Books: Mechanicsburg, PA. Provides writing pages where kids can keep a journal or write expressively. Includes short stories about nature and is chock-full of activities for kids in the summer.

Albert, Toni. (1997). *A Kid's Fall EcoJournal: With nature activities for exploring the season.* Trickle Creek Books: Mechanicsburg, PA. Provides writing pages where kids can keep a journal or write expressively. Includes short stories about nature and is chock-full of activities for kids in the fall.

Byrd, Norma. (2000). Director's *Guide to Best Practices: Examples from the nature and environmental learning center profession.* Association of Nature Center Administrators.

Cohen, Michael. (2004). *Reconnecting with Nature: Finding wellness through restoring your bond with the earth.* Ecopress: Corvallis, OR. Suggests ways to use nature's wisdom to reawaken dormant sensitivities, rebuild spiritual connection with the earth, and enhance wellness.

Cornell, Joseph. (1989). *Sharing Nature with Children II.* Dawn Publications: Nevada City, CA. One of the best general nature books includes activities for adults and children.

Gilbert, Bethe; David Almeras; Sharon Cooper; Sharon Wynne. (2001). *Access Nature.* National Wildlife Federation. (Spiral edition)

Hamilton, Leslie. (1998). *Child's Play in Nature.* Berkley Publishing Group: NY . Games, science experiments, recipes, crafts and other activities.

Kahn, Peter, and Stephen Kellert (Eds.) (2002). *Children and Nature: Psychological, sociocultural, and evolutionary investigations.* MIT Press:

Cambridge, MA. (Incorporates research from cognitive science, developmental psychology, ecology, education, environmental studies, evolutionary psychology, political science, primatology, psychiatry, and social psychology.

Kellert, Stephen, and Timothy Farnham (Eds.). (2002). *The Good in Nature and Humanity: Connecting science, religion, and spirituality with the natural world.* Island Press: Washington. Series of articles.

Lawler, Elizabeth. (1993). *Discover Nature Close to Home: Things to know and things to do.* Stackpole Books: Harrisburg, PA.

Levin, Mark. Courtin, Jeanette. (1998). *Taming the Wild Outdoors: Building cooperative learning through outdoor education.* Good Apple, Inc.

Lingelbach, Jenepher, Purcell, Lisa. (2000), revised. *Hands-On Nature: Information and activities for exploring the environment with children.* Vermont Institute of Natural Science: Woodstock, VT. More than 40 natural science units grouped around five themes: adaptations, cycles, designs of nature, habitats, and earth and sky. Excellent source of activity ideas.

Miller, Lenore. (1986). *The Nature Specialist: A complete guide to program and activities.* American Camp Association: Bradford Woods, IN.

National Wildlife Federation Staff. (2003). *Conservation Directory 2004: The Guide to Worldwide Environmental Organizations.* National Wildlife Federation.

Northwind Press. (1999). *Fun with Nature: A take-along guide.* Northwind Press: Chanhassen, MN. Not really a "take-along" guide since it is a hard back, fairly heavy book. Good information and craft ideas in chapters on: caterpillars, bugs and butterflies; frogs, toads and turtles; snakes, salamanders and lizards; rabbits, squirrels and chipmunks; tracks, scats and signs; and trees, leaves, and bark.

Petrash, Carol. (1992). *Earthways: Simple environmental activities for young children.* Gryphon House: Beltsville, MD. Hands-on nature crafts and seasonal activities to enhance environmental awareness. Some very good activities.

Rogovin, Anne. (1992). *1,001 Activities for Children.* Gramercy Books: NY . Simple games to help a child explore the wonders of nature, the imagination, the senses, art, crafts, music, and more.

Rubenstein, Len. (1997). *The Big Book of Nature Projects.* Thames & Hudson. Developed at the Children's School of Science at Woods Hole, MA, 50+ hands-on projects.

 General Nature Internet Sites

Nature Study on Line.
http://www.earthfoot.org/nsonline/welcome.htm

Backyard Nature with naturalist Jim Conrad:
http://www.backyardnature.net/

Science Reading Room: Nature Study, Nature Writing: Past & Present.
http://www.loc.gov/rr/scitech/SciRefGuides/nature.html

PBS Nature & Wildlife:
http://www.pbs.org/neighborhoods/nature/

Acorn Naturalists, sell resources for science, outdoor and environmental education:
http://www.acornnaturalists.com/store/

NATURE CRAFTS

Philip James Bailey once said: *Art is man's nature: nature is God's art.* It has been said that many mechanical and technological devices increasingly are depriving human beings of creative expression. Work with natural materials, where mechanical devices are at a minimum, offers an opportunity for personal expression. Originality and ingenuity constantly are being challenged. Valuable, too, is the concomitant learning found in this type of craft. Since crafts dealing with native materials have roots in the oldest inhabitants in the country, they can arouse an interest in indigenous people, roots of diverse cultures, and the history of crafts. Creating beautiful and useful articles from pine cones, shells, or acorns is a novel and interesting idea to most groups.

It is often much cheaper to work with seeds and grasses than it is to work with leather and metals. Such materials are inexpensive, frequently free, and usually relatively easy to find near your home, although they may vary greatly from one part of the country to another. When making crafts from native materials, the individual learns to work with raw materials and to feel the response of clay, sand, and other natural materials. Design ideas are everywhere if you can learn to recognize them. Nature in its beauty and variety provides a limitless source of design inspirations, but you must develop awareness in order to become sensitive to the design possibilities. As you become aware of the variety of beautiful shapes, colors, and textures in nature, good aesthetic taste and feeling for making beautiful things will develop.

Even though nature has provided an abundance of colorful and interesting craft materials, it is of utmost importance that persons engaging in these activities have knowledge about environmentally appropriate practices and conservation principles. Acceptable practices that exhibit environmental stewardship change from ecosystem to ecosystem. Ecotourism activities that aim to preserve ecosystems around the world have proliferated, typically supporting responsible use of natural materials by native craftsmen and women.

If individuals are in doubt about the environmental integrity of an activity in a particular environment, they should find definitive information to support their choices or avoid the possibility of harming the environment. Many natural materials are renewable resources, but many specific supplies are protected or at risk. No responsible person wants to jeopardize the future existence of any natural materials.

Groups should be cautioned not to take materials that will result in a lasting injury to an area. The days are long gone when tree products could be harvested wherever they stood. Most all public parks and spaces prohibit cutting live trees, although there are sometimes exceptions in specific areas for gathering or cutting down wood for firewood and other activities. In the National Parks it is illegal to remove any natural material, dead or alive, even from the ground cover. Live bark should not be taken from trees. No materials from trees that are living or dead should be taken unless permission is granted and a plan for environmental sustainability is being followed. Some places once rich with wild flowers and saplings are gone because of ruthless and indiscriminate cutting. Respect for sources of craft materials may be developed by having the group set aside an area in which plants are grown specifically for use in the craft program.

As used here, nature crafts include those objects made by hand using native materials and reproductions of native materials in the various art forms *in an environmentally responsible manner*. This chapter is not meant to be exhaustive, but only suggestive of the vast scope of nature crafts. The following sections are included: (A) Crafts from Trees; (B) Crafts from Plants; (C) Crafts from Nonplant Materials; (D) Reproductions; and (E) Preservation.

SECTION A
CRAFTS FROM TREES

GATHERING MATERIALS

So where do you get supplies in an environmentally responsible manner? There are many options depending on specific circumstances. In general, people are advised to use tree materials that are dead and on the ground. Woods managed commercially are periodically thinned, producing many wood products that are generally discarded. There are many commercial craft shops that sell wood and wood products for carving and crafts. Specific types of wood can also be procured from companies that sell lumber.

Trees can furnish a great variety of materials that can be used effectively in a nature craft program. All parts of the tree including its roots, bark, twigs, nuts, and flowers have been used by native peoples over generations for clothing, shelter, fire, and food. For many craft activities, no substitute material can bring the same satisfactions that working with wood itself does. Following is a list of some woods frequently used in making craft items:

- *Basswood*—best of the carving woods for ease and for beginners. Inner bark is excellent for fiber material used in making cordage; it can be used also for the same purposes as raffia. Green basswood is one of the best woods for making whistles.

- *Cedar* —an excellent whittling wood that has beautifully colored heartwood. Old trees have interesting roots and gnarled sections. Wood is very resistant to decay. Cedar is often used in fire-by-friction sets as fireboard and drill.

- *Hickory* —one of the best woods for making coals for broiling. Inner bark can be used for lashing. Slender green branches can be bent for making toasters and frames. Hickory nuts are excellent food. It is a preferred wood for axe handles. Native Americans used hickory to make bows.

- *Sassafras* —roots are famous as a source of sassafras tea, although there are studies that indicate it may be linked to liver cancer if consumed in large quantities. Small twigs can be cut into beads and easily strung. Bark can be removed and the green wood may be pounded for splints for use in basketry.

- *Willow* —may use young shoots for basketry, particularly where sharp bends are not required. Used for whistles. Bark can be used for binding material on chair bottoms. Straight shoots often are used for making willow beds.

- *Witch hazel* —best of the woods for making "pulled" whisk brooms. (See section in this chapter on "How to Make a Whisk Broom" for instructions.)

Additional woods are listed under whittling and wood carving.

WHITTLING AND WOOD CARVING

Whittling and wood carving belong to the group of truly great crafts that are rapidly disappearing. During pioneer days, almost everyone knew how to use a knife and had developed enough skill in woodcarving to make tools and implements as needed. See Chapter 4, Section D[msh1]: Toolcraft for information about pocketknife handling and safety.

Most people become very enthusiastic about wood carving once they get started and learn some of the basic skills. Following are some tips for beginners:

- When working with beginners or those of varying abilities, using appropriate knives and selecting the right type of wood can be the keys to success and safety, especially for individuals with visual impairments or lack of coordination.

- Get a good quality knife that has several blades of various shapes and sizes. The handle should fit comfortably in the hand.

- Sharpen the knife on a carborundum stone. New knives are not always highly sharpened. You will be less likely to cut yourself with a sharp blade than with a dull one that is difficult to control and can easily catch and/or slip.

- Always cut away from the body, as well as any body parts (thighs, legs, etc.)

- Wrap all fingers around the knife. Avoid using the thumb to push the blade. It may snap shut on the other fingers at the end of a cut. If you need to use the thumb to guide finer cuts, make sure the thumb is entirely on the knife handle and not the knife blade.

- Select a piece of soft wood such as basswood or white pine for your first project. Start with a simple design of an animal and use a jigsaw or coping saw to cut the wood down to its approximate shape. Begin to round off the edges and to shape the wood into the design. While rounding off the edges, you learn quickly how to hold the knife for good control and how the knife cuts better when you cut with the grain of the wood rather than against it. Take bold strokes at the beginning and smaller ones when you are completing the shaping.

- Use sandpaper to smooth out the rough edges. Begin with a medium-grain paper and finish with a fine-grain paper.

- Use a paste floor wax or linseed oil for a finish. Apply directly to sanded surface and rub it in with a soft cloth or your fingers. Repeat this operation until the desired luster is obtained. Avoid using finishes that cover or destroy the natural beauty of the wood. Varnishes and shellacs are suitable, but take time to dry. Shellacs mixed with alcohol (1 to 2) work well and dry faster with fewer bubbles. Surfaces should be sanded lightly between coats. When you are working with groups, remember they are likely to leave messy brushes. Be sure to have an ample supply of the appropriate cleaning fluids. Also there should be a place where projects can be left to dry.

You can experience great satisfaction when you find a piece of wood or a branch in the outdoors and start to work on it. After looking over the piece that you have picked up, you will begin to get some ideas of possible design. You may see in the wood a letter opener or a little squirrel. Only you and your pocketknife can take away the excess wood and release the letter opener or the squirrel from its prison. The following are good whittling woods:

- *Apple*—brownish wood that takes a beautiful polish (hard wood)
- *Basswood*—one of the best for beginners (soft wood)
- *Cherry*—reddish-brown wood excellent for whittling (hard wood)
- *Osage orange*—difficult to carve, but one of the most beautiful carving woods (hard wood)
- *Red cedar*—excellent for whittling, but splits easily (hard wood)

- *Walnut* —a harder wood, but extremely beautiful when polished (hard wood)
- *White pine* —excellent for beginners (soft wood)

 Books On Whittling and Wood Carving

See master publicatons list for cities of Publishers.

Bartlett, Patricia M. (2000). *Driftwood Sculpture from Finding to Fine Finishing.* Waterfront Publications.

Beiderman, Charles, and Johnston, William. (1993). *The Beginner's Handbook of Woodcarving: with Project Patterns for Line Carving, Relief Carving, Carving in the Round, and Bird Carving.* Dover Publications. Lots of patterns included in 8 1/2 X 11 format.

Bodhus, Willard, and Beving, James. (1985). *How to Teach Whittling and Wood Carving.* Almar: Binghamton, NY. (out of print, limited availability)

Buchanan, Joyce. (2000). *Carving Wood Spirits in Tree Bark.* 2nd edition. Fox Chapel Publishing.

Bütz, Richard. (1984). *How to Carve Wood: A Book of Projects and Techniques.* Taunton Press: Newton, CT. Includes chapters on whittling, chip carving, and wildlife carving.

Carstenson, Cecil C. (1981). *The Craft and Creation of Wood Sculpture.* Dover Publications: NY. (out of print, limited availability)

Colletti, Jack. (1977). *The Art of Wood Carving.* Simon & Schuster. (out of print, limited availability)

Fox-Wilson, Frank. (2000). *Carving Nature: Wildlife Studies in Wood.* Guild of Master Craftsman Publications Ltd.

Gottshall, Franklin H. (1980). *Wood Carving for Everyone.* Scribner: NY. (out of print, limited availability)

Green, H.D. (1982). *Patterns and Instructions for Carving Authentic Birds.* Dover Publications.

Higginbotham, Bill, (1982). *Whittling.* Sterling: NY.

Hunt, W. Ben. (1970). *Big Book of Whittling.* Macmillan: NY. (out of print, limited availability)

Ishimoto, Laruso. (1957). *The Art of Driftwood and Dried Arrangements.* Crown Publishers: NY. (out of print, limited availability)

Pergrin, David. (1985). *The Carver's Handbook: Wood Carving Wild Animals.* Schiffer: West Chester, PA.

Phillips, Lois B. (1978). *Wildlife Woodcraft,* Naturegraph. Happy Camp: CA. (out of print, limited availability)

Tangerman, E.J. (1989). *Complete Guide to Woodcarving.* Borgo Press: San Bernardino, CA.

Internet Sites on Whittling and Wood Carving

Suggested search words: whittling/woodcarving/knives/carving wood

National Wood Carvers Association:
http://www.chipchats.org/

Woodworking.com whittling page:
http://www.woodworking.com/
wwtimes_whittling.cfm

Museum of Woodworking Tools:
http://www.toolsforworkingwood.com/

Driftwood

Use driftwood in its natural state. Scrub and clean the wood. It is preferable to leave driftwood in this natural, clean state with no finish; however, it may be rubbed down with oil or wax. *Driftwood should never be painted or varnished.* Use driftwood for decorative purposes or carve into statuary, jewelry, lamp bases, centerpieces, mobiles, or totem poles.

Roots and Burls

Roots and burls (a hard, woody outgrowth on a tree, more or less round in form) can be very difficult to carve and you need a good knife to be successful. They can be carved into jewelry, figures, or used in natural shape (burls) for containers or dishes.

Twigs and Branches

By whittling and carving twigs and branches you can make buttons, buckles, match holders, candleholders, shepherd pipes, soap dishes, camp furniture, coat hangers, birdhouses, whisk brooms, spoons, forks, cooking utensils, animals, name tags, or pins. The possibilities are limitless. Equipment also can be made for various games such as tic-tac-toe and checkers from slices of twigs and branches. Another interesting project is to make a twig belt or necklace. Hiking sticks can be carved from branches. A shepherd pipe, whistle, or a bird or animal call can be made from willow or elderberry.

How to Make a Mushroom on a Log. A simple beginning project using a branch 2 to 3 inches in diameter and 3 to 4 inches long is a mushroom sitting on its own log. Use a dead limb that has bark on it and saw off both ends so that they are flat. Leave the bark on the bottom part as the base approximately an inch to an inch and a half high. Carve the top portion into the shape of a mushroom.

How to Make a Willow Whistle. As always, make certain that you have permission to cut wood (even branches) and that it is environmentally responsible to do so.

Step 1. Cut a 2½"–3" straight section of willow branch, elderberry, or basswood (or other similar wood which will permit the bark to be removed easily) without knots or joints and about ⅜"-½" in diameter. (Late fall and winter are not good times to make whistles as the sap isn't flowing.)

Step 2. Using a closed pocketknife, hammer the whole length of the branch, crushing the cells between bark and wood (inner), until you can slide the bark off in one piece. Be careful not to mutilate the bark, since it will be used as a slide. It should have no cracks through which air can escape as the whistle is blown.

Step 3. With your pocketknife, carefully make a vertical cut about ⅜ " from the smallest end to a point about one-third through the wood and a diagonal cut about ¼ " farther back, completing the notch as shown in diagram above.

Step 4. Now, slide the bark off, removing the core through the larger end, opposite the notch, to avoid splitting the bark.

Remove

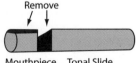

Mouthpiece   Tonal Slide

Step 5. Cut the wood (core removed from bark) into two pieces where the notch was made, as shown. The space left after removing the notched portion serves as the music box. The smaller piece is the mouthpiece and the larger one the tonal slide. Slice a thin piece (1/16" or less depending on the size of branch used) off the top of the mouthpiece for the air channel.

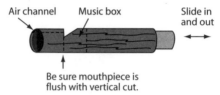

Air channel   Music box   Slide in and out

Be sure mouthpiece is
flush with vertical cut.

Step 6. Replace the mouthpiece in the end of the bark cylinder and the long tonal slide in the other end. Be sure the end of the mouthpiece is flush with the vertical cut in the bark, as indicated in the diagram. Leave the long piece (tonal slide) extended slightly so it can be held for sliding back and forth.

Step 7. Now blow-you should have a whistle! If you slide the tonal slide in and out slowly, you will have a multi-toned whistle of three or more tones depending upon the length you have used. Experiment with whistles of different lengths and diameters.

ACTIVITY

How to Make a Whisk Broom. If it is environmentally responsible to do so, select a freshly cut stick of ash, witch hazel, or sassafras that has a natural handle about ½ inch in diameter and 12 inches long (can vary in length).

Step 1. Cut away bark (peel off) from shaded area shown in the diagram. The length of the upper part of the peeling should be the length of the lower part plus the bark band, and a small amount extra for the fold.

Step 2. At brush end, peel wood fibers back (about toothpick size or smaller) to the band of the bark.

Step 3. Beginning at the handle end, peel around the stick until all the end is stripped into bristles.

Step 4. Begin pulling fibers at the handle point down toward the band of bark. Peel until about halfway through the stick.

Step 5. Now, fold the bristles from the upper portion down over the band and bind with cordage.

Bark band

Peel   Handle

Bark

Bark should not be taken without permission or when it is damaging to the environment. Bark should not be taken from live trees. Bark can be used for pictures, collages, greeting cards, block printing, and containers of all types. Birch bark is the best suited for bark crafts. To secure bark, make a straight cut down the trunk of the tree or limb and work the bark off with a wedge. In preparing it for use, soak it in hot water if you wish to make it pliable. Bark bookmarks, book covers, hatbands, and pocketbooks all are easy to make. Just cut the bark, soak it, punch holes, sew it together with cordage, and then carve your own design. Bark duck floats, animals, whistles, and various bird calls (see willow whistles) can be made with a little effort and interest. See general craft resources at the end of chapter for techniques

 **Internet Sites on Bark**

Suggested search words: *bark/nature bark/bark crafts*

The West Virginia University Tree Bark Website:
http://www.caf.wvu.edu/bark/

Make a Bark Rubbing:
http://www.21stcenturyadventures.com/AdventureKids/ naturecraft.html

Making Cordage

Bark and plants should not be taken without permission or when it is damaging to the environment. The inner bark of some woods, such as basswood, elm, and roots of certain trees (white spruce for example) and shrubs, as well as plants such as Indian hemp, milkweed stem, yucca, and stinging nettle, provided Native Americans with materials for making cordage for lacings, rope, nets, and fish lines. See general craft resources at the end of chapter and resources for campcraft at the end of Chapter 4 for techniques.

 Internet Sites on Cordage

Suggested search words: cordage/rope making/rope crafts

Native American Cordage, Nativetech page:
http://www.nativetech.org/cordage/

Rope Works:
http://www.northnet.org/ropeworks/

Rope Maker:
http://www.rope-maker.com/index.html

Nuts

Nuts, such as walnuts, hickory nuts, butternuts, and acorns can be used for jewelry, belts, lapel pixies, and so on. Lapel pins may be made by gluing nut shells together or by carving them. Nut buttons are made by using the whole nut or by cutting it into sections. Belts can be made by slicing a nut with a hacksaw, holding the nut in a vise. Clean the nut first with a wire brush. Sandpaper the cut edges and then wax, oil, or shellac. For belts, string on rawhide thongs. Bracelets, brooches, and earrings in matching sets also may be made from nuts.

Pine Needles (Long)

Use long dry pine needles, where it is environmentally appropriate to gather them, for weaving basketry and making pillows and brooms.

Basketry

Making useful and beautiful containers from native materials is one of the oldest known crafts. Primitive people had few tools but were able to make many things by twisting and knotting pliable plants. Native materials suitable for making baskets can be found in every country. Because materials are readily available, basketry has become an important part of many nature craft programs.

Some of the materials found in the United States include honeysuckle, willow, woodbine or Virginia creeper, pine needles, and such nontree materials as cornhusks, sweet grass, rye, broom straw, cattails, and rushes. Most of these materials should be gathered while they are still green and then dried slowly, turning them at frequent intervals. Most of these will have to be moistened when it is time to use them. The following woods may be pounded to make splints for pack baskets and other similar basketry weaves: black ash, sassafras, American ash, hickory, and basket oak.

There are three basic techniques used in the construction of baskets: braiding, plaiting, and coiling.

 **Books on Basketry**

See master publicatons list for cities of Publishers.
Bernick, Kathryn. (1998). *Basketry & Cordage from Hesquiat Harbour: British Columbia.* University of British Columbia.
Christopher, J. Frederick. (1952). *Basketry.* Dover Publications: Mineola, NY.

Gillooly, Maryanne (editor). (1992). *Natural Baskets: Create over 20 Unique Baskets with Materials Gathered in Gardens, Fields and Woods.* Storey Books: Pownal, VT. Excellent illustrations and good directions.

Hart, Carol, and Dan Hart. (1977). *Natural Basketry.* Watson-Guptill Publications: NY. (out of print, limited availability)

Lonning, Kari. (2000). *The Art of Basketry.* Sterling Publications.

Mallow, Judy. (1997). *Pine Needle Basketry: From Forest Floor to Finished Project.* Lark Books.

Meilach, Dona Z., and Dee Menagh. (1979). *Basketry Today with Materials from Nature.* Crown Publishers: NY. (out of print, limited availability)

Navajo School of Indian Basketry (1971). *Indian Basket Weaving.* Navajo School of Indian Basketry. Dover Publications.

Emberton, Jane. (1979). *Pods, Wildflowers and Weeds in their Final Beauty.* McMillan Publishing, Co. (out of print, limited availability)

Steitz, Quentin. (1987). *Grasses, Pods, Vines, Weeds: Decorating with Texas Naturals.* University of Texas Press.

 Internet Sites on Basketry

Suggested search words: basketry/native baskets/nature baskets

Basketry Information:
http://www.beebes.net/basket/index.html

Native Basketry: Survival, Beauty:
http://www.kstrom.net/isk/art/basket/baskmenu.html

National Basketry Organization, Inc:
http://www.nationalbasketry.org/

Hopi Basketry:
http://www.nau.edu/~hcpo-p/arts/bas1.htm

Nativetech.org Basketry page:
http://www.nativetech.org/coil/

Boy Scout Basketry Merit Badge:
http://www.meritbadge.com/bsa/mb/027.htm

Pine Cones

Christmas tree ornaments, animals, mobiles, bird feeders, dolls, and collages can be made with pinecones that can be used in block printing, too.

ACTIVITY

How to Make an Owl Pin. A simple but attractive pin can be made by breaking off pinecone petals in graduated sizes to make an owl pin. Glue three petals in ascending size on a twig the size you prefer for a pin. With dots of white paint, make eyes on each petal. Glue a pin clasp to the back of the twig.

Nature Pixies. Making nature pixies is a delightful craft that challenges the creativity of both the young and the old. Nature pixies are animals made by combining a variety of seeds, pods, and other natural items.

Dried Nut — Feathers — Seed — Seed Hull — Pinecone

Making the pixies is not difficult, but you should have a generous supply of materials on hand before beginning, such as pine cones, acorns, hickory nuts, melon seeds, twigs, cornhusks, bark, feathers, and so on. Other materials and tools that can be used to put the pixies together are pipe cleaners, fine wire, quick drying glue, thin-nosed pliers, a hand drill with small bits, and a hacksaw. A wire brush is useful to use on hickory nuts and walnuts.

It is good to have an idea in mind before you begin to explore the possibilities of putting the materials together to make the figure. Large pine cones make wonderful turkeys, while small pine cones make interesting mice, rabbits, and birds. Swans may be made from milkweed pods.

SECTION B

CRAFTS FROM PLANTS

There is quite a variety of plants other than trees, such as berries, cattails, corn, fungi and lichens, gourds, grasses, mosses, seed pods, and seeds, that can be used for crafts. Perhaps the best known are grasses. Making crafts from plants is a three-step activity: (1) gathering, (2) preparing the plant material, and (3) making the craft.

Field trips can be taken to collect materials. Be sure to obtain necessary permissions to collect from any public or private site. Good conservation practices should be carefully observed so that plant materials remain available in the future.

Before making crafts from plants, you must prepare the plant material so that it holds up, that is maintains color, pliability, and other natural characteristics and does not deteriorate easily. This ensures that the craft made from plant material has a particular level of quality and will last.

BERRIES

Use berry juice for dyeing or staining. Different berries produce different colors. (See the section on dyeing). String them for ornaments.

CATTAILS

Cattail leaves can be used for weaving, basketry, or decorative arrangements. The tails can be used in decorative arrangements.

CORN

Cornhusks can be used to make braided sandals, baskets, flowers, brooms, dolls, and so on. The best cornhusks for craft work are those from the inner layer of husks next to the silks. Dry husks in the shade for a soft green color, or in the sun for a bleached white color. Husks are readily dyed with fabric dye or with native dyes. Hair, eyebrows, and moustaches for dolls may be made out of corn silks or yarn. Baskets are made by taking strands of braided cornhusks and sewing them together. Even brooms can be made from the husks. Corncobs can be used for dolls, puppets, animals, buttons, and even block printing. Whistles, animals, and furniture can be made from cornstalks.

FUNGI AND LICHENS

As with all living things, care must be used when taking fungi and lichens from the wild. For the most part, only specimens that are not alive should be collected. Lichens should not be disturbed unless they are loose on the ground. As always permission must be secured and only things that fit in the environmental sustainability plan should be collected.
Use flat bracket fungus for small, decorative shelves or name plaques. If the fungus is gathered before it begins to dry out, you can write your name or some message on it that remains after it is dried and shellacked for preservation.
Collect turkey-tail fungus from dead branches or logs, the small shell and larger gray lichens. Dye in permanent ink or use a fabric dye. *Do not try dyeing with tempera, paint, or shellac* because the texture will be ruined. When dyed with ink or fabric dye each fungus has two intensities of color in rings. Trim fungus end that was attached

to the log. Make flowers, such as pansies, for a brooch and matching earrings. Glue pin on back. If a preservative is desired, use a light coat of clear plastic spray.

GOURDS

The shape of the gourd will suggest the object into which it will be made. Table pieces, dishes, salt and pepper shakers, birdhouses, rhythm band instruments, and decorations can be made from gourds.

GRASSES

Common wayside grasses may be used to weave beautiful placemats, baskets, or sit-upons. The tall grasses, such as sedge grass, swamp grass, or slough grass, are preferred, but over fifty kinds of related grasses found in every part of the United States can be used. The grass should be cut close to the ground to get long lengths of stem. It is best to cut the grass in the summer or fall after it has matured. It should be laid out to dry in a shady place for several days and then can be tied into bundles and stored until you are ready to use it. Grass may need to be soaked before use because of brittleness caused by drying.

The grass is prepared for weaving by cutting off the wiry tops and peeling the leaves from the stem. A floor or table loom is nice, but a cardboard loom can be substituted for the weaving of place mats. Use a coarse crochet thread or carpet warp for the warp. The weaving process is the same as that used in weaving oat, wheat, or rye straws and long pine needles.

Grasses also can be used effectively in making dry nature arrangements, basketry, and nature prints. For these purposes you will want to include some of the smaller, finer, and colorful grasses. Grasses can be dyed, although whenever possible the natural color should be retained.

Caution: Some people have allergies to certain grasses.

 ACTIVITY

How to Make a Navajo Loom. Use this loom for weaving solid stemmed rushes, cattails, sedges (triangular stems), or any tall grass.

Step 1. Cut two 48″ sticks and at least four 18″ stakes. Number of stakes used depends upon desired size of the mat and closeness of weaving.

Step 2. Lash one of the long sticks to a tree about 18″ to 24″ from the ground. Tie 8 pieces of twine to the stick at equal intervals (alternating 4′ and 5′ pieces.) Use a clove hitch to tie pieces to the stick.

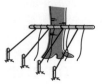

Step 3. Drive stakes into ground; be sure that at least 12″ is sticking out of the ground. Tie the shorter twine lengths to the tops of the stakes. Tie the longer strings to the other 48″ stick. When the strings are tied and pulled taut, the stick should be about 6″ beyond the stakes.

Step 4. Holding the big stick and its four strings up, lay in grass or whatever material is being used and push up tight against the stick attached to the tree.

Step 5. Lower the stick to the ground and put in another bunch of grass tightly against the next; then raise the stick. Continue with this procedure until mat is finished.

Step 6. Cut strings from sticks and stakes and tie ends in pairs with square knots, holding the grass together firmly.

You can make a thinner coaster by using single pieces of rushes or sedges, or thicker mats by using larger bunches of grass, and bigger mats by extending the length of twine and number of sticks. Be careful to use a sufficient number of strings to hold the grass firmly.

MOSSES

As with fungi and lichens, mosses must be gathered in an environmentally responsible manner. Never take mosses without permission or in a manner that may damage the environment. Mosses can be used for models, pictures, and displays.

SEED PODS

Use seed pods to make into jewelry, holiday decorations, rhythm instruments, and mobiles.

SEEDS OTHER THAN NUTS

Animals, dolls, beanbags, buttons, jewelry, rhythm instruments, mosaics, collages, blueprints, rubbings, murals, pictures, and signs can be made from seeds.

S E C T I O N   C

CRAFTS FROM NONPLANT MATERIALS

Nonplant materials offer a great variety of craft opportunities. Clay and rocks, especially, can become lifetime art forms, when clay becomes pottery and rocks become jewelry through lapidary. This section includes a selection of a few of the nonplant materials that can be found in natural settings. As with all things in nature, the collector should know and practice environmentally responsible collection.

BONES

Objects such as pirate ships can be made from the breastbones of chickens or other fowl. Neck bones can be used for neckerchief slides, animals, napkin rings. Bones also can be used for sculpting.

CLAY

Clay must be dug in an environmentally responsible manner to avoid erosion or disturbance of the environment. Dig clay from stream beds, lake beds, and excavations. Remove foreign matter. Mix in one tablespoon of dextrin to help the clay to harden. Mix well; add enough water to make thick modeling clay. Keep clay covered with wet cloths until used. A primitive kiln can be made for firing.

FEATHERS

Use feathers for backing of pictures, brooches, decorative arrangements, and decorations on objects. Only those feathers that have been shed and can be picked up easily should be used. Possession of feathers from certain protected birds and song birds may be illegal and result in significant fines. Eagle feathers are protected by federal law and may not be owned without proper permits. Check with your state or county natural resource or conservation office to determine what species are protected.

HORNS

Horns and antlers can be used in various ways, particularly as neckerchief slides and napkin rings. Large horns may be used for ornamental decorations, lamps, and so on.

ROCKS

Lapidary, the polishing and cutting of stones for jewelry or ornamentation, has been popular craft for many years. Chipping flint knives and arrowheads also can be an interesting hobby. Other projects include limestone carving, stone mosaics, and rock pictures (using different colors of soft rocks as chalk).

 Books on Rocks

See master publicatons list for cities of Publishers.

Kraus, Pansy D. (2003). *Introduction to Lapidary*. Chilton/Haynes.

Wellford, Lin. (1994). *The Art of Painting Animals on Rocks*. North Light Books.

Wellford, Lin. (1998). *Painting More Animals on Rocks*. North Light Books.

 Internet Sites on Rocks
(Lapidary, Chipping)

Suggested search words: rocks/lapidary/gem polishing

The Eclectic Lapidary (free publication written by and for rockhounds, mineralists, gemologists, and lapidary enthusiasts):
http://www.bovagems.com/eclectic/

Lapidary Journal:
http://www.lapidaryjournal.com/

Atlas of Igneous and Metamorphic Rocks, Minerals & Textures (part of the virtual geology project at the University of North Carolina):
http://www.geolab.unc.edu/Petunia/IgMetAtlas/mainmenu.html

Rocks for Kids (of all ages):
   http://www.rocksforkids.com/

Rocks and Minerals (The Franklin Institute online):
   http://sln.fi.edu/tfi/units/rocks/rocks.html

Collecting Rocks (US Geological Service):
   http://pubs.usgs.gov/gip/collect1/ collectgip.html

Fossils, Rocks and Time (US Geological Service):
   http://pubs.usgs.gov/gip/fossils/ contents.html

SAND

Most youngsters at one time or another have built castles and other objects in the sand. For crafts, however, sand is used primarily as a casting material for reproductions and for sand painting. (See Section D in this chapter for sand-casting techniques.)

 ACTIVITY

Sand painting. Obtain *fine*, preferably white, clean sand on a collecting trip. To dye the sand use regular all-purpose dye, food coloring, or tempera paints. Experiment with dyes and the amount of water needed until you get the colors you want. Remember that when the sand is wet it will be much darker than when it dries. Dry sand by spreading it out in the sun. Store in clear plastic containers or jars (so you can see the colors) or in boxes.

How to Paint

Step 1. Draw the picture you want to paint in outline and decide on colors.

Step 2. Mix glue (such as Elmer's Glue) with equal parts of water.

Step 3. Brush glue on design, covering only the area for one color at a time, then sprinkle that color of sand on the design.

Step 4. Let stand a few seconds to dry and shake off excess sand onto a piece of paper so that it may be returned to the storage container for reuse. Put lighter colors on first. Continue brushing glue and sprinkling sand until all colors are on.

SHELLS

Trays, artificial flowers, jewelry, animals, Christmas tree ornaments, mobiles, mosaics, and block prints are all possible projects using shells. Spoons can be made easily from clam and mussel shells.

SECTION D
CRAFTS THAT ARE REPRODUCTIONS

Three types of reproductions are included in this section: (1) nature prints of leaves, flowers, ferns, and grasses; (2) casting; and (3) sketching.

NATURE PRINTS OF LEAVES, FLOWERS, FERNS, AND GRASSES

Although spatter prints, blueprints, and ozalid prints are easy and inexpensive forms of nature printing, they show less detail than other types and are not as useful for identification or notebook collections. Crayon prints and oil and smoke prints can be used for identification, for making attractive note paper, and for making coverings for boxes and containers. Christmas cards, program decorations, and leaf scrapbooks also can be made. Block prints and spray, oil, and spatter prints may be made directly on fabric if suitable inks or paints are used. Heavy materials and materials with a coarse weave do not take the prints as satisfactorily as lighter weight materials. Ink-pad prints are a handy method if for some reason you want to make prints in the field. Leaves also may be reproduced by hammering on cloth, photographic printing, and carbon paper printing.

 ACTIVITY

How to Make Hammered Leaf Prints.

Step 1. Assemble the following supplies:

- Prewashed 100% cotton fabric (without permanent press finish). Muslin used by quilters is cheap and works very well.
- Smooth panel (old thin board or cutting board). Best results are obtained when board is on a very hard surface.
- Canning salt solutions (mix 1 tbsp per gallon of water); available in grocery stores or wherever canning supplies are sold.
- Sink or buckets (LOTS OF WATER)
- Paper towels or brown paper
- Hammer (with a flat surface)
- Glue stick
- Masking tape

Step 2. Start with prewashed plain cotton fabric (later you can experiment).

Step 3. Spread paper or paper towel over smooth board. Tape paper down.

Step 4. Place freshly picked leaf on paper, vein side up. You can use a bit of glue stick if necessary to hold the leaf in place

Step 5. Place fabric on top of leaf. (If it is windy, tape can help keep things in place.)

Step 6. Use a hammer to pound the leaf into the fabric. Hold the hammer 2 to 3 inches above fabric, using quick firm, gentle strokes, beginning in the center of the leaf and work outward. Note: If pounding is too gentle, the leaf will not release its tannin content into the fabric, and if pounding is too hard, you can tear the fabric.

Step 7. Allow leaf to dry, then pull the layers apart. Remove ALL the leaf bits. Pull the fabric on the bias to help release the flakes of leaf.

Step 8. Quickly dunk fabric into a solution of canning salt (mix 1 tbsp canning salt per gallon of water). Rinse fabric in running water or water in a bucket until it runs clear. Best results obtained with rinsing immediately. *Do not stack the prints-they will bleed onto one another.* Wring out excess water.

Step 9. Wash in warm water and mild soap. Press with iron on medium heat. This helps set the color.

ACTIVITIES

Blueprinting. You can purchase blueprint paper from shops handling drafting supplies or on the Internet. A 5"x 7" size is preferable.

Step 1. Make a 9" x 12" frame by placing a piece of glass and a cardboard of the same size together and binding with masking tape at one end. All edges of the glass should be bound with masking tape for safety.

Step 2. Place object to be printed between glass and cardboard, with blueprint paper next to cardboard with the blue (sensitive) side up.

Step 3. Hold frame, glass side out, in the sun for several minutes, or until paper is greenish-gray. You will have to experiment on the proper amount of time according to the sun's intensity.

Step 4. Take into the shade and remove paper; immerse in pan of water, exposed side down. A drop of hydrogen peroxide in the water will help bring out the blue color. Be sure the paper is thoroughly wet; leave in the water 15 to 60 seconds. Some blueprint papers need a chemical to fix the color; check on this when you purchase the paper. Take paper out and press on blotter pad of newsprint to absorb water. Dry in shade, weighting down corners to keep flat.

CAUTION: Blueprint paper is highly sensitive to light so you must work with it in the dark, until ready to expose to sun. Extra blueprint paper must be wrapped in heavy paper and kept in a dark place.

Ozalid Printing. Ozalid paper used to be common and there were specialized machines used to make copies with it. Over the years copiers have evolved to sophisticated digital machines. The old style ozalid paper (also called Diazo paper) can be found on the Internet at eBay and other specialty stores. It is a "dry" process and can be developed into three colors depending on the processing.

Step 1. Follow the procedure for blueprints in the previous paragraph, testing the exposure time approximately 15 to 25 seconds for red, 20 to 35 seconds for blue, 40 to 50 seconds for black.

Step 2. Remove print from frame in the shade, roll into cylinder, print-face inside, and place in a half-gallon glass jar containing enough concentrated ammonia (strong ammonia-about 28%, purchased at a drugstore) barely to cover the bottom and a layer of marbles to keep the paper from getting into the ammonia. The ammonia also may be placed in a small jar, like an ink bottle, and set uncapped inside the big jar. Another method is to turn the large-mouthed jar upside down to prevent loss of fumes. Ammonia is placed in a container on the table with the jar over it. The ammonia fumes develop the print by bringing out and setting the color. Ammonia cannot be saved and reused. Use a fresh supply when you wish to print on another day.

Step 3. Remove the print after 3 to 4 minutes when proper color appears. Underfuming makes prints pale; overfuming makes them harsh and dark. Developing should be done outside or in a well-ventilated room.

Oil Printing. Provide plenty of newspapers plus several sheets of waxed paper or cardboard that will not soak up ink readily.

Step 1. Put a pea-sized dab of printer's block printing ink on the waxed cardboard or paper. You can use either water-base or oil-base ink. The oil-base makes nicer prints, but water-base is better for youngsters since they tend to get it on their clothes.

Step 2. Spread ink out to just a bit bigger than the leaf, using a wadded piece of newspaper as the spreader. The ink should be even and not very thick.

Step 3. Place leaf vein-side (back or underside) down on ink. Place another piece of paper over the leaf and rub thoroughly every vein and edge of leaf to help ink adhere evenly.

Step 4. Remove paper; lift the leaf carefully by the end of its stem. Lay carefully on notepaper or whatever paper or fabric you wish to decorate. Put a clean piece of newspaper over leaf *being sure that the leaf does not move.* Holding your finger down on center of the leaf, rub thoroughly every vein and edge. Remove paper and leaf carefully. There's your print!

Step 5. Now, take your spreader and even out the ink on the waxed cardboard or paper. Place leaf vein-side down again and repeat the process. When ink becomes too light, add a *very small amount* of ink. If prints do not show veins, but just a blotch of ink, the ink is too heavy. You can mix inks to get fall colors.

If textile extender is used in the oil ink and the ink then properly set, printing can be done on fabric. Fabric paints are available at art stores and over the Internet. Deka permanent fabric paints work very well, but are hard to come by except on the Internet on eBay.

Smoke Printing

Step 1. Cover a piece of typewriting paper or a smooth-surface notepaper with a thin layer of lard, shortening, or Vaseline petroleum jelly. You can also use a greased paper.

Step 2. Light a candle and smoke the greased paper by moving it back and forth over the flame so that soot forms on the paper. Keep the candle moving so the paper does not catch fire. (Have a bucket of water ready, just in case.)

Step 3. When the surface is black with soot, place soot-side up on a table and lay the leaf vein-side down on the blackened surface. Cover the leaf with another piece of paper, such as newspaper, and rub every vein and edge of leaf well to make soot stick to the leaf.

Step 4. Lift leaf carefully by end of stem and place smoked side down on fresh piece of paper. Lay another piece of paper over it and, holding with finger in center, rub entire leaf carefully.

Step 5. Remove top paper and leaf with care. Smoke prints are delicate. They may be preserved from smudges by spraying lightly with clear plastic spray. Smoke also may be gathered on glass if care is used with the flame so that the glass will not crack.

Spatter Printing. Cover working area with several layers of newspaper. Select a leaf, flower, fern, or other material to spatter. It is preferable to have previously pressed the object flat. Choose paper and contrasting ink. Pin leaf on cardboard (on top of newspapers), putting pins at points and depressions so that the leaf lies very flat against the paper. Slant pins toward center of leaf or away from edge so pins will not retard spraying. Small stones or pennies can be used instead of pins. Spatter by one of these methods:

Step 1. With toothbrush and knife or toothpick: Dip toothbrush in water-based ink or paint mixed to a thin, cream consistency; shake off excess. Hold near paper and leaf. Draw knife blade (or toothpick) across the brush with bristles at slight angle, bringing the knife toward you making a spray of ink. Move the brush and knife around so ink sprays in desired places and gets desired intensity. Practice will be necessary to get even spattering without blobs. Avoid getting too much ink or paint on brush.

Step 2. With toothbrush and screen: Dip brush in paint; shake off excess. Hold piece of fine wire screening in place and "scrub" or brush, moving around as above. Practice! A good method for screening that is not quite so messy is to make a frame from a cigar box or other box of similar size; remove top and bottom, using just the sides for a frame. Attach screening to top of box only. Place the open bottom of box down on paper. Brush across screen, moving brush only to get spatters all over. If paint quickly and thickly fills squares of the screen, there is too much paint on the toothbrush. To get rid of excess paint on the screen, lay it on newspaper and rub, blotting off the excess paint. Delicate looking leaves with interesting edges and compound leaves make interesting designs. For a shadowing and depth effect overlap leaves with different colors.

Step 3. An atomizer of washable spray paint also can be used.

Spore Printing. This is a very different kind of printing.

Step 1. Spread a thin coat of a half-mucilage, half-water mixture (or slightly beaten egg white) onto a piece of thin cardboard or poster board.

Step 2. Cut off the stem of a mature, fully opened mushroom directly under the cap. Place the cap, bottom down, in the middle of the cardboard. Cover the layout with a turned-over glass dish and leave undisturbed for 24 hours.

Step 3. Remove both the dish and the mushroom and air dry. *Caution: Some people may have allergies to certain spores.*

CASTING

Another method of preserving designs and imprints is through "castings." Casts can be made from a variety of materials, such as plaster of Paris, plastic, or paraffin wax. The casting material is in a liquid form and is poured into the mold. The hardening qualities of these materials cause it to "set" after which the mold can be removed. The result is three-dimensional reproduction that can be handled and studied. The clear plastic casts permit the preservation of insect and plant life by imbedding them in their natural state in such a manner that they can be viewed from all angles. The discovery of an imprint of the paw of an animal and the making of a cast can be an interesting and educational experience for children and adults alike.

 ACTIVITY

Plaster Casting. Plaster casts of animal tracks, snakes, mushrooms, leaves, fish, and so on may be used for wall plaques, bookends, paperweights, identification boards, and the like. Single tracks are best for plaster casting.

Step 1. Look for distinct tracks along streams, in sand or mud. Put a round or oblong form, or "collar" made of 2″-wide strips of tin or cardboard (cut before you go into the field) around the track to hold the plaster in place. The form should be 2 to 3 inches wider than the print to be cast.

Step 2. Push this down into the mud or sand, leaving about one inch above the surface. Mix the plaster of Paris and water, pouring the plaster into the water, to a thick, soupy consistency. Pour the plaster into the track, filling the form to about one inch in depth.

Step 3. Leave this in place for 2 to 3 hours to harden. The thicker the mix, the quicker it hardens. But if you get it too thick, it may harden before you can pour it! To reverse the track, put a cardboard mold around the plaster of Paris track that has been well greased with petroleum jelly. Pour in some plaster of Paris. Let it harden, and then knock it out. (It should drop out because of the petroleum jelly.) Now you have a track as it appeared in the sand or mud.

Some tips: Stir plaster of Paris with a disposable stick, not a spoon. Sift plaster of Paris into water without stirring, letting it sink to the bottom until no more will sink below the water surface, then add a little more for good measure and stir. If you start to stir right away, you may have a more difficult time adding more plaster of Paris. If the mixture becomes too hard before pouring, throw it out! Adding salt will hasten setting; vinegar will retard. You can tint casts of leaves and flowers with poster paints while plaster of Paris is still moist, or when dry with thinned oil paints. Air bubbles sometimes are formed in the plaster in the process of stirring and pouring. Jarring the cast while wet will help break many of these. To help keep the cast from retaining so much sand or mud, shake talcum powder into the track before pouring plaster.

ACTIVITY

Sand Casting. Put sand in a box of sufficient size to hold the object to be cast and still leave a border on the sides.

Step 1. Dampen sand so the grains will stick together. Finer sand sticks together better.

Step 2. Draw or carve design in sand, or sink object to be molded. Use equal amounts of water and plaster of Paris-first placing water in container that can be thrown away and sifting plaster in slowly so air bubbles will come to the top. Stir until it starts to thicken. When you have a thick "gravy," pour plaster into design, filling deepest depressions first. If you are making plaques, a twisted wire stuck in the back will make a wall hanger.

Step 3. Remove plaster when hardened, usually about an hour. Some sand will stick to the plaster. It may be left for texture or may be removed with a brush.

Color (dry tempera) may be added to the plaster of Paris if a colored object is desired. Substituting wax for the plaster of Paris results in beautiful sand candles. Add a crayon to the melted wax for color and string for a wick as the wax starts to harden.

Plastic Casting. The use of plastics in the preservation of insect and plant specimens is one of the more recent developments to gain widespread popularity. These products can be purchased in craft stores. The product can be used either for study or as a memento of an occasion or may serve as a paperweight. The plastic is purchased as a liquid to which a hardener is added, causing it to jell and become hard. The mold is half filled with the liquid; the insect or plant is then placed into the mold and more plastic is poured over the top. Thus the flower or insect is completely surrounded with a protective layer of clear plastic. Be sure that the mold is large enough. Keep the design simple and avoid overcrowding.

SKETCHING

Charcoal sketching can make use of native materials. Burn thin hardwood sticks in the campfire and then cover them with earth before they are consumed by the flames. This shuts off the air and allows the wood to char completely through. Finger sketching can be done with paints made from berries. Soft limestone and other rocks also can be used for drawing. Plant materials such as leaves and dandelion heads also yield colors when rubbed on drawing paper.

 Books on Sketching

See master publicatons list for cities of Publishers.

Maltzman, Stanley. (1995). *Drawing Nature: Capture the Beauty of the Outdoors Using Pencils and Other Drawing Materials.* North Light Books: Cincinnati. Good illustrations and presentation of techniques. Specifically covers trees, clouds, snow, barns, grass, rocks, and water.

Ross, Michael. (2000). *Nature Art with Chirua Obata.* Carolrhoda Books: Minneapolis. This small book is a treasure, excellent illustrations and ideas and truly nature-oriented.

SECTION E

PRESERVATION

There are many rare and endangered wildflowers and plants. To be environmentally responsible, one must know which plants are rare or endangered and be familiar with the ecosystem to know when it is appropriate to pick wildflowers. If you don't know, don't pick! Of course, common garden flowers can be used instead of wildflowers.

There are a number of different methods of preserving wildflowers and plants. In this section the following methods are presented: drying flowers, pressing flowers, sunbaking flowers, parchment, and dyeing.

DRYING FLOWERS

Flowers to be dried should be picked in prime condition just before the peak of bloom, although they may be dried in any stage of development before full bloom. If colors are to be retained, the flowers must be fresh and should be picked when they are free of moisture (e.g. dew, rain). You may want to make new stems of florist's wire.

There are two primary materials for drying most flowers—silica gel or borax and corn meal. Silica gel is preferable as it absorbs moisture rapidly and thus retains color better. Also, while the initial cost may be more, it can be used again and again. When it loses its absorbency, it can be placed in a warm oven to restore this quality. It may be purchased at most garden centers and craft stores and is sold under the trade name of FlowerDri®. When using silica gel, place the flower in a slanting position in a container with a lid covering the flower entirely with silica gel. Secure the lid and leave in a dark place for five to seven days.

For borax drying, pour about one inch of borax (or two inches of borax and corn meal mixture in 1:6 ratio) in a plastic bag or paper sack and place the flower upside down or face down on the borax. Pour more borax (mixture) gently around the flower until well covered (1″-2″). Place flowers so they do not touch each other. Flowers and more borax may be added until the bag is almost full. Gather the top of the bag, squeeze the remaining air out of it, and tie with cord. Put in a dry, dark place for one to four weeks, depending on how much water the petals originally contained. Flower petals turn crisp when they are dried. Remove the flowers as soon as they are dried; they will lose their color if left too long. This method works well on marigolds, pansies, single roses, sweet peas, and similar woods flowers.

PRESSING FLOWERS

Simply place flowers, ferns, or leaves between sheets of absorbent paper under a weight. Leave for several days in a dry place. You may want to change absorbent paper (e.g. papet towel) occasionally. May be mounted, as on lampshades, and sprayed with clear plastic.

SUNBAKING FLOWERS

Remove all leaves from the stems of the flowers. Pour one to two inches of sand in a shallow box and then place the flowers upside down on the sand, carefully pouring more sand over each flower to cover to a depth of about one inch. Be sure the flowers do not touch. Place the box of sand and flowers to bake in the sun. Two or three days will be ample. This method works well on the flowers mentioned above for borax drying.

 ## Books on Flower Preservation

See master publicatons list for cities of Publishers.

Dinoto, Andrea, and David Winter. (1999). *The Pressed Plant: The Art of Botanical Specimens, Nature Prints and Sun Pictures.* Stewart, Tabori & Chang: NY. Although a large book and a bit expensive ($30), it has excellent illustrations and information. A good reference for libraries and groups.

Hillier, Malcolm. (1987). *Book of Dried Flowers: A Complete Guide to Growing, Drying, and Arranging.* Simon & Schuster.

Klutz Press (Editors). (2001). *Squashing Flowers Squeezing Leaves.* Klutz Press: Palo Alto, CA. (A Nature Press Book). Excellent projects plus the sturdy book includes leaf and flower press and supplies so you are ready to go.

MacFarlane, Ruth B. (1985). *Collecting and Preserving Plants.* Dover Publications: NY. Fairly comprehensive for preserving plants for scientific, craft, or ornamental use. Good illustrations for "how-tos." Shows how to make a herbarium (essentially a library of preserved plants).

Miller, Cathy. (1997). *Harvesting, Preserving & Arranging Dried Flowers.* Artisan Sales.

Squires, Mable. (1958). *The Art of Drying Plants and Flowers.* M. Barrows and Company: NY. (out of print, limited availability)

Whitlock, Sarah, and Martha Rankin. (1977). *Dried Flowers: How to Prepare Them.* Dover Publications: NY.

 ## Internet Sites on Flower Preservation

Suggested search words: dried flowers/drying flowers

Clemson Extension, Drying Flowers:
   http://hgic.clemson.edu/factsheets/HGIC1151.htm

GardenGuides.com, information on drying flowers:
   http://www.gardenguides.com/TipsandTechniques/drying.htm

A Flower Arranger's Garden, Preserving Flowers:
   http://www.gardenguides.com/TipsandTechniques/drying.htm

Kid's Valley Garden, Drying Flowers:
   http://www.raw-connections.com/garden/showing/drying.htm

University of Minnesota Extension Service: Drying Flowers:
http://www.extension.umn.edu/info-u/plants/BG408.html

PARCHMENT

A method of preserving nature specimens to make useful products such as lamp-shades, note cards, booklet covers and so on is to make a semitransparent parchment. Place upon a piece of household waxed paper various nature specimens (leaves, ferns, grasses, flowers, etc.) in a pleasing design. It is preferable to have these objects pressed flat. Cover with a single piece of rice paper. A single facial tissue (separate the ordinary tissue into its layers) may also be used with good success. Using a stiff-bristled pastry brush or other suitable brush (or your finger), saturate the paper evenly with a tapping motion while applying a diluted mixture of white glue-50 percent water and 50 percent Elmer's or other similar glue. Dry thoroughly. Iron between layers of brown wrapping paper with iron set for "silk," or press between weights to flatten. Ironing is preferable because it sets the wax into the parchment. Trim edges; a deckle edge can be made by tearing excess, using a straightedge.

Two pieces of rice paper can be used. "Wash" paper with glue after placing specimens between sheets and hang by clothespins to dry. Makes good opaque "glass" for a door or other object.

DYEING

There is satisfaction and charm in making and using native dyes that are easily obtained from many vegetables, fruits, and trees. Following is a guide to plants and the colors they will produce.

onion skins: red or yellow	goldenrod: yellow
raspberries: dark red	pear leaves: dull yellow
bloodroot: red	sumac roots: yellow
beets: red violet	celandine: yellow
strawberries: red	tanglewood stems: yellow
mountain ash berries: orange	citron: yellow
larkspur flowers: blue	blackberries: blue
pokeweed berries: purple	dandelion roots: magenta
sassafras roots: pink	butternut bark: brown
walnut hulls: rich dark brown	sumac bark: brown

Books on Natural Dyeing

See master publicatons list for cities of Publishers.

Adrosko, Rita. (1976). *Natural Dyes and Home Dyeing.* Dover Publications: NY.

Bessette, Arleen, and Alan Bessette. (2001). *The Rainbow Beneath My Feet: A Mushroom Dyer's Field Guide.* Syracuse University Press.

Brooklyn Botanical Garden. (1984). *Dye Plants and Dyeing-A Handbook.* Brooklyn Botanical Gardens. (out of print, limited availability) Includes plants from throughout the world.

Buchanan, Rita. (1999). *A Weaver's Garden: Growing Plants for Natural Dyes and Fibers.* Dover Publications.

Dean, Jenny. (1995) reprint edition. *The Craft of Natural Dyeing.* Search Press Ltd: Tumbridge Wells, Kent, England. Ms. Dean does excellent work in directions, pictures and pointing out safety considerations. Very good book for those who wish to seriously pursue dying yarns and other materials.

Dean, Jenny, Casselman, Karen Diadick,[msh2] and Janny Dean. (1999). *Wild Color.* Watson-Guptill Publications: NY. Very comprehensive with detailed directions, excellent pictures.

Liles, J.N. (1990). *The Art and Craft of Natural Dyeing: Traditional Recipes for Modern Use.* University of Tennessee Press: Knoxville. Excellent detail and directions, very comprehensive. No pictures.

Senisi, Ellen. (2001). *Berry Smudges and Leaf Prints: Finding and Making Colors from Nature.* Dutton Books: NY. Excellent pictures, easy to read and good projects.

Schultz, Kathleen. (1975). *Create Your Own Natural Dyes.* Sterling Publishing: NY. (out of print, limited availability)

 Internet Sites on Natural Dyes

Suggested search words: natural dyes/native dyes

Joy of Handspinning, natural dyes:
http://www.joyofhandspinning.com/natural-dyes.html

Pioneer Thinking, Making Natural Dyes from Plants:
http://www.pioneerthinking.com/naturaldyes.html

NativeTech, Matching Game: Natural Dyes & Porcupine Quills:
http://www.nativetech.org/games/porcupinequill/

GENERAL RESOURCES ON NATURE CRAFTS

Selected resources have been provided following certain sections; however, the following list includes general nature resources. These resources have ideas and projects relating to all of the sections in this chapter.

Copies of most all of the books cited have been reviewed, as have all of the Internet sites recommended. Brief annotations are provided for some of the resources.

Some references that are older and out of print have been purposely included when they provide excellent information. Frequently these resources can be found in public/school libraries or on the Internet. County extension agents frequently have a variety of helpful resources including pamphlets, software, and booklets.

The resources and information available on the Internet are ever expanding. A few sites have been suggested and although we have tried to select sites from well-established organizations or agencies (public, private, and governmental) that are likely to remain over time, there are always changes. We have provided suggestions for search words that we have used with some success when looking for information about specific topics

Lists of ever-evolving, new materials can be found in periodicals and publication catalogs. Nature centers, conventions and workshops, and bookstores are also good places to check out the latest resources. Caution: be sure to check that crafts, games, and other activities are nature-oriented; too many suggestions in popular resources misuse nature materials or do not involve environmental education.

Many of the general nature resources included in Chapter 1 resources also include craft activities. Look under each section in the text for resources specific to that topic.

CHELEY COLORADO CAMPS, CHELEY, CO.

General Books on Nature Crafts

See master publicatons list for cities of Publishers.

Cusick, Dawn. (1995), reprint ed. *Nature Crafts with a Microwave: Over 80 Projects.* Lark Books.

Daitz, Myrna. (1997). *Crafty Ideas from Nature.* Exley Giftbooks.

Diehn, Gwen, and Terry Krautwurst,. (1997). *Kid Style Nature Crafts: 50 Terrific Things to Make With Nature's Materials.* Sterling Publications, NY, 1997. Nature crafts divided by the seasons, excellent activities, good directions and pictures.

Fiarotta, Phyllis, and Noel Fiarotta. (1975). *Snips and Snails and Walnut Whales: Nature Crafts for Children.* Workman Publishing Company.

Forte, Imogene. (1986) *Puddles and Wings, and Grapevine Swings: Things to Make and Do with Nature's Treasures.* Incentive Publications: Nashville.

Hammett, Catherine, and Carol Horrocks. (1957). *Creative Crafts for Campers.* Association Press, NY, 1957. (Republished in 1987 by the American Camp Association.)

Jaeger, Ellsworth. (1992). *Wildwood Wisdom,* 2nd ed. Shelter Publications. Cordage, barkcraft, and camp furnishings only.

Jollands, Beverly. (1997). *Topiaries and Pomanders* (Gifts from Nature Series). Lorenz Books.

Koontz, Robin. (1998). *The Complete Backyard Nature Activity Book: Fun projects for kids to learn about the wonders of wildlife and nature.* McGraw-Hill: NY. Although certainly not "complete," there are some good projects. Some, such as bat houses, require some woodworking skills.

Martin, Laura C. (2003). *Nature's Art Box.* Storey Books.

Metcalf, Harlan G. (1977). *The Pioneer Book of Nature Crafts.* Lyle Stuart.

Musselman, Virginia W. (1969). *Learning about Nature through Crafts.* Stackpole Books: Harrisburg, PA. (out of print, limited availability)

Needham, Bobbie. (1999). *Ecology Crafts for Kids: 50 great ways to make friends with planet Earth.* Sterling Publishing.

Perkins, John. (2000). *Build Your Own Birdhouses and Feeders: From Simple, Natural Designs to Spectacular, Customized Houses and Feeders.* Firefly Books.

Ross, Kathy. (1998). *Crafts for Kids Who are Wild about the Wild.* Millbrook Press.

Sohi, Morteza E. (2000). *Look What I Did With a Shell!* Walker & Co.

Vinal, William G. (1963). *Nature Recreation,* 2nd edition. Republished in 2000 by Dover Publications: NY. (Out of print, but a gem if you can find it!)

Williams, Joy. (2002). *Nature Crafts* (Creative Kids). North Light Books: Cincinnati, OH. (Excellent nature-oriented selection of crafts. Written for kids with notes to parents/leaders. Pictures and directions are easy to do and fun to make.

Yow, Cathy. (1999). *Jewelry from Nature: 45 Great Projects Using Sticks & Stones, Seeds & Bones.* Lark Books.

 ## Internet Sites on Nature Crafts (General)

Suggested search words: native crafts/natural crafts/nature crafts

Backyard Nature:
http://www.backyardnature.net/index.html

Freekidscrafts.com:
http://www.freekidscrafts.com/nature_crafts.htm

The Treehouse:
http://www.seedsofknowledge.com/naturecrafts.html

Better Homes & Gardens, garden and nature crafts:
http://www.lhj.com/bhg/category.jhtml?categoryid=/templatedata/bhg/category/data/c_108.xml

Earlychildhood.com crafts:
http://www.earlychildhood.com/Crafts/index.cfm?CatID=203

Nature Crafts supplies:
http://www.allcrafts.net/nature.htm

BRYCE HUNT, McMILLEN PROGRAM CENTER,
GIRL SCOUTS OF LINBERLOST COUNCIL, FORT WAYNE, IN

3

NATURE GAMES

Nature-oriented games can serve several useful functions, provided they are used appropriately. Games are not a substitute for the study of nature, nor should they be considered a necessary device to sugarcoat or entice youngsters to learn about nature, implying that nature is not interesting in and of itself. Games can be used in many settings with youth and other groups, but they should always be used in a supplementary manner to the actual nature study and direct activity.

Safety, as well as environmentally responsible behavior, should be a consideration for all games. Safety includes having qualified leaders who know activity-specific safety requirements; the needs and abilities of the group; and the characteristics of the setting that may impact safety or environmental protection.

In assessing the activity-specific safety requirements for each game, factors to consider are: the need for special equipment requiring skill and safe handling; the competency level of participants; and the need to space out or cordon off activity areas. Knowledge of the group includes an accurate assessment of: readiness skills; the maturity level of the group that may impact decision making; and the group's social skills that determine their ability to work effectively together and to follow directions.

In regard to the setting, in hiking and trailing games for example, questions to consider include:

- How do you ensure that no individual or group becomes lost?
- Will you use GPS systems (see Chapter 7, Section H) or cell phones for emergencies?
- Will leaders familiar with the area be assigned to each group?
- Will groups be required to stay together or a buddy system used?
- Is environmentally responsible behavior emphasized—both the use of natural materials and appropriate use of natural areas? Leaders should know appropriate use of natural materials in specific settings. Natural environments should

be protected and careful consideration given to environmental protection when selecting settings and boundaries.

The emphasis should be on learning, not on winning, although healthy competition can also teach valuable life skills. Three functions that games can serve in the nature-oriented program are:

1. Providing fun in a recreational period or during free time

2. Teaching information, skill, and appreciation

    a. Stimulating new interests by introducing new areas or advanced levels of knowledge and skill

    b. Reinforcing prior learning

3. Providing opportunities for inclusion

    a. Leveling the playing field by removing or lowering barriers between those with different abilities

    b. Engaging a wide variety of people including intergenerational groups, different ethnic and cultural groups, and many other diverse groups

There are five sections of games in this chapter: (A) Map and Compass Games (see also Chapter 7, Section H: Navigating in the Outdoors); (B) Campcraft Games (see also Chapter 4: Outdoor Living Skills); (C) Hiking and Trailing Games (see also Chapter VI, Section G: Hiking and Backpacking); (D) Searching and Seeking Games (see Chapter 6: Projects and Hobbies); and (E) Quiet Games. For the most part, these sections are supplemental to activities presented in later chapters.

S E C T I O N   A

MAP AND COMPASS GAMES

Chapter 7, Section H: Navigating in the Outdoors provides basic information on using maps and compasses, as well as global positioning systems (GPS).

 A C T I V I T I E S

Area Identification. Lay out a compass course along a circular path, so that when the course is completed, the participants end up at the starting point. At the starting point, provide compass bearings to find the next point.

At point #1 have the person list all the objects within a designated area that are foreign to the environment, such as pieces of paper, foil, cloth, marbles, etc. Provide a compass bearing for point #2. At point #2 have person identify the leaves within a marked circle. Provide a compass bearing for point #3. Have cardboard animals or casts of animal tracks along the path to point #3 and identify the animals that are native to the area. Provide a compass bearing to return to the starting point. At each point make appropriate connections to the ecosystem.

Many other points for different types of identification can be added. Make sure signs and pictures are large enough to read, so that people of various abilities and ages can see them clearly.

Compass Relay. Lay out a compass course with points that match the total number of players on a team (three to eight is good) and are out of sight of each other. Select team members and station each team member at the designated points along the course, with their locations unknown to the other team members. The first runners have the readings for the entire team. The first runner takes the first reading that will lead to the second runner, who takes the next reading and runs to the third team member, etc. The final team member has a bearing back to the original starting point. Boundaries should be predetermined and a maximum time limit should be set.

Compass Treasure Hunt. Individuals are given a list of compass bearings (of similar difficulties and distance) that go different ways but all end at the same place. At the end there is a prize for the first one who gets there.

Compass Line Game. This game may be played individually or in teams. On a 100′ line, beginning positions are marked 1 to 20. Each player has a card with a series of three different compass readings and number of paces or steps to take that will bring them back to the beginning position on the line. Each player or team begins with 100 points. In scoring, one point is subtracted for each foot that the player is away from the finish point on the line.

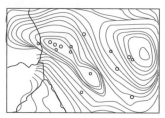

Map Search. Teams of two players are given a topographical map and the coordinates of a location on the map. Each team is instructed to use the compass to locate the designated point. First team to find that point wins.

Map Symbol Quiz. Give each player a series of map symbols to identify. The winner is the one who has the most correct. For variation, provide the names of map symbols and ask the participants to draw the symbols.

Square Play. In a large outdoor area, each player walks in a straight line 400 feet; turns left 90 degrees and walks 400 feet; turns left again and walks 400 feet; and once more repeats the procedure. The player coming closest to the starting point is the winner. You may also use the same procedure with a triangular pattern— 40 degrees for 100 feet; 160 degrees for 100 feet; and 280 degrees for 100 feet. Be sure the starting point, that is also the ending point, is not an obvious landmark that the participants can recognize readily and walk to regardless of the compass readings. A twig, small rock, or golf tee pushed into the ground are suitably   inconspicuous.

 Books on Maps and Compass Games

See master publicatons list for cities of Publishers.

Disely, John. (1979). *Orienteering.* Stackpole Books: Harrisburg, PA.

Kjellström, Björn. (1994). *Be Expert with Map and Compass.* John Wiley & Sons: Hoboken, NJ.

SECTION B

CAMPCRAFT GAMES

Chapter 4: Outdoor Living Skills includes related information about firecraft, ropecraft, and toolcraft, while Chapter 5 discusses outdoor cookery. With all nature-oriented activities, but especially with campcraft activities, special care should be taken to protect and conserve the natural environment. Environmentally sound practices can vary greatly among different ecosystems. At least in the beginning stages, it is probably best to teach standard conservation practices regardless of the nuances of specific environments. For example, in the three games that require building fires, only the minimum amount of fuel needed for the task at hand should be used. For games requiring chopping logs or lashing sticks only dead or down logs and sticks should be used.

Safety is also essential in conducting campcraft games, especially among groups that do not have familiarity with or exposure to tools of any sort. Most contests should not be conducted until participants have learned and demonstrated safety knowledge and skills specific to the activity and tools. In timed events, the length of time should be set so that the pressure of time does not lead to unsafe practices. Also persons with beginning abilities should be encouraged to use correct techniques and should not be unduly rushed by time.

 **ACTIVITIES**

Bucking Contest. This is a contest to see who can saw a log the fastest with a bucksaw. Use an 8-inch log about 12 feet long resting on two sawbucks. Buckers take turns sawing against time. Each person saws off two pieces—one from each end of the log. After sawing one end, the contestant runs quickly to the other end of the log and repeats. (Try to have saws of comparable sharpness!)

Endless Rope. Players stand in circles of six to eight players each. Each player has a small length of rope about 2 feet long. The leader calls out a specific knot. The first player ties rope to the second player's rope using the knot called out by the leader. The second player ties rope to the next, etc. around the circle. When a continuous rope circle is completed, the rope is held up. Time and the correctness of the knots determine the winning circle.

Fire-Building Contest. Players are given two matches each. They must find their own tinder and kindling, paying heed to environmental considerations appropriate to the area. The first to lay a fire that burns for two minutes (without adding wood after the fire has been lit) is the winner.

Fuzz Stick Contest. A fuzz stick is used to start fires. It is a way of making a larger stick burn more easily by making a number of thin shavings most of the length of the stick. To make a fuzz stick, with a sharp pocket knife, shave and lift slivers off a stick, but do not remove them. Long (8″ is good) and thin slivers are best. When used to start a fire, stand each fuzz stick up as part of the firelay.

Participants are given pieces of wood 1/2 inch to 1 inch in diameter (or asked to find their own wood, paying heed to appropriate environmental considerations). They are given a limited amount of time to make a "fuzz stick" with their own pocket knives. Judges decide which individual made the best fuzz stick according to number and length of shavings. Prior to any contest, participants should be taught, and be able to demonstrate, safe knife-handling techniques. The time allotted should not be so short as to foster unsafe knife practices. Violation of safety procedures should result in disqualification of the participant.

Knot-Tying One Step Forward. Players are arranged along a starting line, each with a length of rope 18 inches to 24 inches long. The leader calls the name of a knot and begins to count, setting time limits according to the difficulty of the knot. At the end of the count, players must lay their ropes on the ground in front of them. If the knot is tied correctly, they may advance one step. The player reaching the finish line first becomes the next leader.

Knot-Tying Relay. Players stand in a circle each holding a length of rope approximately 2 feet long while one player ("It") walks around the outside of the circle. "It" calls the name of a knot and taps one of the players. Both run, in opposite directions, around the circle tying the knot on the way. The last player to return to the open space is "It," if the other player's knot is tied correctly.

Lashing Contest. Teams of two people complete various types of lashings as instructed. Those finishing first with the neatest job receive a point. Winner is the team that accumulates the most points.

One-Hand Tie. Two players on a team tie the knots indicated by the leader, each using only one hand. Players cannot switch hands after starting. Team that completes the knot first wins. Game can be made competitive by choosing the best knot from each group and having a contest with a series of five or more knots.

Overhand Knot. Each player is given a small length of rope (14"-18" long). They are instructed to make an overhand knot without releasing either end of the rope. (The trick is to cross your arms, pick up both ends of the rope, and straighten arms.)

Pole-Chopping Contest. Cut an 8 inch-diameter log into 6-foot lengths. Either a hand axe or a regular axe can be used (reduce size of log for hand axe). The person chopping through the log with the fewest strokes wins.

Skudding. Teams of four "snake," or drag, a log with a rope for 100 yards against time. The log should be 1 foot in diameter and 10 feet long. (The size of the log can be modified based on the size of contestants.) Tie the rope to the log with a timber hitch.

Square Knot Gamble. Players sit in a circle, each with a short length of rope (approximately 18"- 24" long) that they hold behind them. They then tie their ropes together behind their backs, using square knots. When all are finished, they lean

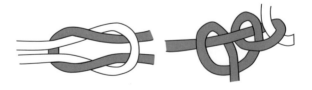

SQUARE KNOT   SAILOR KNOT

back on the completed rope circle. If they all have tied the knot correctly, the rope will hold. If one has tied a "granny," the rope will not hold.

String-Burning Contest. Stretch string or binders twine 12 inches horizontally above the ground (in a prepared fire-site area). The string must be long enough for four to six contestants at a time. Contestants lay fires of their choice beneath the string. The fire can be built as high as the string, but no higher. After the fires are laid, remove the 12" high string and replace it with an 18-inch high string in the same place. At the leader's signal, contestants light their fires. Additional fuel may be added after the fires are lit. Whoever burns through the string first wins.

Tent Peg and Sliver. Each person must have an axe, a piece of dead wood 2 inches thick and 15 inches long, and a chopping block. Judges determine who made the best tent peg and the thinnest sliver in a given length of time. This game is only for participants who have demonstrated skill and safe use of the axe. Remember, the length of time should be set so that safety is not compromised.

Tent Pitching. Give teams of two or three participants two-person trail tents. Have a contest of speed and soundness of pitching a tent. For a real challenge, give each team a tent and do this with the entire team blindfolded.

Water-Boiling Contest. Each player is given two matches and a cupful of water in a container that can be used over an open fire. The one who builds a fire and boils the water first is the winner. For ease of judging, add one tablespoon of a sudsing detergent. It will foam and boil over the can. Always emphasize fire safety and take precautions to ensure that the boiling water is not likely to be accidentally spilled on ankles and feet.

Campcraft Tournament. Suggested events include contests described in this section of campcraft games. Select those suitable to the skills of the participants and the length of time available. Tournaments may be designed for team or individual participation. As always safety is a key concern. Appropriate use of the environment, adequate supervision, matching of skill levels to events, and safety should be carefully designed and monitored throughout the events.

SECTION C
HIKING AND TRAILING GAMES

Chapter 7, Section G: Hiking and Backpacking includes general information related to this section. With hiking and trailing games, one of the primary safety concerns is making sure that groups do not get lost. Proper planning and supervision can eliminate this unwanted outcome. Selection of familiar areas, setting boundaries, and including supervision of groups by good leaders familiar with the setting can avoid most problems. It is good practice to carry appropriately stocked first aid kits on hikes away from central camp.

HIKING GAMES

 ACTIVITIES

Beeline Hike. Participants take a compass bearing and follow it to the predetermined destination. Objects in the path must be climbed over or under, or be pushed through.

Heads and Tails Hike. One person flips a coin at the junction of each trail, road, or street to determine a new direction. Heads go to the right; tails go to the left. The hike, of course, is in a familiar area or with a leader who can return the group safely to the original location.

Hold the Front, or Number One, Spot. The leader is followed by the hikers in single file as they hike along the trail. The leader asks questions about things observed such as: "What is the name of that bird, tree, rock, flower, or other stationary object?" If the first person (No. 1) in line answers correctly, that player stays in the number one position. If the answer is incorrect, the person moves to the rear of the line and No. 2 attempts to answer the question. Each player who fails to give the correct response goes to the rear of the line. The object is to stay in the No. 1 position as long as possible.

BEN DEERING, CATALINA ISLAND CAMPS, HOWLANDS LANDING, CA

Variation: Sentinel. Hikers walk single file. The lead person is the "Sentinel." The Sentinel may find a tree, rock, flower, weed, or any nature object that can be positively identified. The Sentinel stops. Each hiker passing by must either whisper correctly the name of the object or go to the end of the line. The new leader becomes the Sentinel and the old Sentinel goes behind those who answered correctly but in front of those who answered incorrectly. The object of the game is to get as near the head of the line as possible and to become Sentinel as often as possible.

I Spy. (For primary grades.) The leader spots an item of interest. in nature For example if it is a robin, the leader says: "I spy a robin." All children who see the robin squat; the rest remain standing. The leader then points out the robin or asks one of the squatting children to do so. The group continues hiking until another object of interest is seen. Be sure to select objects that all children can successfully identify and find at one time or another.

Variation: Pebble Cribbage. Each person picks up 10 small stones to carry in hand or pocket. As the group hikes along, the leader points out a nature object. Everyone tries to identify the object. When the correct name is determined, all those identifying it correctly in their minds may drop a stone. The one who has dropped all stones first wins. All must agree to play fair!

Nature Far and Near. Make a list of 20 or 30 items that can be found along the hiking route with a score for each, for example:

Points should reflect the difficulty of finding the specific item. First player to observe one of these items and report it to the leader gets the points.

Item	Points	Item	Points
Bird's nest	10	Frog	60
Live snake	15	Animal track	15
Butterfly	5	Flying bird	5

Nature Scouting. Designate several points on a map of a camp, park, or other area approximately equal distance from the starting point. Divide the group into teams and send each team on a scouting trip to a different point. About 15 minutes should be allowed for the trip. When the teams have returned, they are asked to give a report to the group on what they have seen. This serves as an excellent basis for planning a campfire program. The reports are particularly interesting when the groups can describe the things they saw with such clarity that the leader or someone else can make identifications.

Variation: Signs of History. Find signs of history that are typical to the area. Such historical objects may include: old roads and bridges, deserted buildings, old stone fences, rock piles and contents, old trees (must be able to tell how old trees are), arrowheads, cemeteries, patches of daffodils or lilies where a homestead once stood, apple trees, historical markers, pieces of glass and metal, and old paths.

Variation: Observation. Children are given a list of things to look for on a hike, perhaps with questions. They write down what they see and where and answers to the questions. When they return they discuss their observations and answers to the questions.

TRAILING GAMES

Use with Chapter 6: Projects and Hobbies, Section A: Animals and Section B: Birds.

Hare and Hounds. One player, the "hare," is given a 10-minute start on the "hounds" and lays a trail by dropping corn, acorns, leaves, or other natural objects. The hounds follow the trail and try to catch the hare.

Tree Trailing. Hide messages in various places and send out groups 15 to 30 minutes apart. The first message may read, "Take the valley trail to the east until you see a large yellow willow." Additional messages of this kind follow in order. The object of the game is not to complete the trail in the fastest time, but to follow the trail the greatest distance, so the trail routing and clues should grow more difficult as it goes along. As always boundaries should be set in advance and proper planning and supervision will prevent the possibility of groups getting lost.

SECTION D

SEARCHING AND SEEKING GAMES

As with hiking and trailing games, it is important to make sure that groups do not get lost. Proper planning and supervision can eliminate this unwanted outcome. Selecting familiar areas, establishing boundaries, and including supervision of groups by good leaders familiar with the setting can avoid many problems. It is good practice to carry appropriately stocked first aid kits on hikes away from facilities.

 ACTIVITIES

Find the Trees. Players are in groups of six. Give each group the pictures but not the name of 10 trees that are in the immediate area. Have a balance between common and lesser known trees in each set so that every group will have an equal chance to locate them, or have the same trees in each group.

On signal, each group carefully examines the pictures and then tries to find the corresponding trees in the wooded area. If the players do not know the tree's name but can identify it from the picture, they receive 5 points. For a tree that they can both identify and name, they receive 10 points..

After a designated time, call the search to an end. Reassemble the players. Ask the group finding the assigned 10 trees, or most of them, to "prove" their answers by showing the other players the location of each tree for which the members have a picture.

Variation: Bird Nest Hunt. Divide the group into teams. In a limited time, see which team can locate the most bird's nests. Teams receive 3 points for each nest. If they can identify the kind of bird that built the nest, they get an extra 5 points.

NOTE: Nests should not be disturbed.

Variation: Curio Collector. The leader gives the group the name of something to be found, for example, a stump of a tree more than 100 years old or a tree struck by lightning. The participants scatter to find the object. The first person to find it calls the rest of the group to see the curio. The leader then names the next curio to find and the search begins anew.

Photography Treasure Hunt. Teams of two go out on photographic expeditions very similar to the scavenger hunt. Each team has a camera. They are instructed to get pictures of still life (for example: landscapes, trees, wildflowers) and animal life (for example: birds, dog). As an alternative, the picture taking may be focused on a particular category, such as trees, wildflowers, and insects. The teams return after a specified time to process their pictures and put them on display. If digital cameras are used and the computer/printer is available, this can occur immediately. Guidebooks or the Internet may be used to discover more facts or information about the pictures. Slide shows can be created or web sites designed that provide learning environments for others or tell a story.

Scavenger Hunts. Participants are divided into pairs or small groups of four to six people. Groups must stay together throughout the search. Each group is given an identical list of things found in nature. The first group back with a correct and complete list of collected items wins. To emphasize environmental stewardship, at the end of the game you may have groups return the items to the places where they were found.

Note: Stress conservation practices. Adapt length of list and/or distance with those less mobile or of differing ability levels.

Some suggestions regarding scavenger hunts:

1. Have rules that reflect environmental responsibility specific to the ecosystem the hunt occurs in, such as not disturbing living plants and animals.
2. Have safety rules that include specifying boundaries and recognizing and avoiding potentially dangerous plants and animals.
3. Have the participants use what they can find in the immediate environment.
4. Have some things easy to find and others more difficult so that it is a challenge.
5. Provide identification books to aid participants in identification.
6. Decide on the length of time and then call players in promptly.
7. Supply containers to put things in.
8. Make sure that the groups are divided fairly as to daring, physical vigor, and knowledge about nature.

9. Use the facts previously learned on hikes or in nature study groups.

10. Do not send players anyplace where there are hazards, such as poison ivy, marshes, and cliffs.

11. Provide at least one adult leader for each group of six to eight children.

12. Suit your hunt to the group's abilities.

13. Specify only things that are within the area and able to be secured within the time limit set.

14. At the end of the hunt, have the participants identify and comment on the items collected, returning them to their natural setting when appropriate. Much of the learning occurs during the debriefing period.

15. Do not give names only, but sometimes use other identifying factors to elicit more interest or comment.

The following items have been used in nature scavenger hunts with fifth- and sixth-graders and older children in a summer camp:

tendril from grape vine	dwarf sumac leaf
3 different-shaped leaves from same tree	beetle
pickerelweed leaf	mullein leaf
2 kinds of willow leaves	pebble/rock showing effects of erosion
leaf with vein parallel to margin	black locust thorn
leaf with more than 9 leaflets	8-legged animal
tail of a cattail	flower of Queen Anne's lace
evidence of fossils	twin cap of acorn
fly	leaf, white on underside with flat stem
mosquito	dogwood leaf
thorn from hawthorn	oak leaf with bristles
fungus	sprig of fern
leaf with 5 leaflets	red seeding top of sumac
ant	elm leaf
cicada skin	sycamore leaf
leaf of water lily	mayfly
moth	cloverleaf or flower
5-leaf grouping	milkweed pod
burdock	moss
grass gone to seed	seed from elm tree
fragrant seed from tree	dragonfly
3-leaf plant that's harmless and good cattle feed	

Variation: Observation Scavenger Hunt. This hunt is similar to other scavenger hunts, except that instead of collecting items and bringing them to a central location, the participants record the sighting of the object, noting its location. While it is difficult to check on the veracity of the group's report, it is not as apt to harm the natural environment as the other scavenger hunts. Digital cameras can be used and pictures uploaded to computer at the end of the hike to check on score. For a greater learning experience, instead of just recording the object, also record some unique characteristic of the item. Make it truly an "observation" hunt.

Variation: Alphabet Scavenger Hunt. Participants locate objects for each letter of the alphabet, beginning with "A" and proceeding to "Z."—acorns, buttercups, cones, and dogwood leaves, for example. First player to find all items wins. Creativity and imagination for the harder letters helps.

Variation: Sensory Scavenger Hunt. Focus is placed on challenging participants to find as many nature items with specific characteristics as possible. Characteristics could include such things as different shades of green, a rough texture, smooth or serrate edges. This adds a dimension of sensory awareness and design.

SECTION E

QUIET GAMES

Some of the games can be used with environmental projects described in Chapter 6. Quiet games included are observation, active, and paper and pencil.

OBSERVATION GAMES

ACTIVITIES

Animal Tracks. Use a set of plaster cast animal tracks to see how many animals can be identified by their tracks. Pictures of animal tracks could also be used if casts are not available.

Bird Silhouettes. Hold up flash cards of bird silhouettes. Groups may call out the name, and the first group to answer correctly gets a point; or each group may write down its answer, and at the end, the one with the most correct answers wins. This may also be done with tree silhouettes.

BALD EAGLE   HERON   WOODPECKER

Variation: Card Flash. The picture of some nature object is "flashed" before the group for a brief period and then removed. The members of the group attempt to describe it correctly. After a short time it is shown again to the group. This time they try to see what they missed the first time or what erroneous impressions they received.

Kim's Game. The leader places about 20 nature objects on a table and puts a cover over them. Bring each team to the table and remove the cloth for one minute. The team returns to its place and lists all the objects it can recall. A point is given for each correct object and a point is subtracted for each incorrect object.

Variation: Name Me. Scatter interesting natural objects, each with a number, around the room. Each player tries to specifically identify as many as possible. The person with the greatest number of correct names wins.

Mystery Bag. Have nature items hidden in boxes or bags where participants cannot see them. Assure players there are no sharp, slimy, or unpleasant contents. Have each person feel the item in each bag and write down what the object is thought to be. The player with the most correct identifications wins.

Variation: Blind as a Bat. Players work in pairs. One is blindfolded and the other is the "keeper." The blindfolded player is led by the keeper to various nature items about the room. The blindfolded person touches objects and tells the keeper what the item is. The player with the most correct identifications wins. Several people are blindfolded at the same time. The keepers may not talk to their partners to give hints.

Variation: Shadowgraph. Suspend a white sheet as a curtain with a bright light behind it. Pass several objects behind the sheet so that a shadow is cast. Use nature objects such as a small pine tree, a pine cone, a cattail, or a large leaf for the audience members to identify. Audience members individually write down their answers.

Observation Lotto. Players are given a card similar to the one shown in the diagram at the end of this paragraph. (You can make your own cards with objects suitable to the interests or age group.) For example, for a gardening group, the items all could be flowers or vegetables; for bird watchers, all birds; etc.) When an item on the card is spotted, the player puts an X in the appropriate square (or use a marker from nature such as a pebble). Play as in lotto or bingo-the first to fill a row horizontally, vertically, or diagonally wins. The game may be continued to determine 2nd, 3rd, etc., places. Objects may be found in several ways. Outdoors while taking a hike, players look around and call out the objects on the card as they are found. Or photos could be held up. Or the leader could just name the various objects from shuffled cards.

Rabbit	Wild Mustard	Birdhouse	Robin
Stream/River	Bird Feeder	Flock of Sparrows	Reforestation Area
Pine Tree	Squirrel	Bird Bath	Eroded Land
Blackbird	Oak Tree	Deer Crossing	Vulture

Sounds. While resting, hikers may sit quietly and write down all the natural sounds they hear in a designated period of time. The hiker with the longest list wins. This is sometimes called "Seaton Watching," because it was practiced by Ernest Thompson Seaton, an early naturalist and founder of the Woodcraft Indians youth movement, a forerunner of the Boy Scouts.

What Is Wrong with This Picture? Announce that a certain nature object is to be described and, although most of the characteristics given will be true, a few false ones will be included. See how many participants can detect the incorrect ones.

Indoor Woodcraft Hike (Indoor). Place pictures of birds and constellations, prints of leaves; and actual plants, twigs, and rocks around the room. Participants are divided into teams of three. The leader explains that all are to take a hike in the room. The teams draw to see which one starts first. They set off at intervals, the team captains armed with pencils and paper. Each team makes up a "yarn" (story) including all items they saw on their "hike." All the items must be included in the story. At the end of the hike, the stories are shared with the entire group.

ACTIVE GAMES

 ACTIVITIES

Bird Description. See who can imitate the call or song of the most birds. Have someone give a description of a bird and see if others can identify it. Describe birds seen on the trail and ask who saw each bird, what kind of flight it had; shape and size of its beak; and other questions. Also, facts can be told about it.

Variation: Who am I? Pictures of a bird can be placed on each person's back without telling what bird it is. Participants ask questions of others trying to identify what bird they are Questions can be answered only by yes or no. Other natural categories can be substituted for birds, such as fish, animals, and insects.

Flower Authors. Use a set of 48 cards with 12 pictures of flowers with corresponding 12 pictures of the leaves of the flowers, 12 family names of the flowers, and 12 cards with place and time of flower's blooming. Four teams are each given 12 cards and the names of three of the flowers. The team selects from its own cards those with characteristics of their assigned three flowers. Not all characteristics will be found among their own cards, so they go to other teams, trying to trade cards to complete their full three sets for their three flowers.

BLACK EYED SUSAN
Rudbeckia hirta (Asteraceae)

Blooms: June-August
Native to eastern U.S.,
but can be found nearly
anywhere in North America.
Most common of all
American wildflowers.

Grows 2-3 feet high and thrives
in most soils in full sun.

SCARLET SAGE
Salvia coccinea (Lamiaceae)

Blooms: April through first
frost Native to Texas and found
throughout the southern portion
of the United States.

Grows 1-3 feet tall.
Prefers sandy to gravelly
soil in full sun to partial shade.

GOLD YARROW
Achillea filipendulina (Asteraceae)

Blooms: May-November
Native to Europe, but has
naturalized throughout
North America.

Prefers light, rich soils in full sun.
Grows 2-4 feet tall

Nature Charades. Played like regular charades, either in teams or individually, by acting out the word. Some examples of nature categories:

Flowers

carnation	car-nation
sweet pea	sweet-pea
dogwood	dog-wood
marigold	Mary-gold
lady slipper	lady-slip-her
lady finger	lady-finger
foxglove	fox-glove
touch-me-not	touch-me-not
primrose	prim-rows
four-o'clock	four-oh-clock
bittersweet	bit-her-sweet

Birds

sparrow	spare-row
thrasher	thrash-her
towhee	tow he
warbler	war-blur
woodpecker	wood-peck-her
vireo	very-oh
kingfisher	king-fisher
killdeer	kill-deer
pintail	pin-tail
catbird	cat-bird
grosbeak	gross-beak

Trees

basswood	bass-wood
hornbeam	horn-beam
buckeye	buck-eye
catalpa	cat-tall-pa
sycamore	sick-ah-more
walnut	wall-nut
tulip tree	two-lip-tree
tamarack	tam-ah-rack
mulberry	mull-berry
chestnut	chest-nut

Variation: Animal Antics. The group is divided into small teams of six to eight players. The leader tells the name of a mammal, bird, or reptile to two players from each team. First player on the team imitates the locomotion of the animal, the second person the call. The rest of the team attempts to identify the animal. First to do so receives one point. For variation, players may draw or sketch the animal instead of imitating it.

Variation: Rabbit Race. Each player arranges four large leaves in a Y formation on the ground, with one leaf for each upper prong and two on the single stem. Tell the players that the first two leaves at the top represent the location of rabbit's rear feet. Have them race to see who can get in correct rabbit position first (feet on two top leaves with hands between legs on stem of Y.) When all are in proper position, ask them to practice running like a rabbit (put hands down in their respective tracks in front and then jump so feet will overreach hands, forming a Y again just ahead of the old one. Then race in this manner, doing the hop sequentially.

Nature Crows and Cranes. Group is divided into two teams facing each other and standing behind two parallel lines 10 feet to 12 feet apart. Twenty-five feet or more behind each line is a goal. The crows are "true" and the cranes "false." The leader makes a statement. If it is true, the "trues" chase the "falses"—the crows chase the cranes. Any cranes caught by crows before crossing their own goal line become crows and must join the other side. If the statement is false, cranes chase the crows. Winner is team with most players at the end of the game or when one team has accumulated all the players. Sample statements:

1. The firefly is a beetle. (T)
2. All bats are blind. (F)
3. All snakes are poisonous. (F)
4. A toad swallows his own skin when shedding. (T)
5. Spiders are insects. (F)
6. Mosquitoes have four wings. (T)
7. The North Star is the brightest star in the sky. (F)

8. The earth is the largest planet. (F)
9. Chipmunks sleep in the winter. (T)
10. Toads cause warts. (F)
11. Sheep chew cuds like cows. (T)
12. White pine trees have fine needles in a bundle (fascicle). (T)
13. Only the male mosquito bites. (F)
14. Snakes are slimy. (F)

Be sure each individual knows the correct answer before asking another question.

Variation: Tree Tag. One or more persons are "it." Players are safe only when they are touching a tree of a particular kind designated. Change the kind of tree from time to time.

Star Groups. You can use 18 to 36 players. Players use outlines of constellations formed by flashlights around the campfire. Divide into two teams, each team having eight or more players and a captain. A leader with knowledge of astronomy is the judge. Each player should have a good flashlight, the light end loosely covered with a piece of yellow crepe paper held in place by a rubber band. When the leader calls Lyra, each team runs to the fire and holds the flashlights above their heads. Each player takes the position of one star in the constellation named. Captain uses two or three players to form the brightest star in each group, such as stars of the first and second magnitude. When the team captain has the constellation formed and the players who are not required are sent back to the edge of the circle, the captain calls: "ready." The judge then examines the group to check the correctness of the formation for shape, the number of the stars, and star spacing. The first team to form the most nearly correct group wins 2 points.

Variation: This may be done indoors using holes punched in paper and projected on the ceiling. Paper cups, pebbles, or other objects can be used as stars to make the constellations on the floor.

What Am I? A player leaves the room and the group selects an animal or other nature object. The player returns and tries to discover what the object is by asking questions on characteristics that may be answered by yes or no. The person whose answer led to identification of the object leaves the room next.

Variation: Ask a player to think of an object and write it down on a slip of paper. The rest of the group may then ask questions that can be answered yes or no until they find out what the object is.

Variation: Have a panel of four ask questions. They may play like "20 questions" and ask only 20 questions, taking turns, or they may ask any number of questions.

Variation: Have a number of clues describing a nature object written on a card, with the most difficult clue listed first, and each subsequent clue becoming easier or more obvious. Read the clues one at a time until someone guesses what the object is. The player guessing correctly gets to keep the card. If an equal number of clues is used for all objects, one might give scores by the number of clues it takes to guess the object.

PAPER AND PENCIL GAMES

ACTIVITIES

Astronomy Test. What planet, star, or constellation does each of the following describe?

1. Worshipped by the Phoenicians as a god. It is a constellation near Vega. It was called "The Phantom" or "The Kneeled" by the Greeks. A hero of Greek mythology who was noted for his strength.

2. A planet discovered in 1846 that is not visible to the naked eye. A Roman god of the sea.

3. The planet nearest to the sun. This smallest planet can best be seen in March, April, August, and September. A mythical god of the Romans who carried messages.

4. This constellation is composed of six stars forming a bowl. It appears to be about halfway up the southern sky in the spring. The opening at the top of a volcano.

5. This constellation contains a cluster of stars known as "The Beehive." It is sometimes known as "The Crab." A dreaded disease.

6. A constellation located in the Milky Way. It is sometimes called the "Northern Cross." The flying swan.

Answers: 1. Hercules, 2. Neptune, 3. Mercury, 4. Crater, 5. Cancer, 6. Cygnus

Buried Birds (Flowers, Trees). Give each team a series of sentences. Within the sentences are names of birds. The object is to underline the name of the bird that is "buried." Names should be either in one word or adjacent words. For example, in Statement 2, "robin" is found in the words "rob" and "in." Flowers, trees, and birds are given as examples. You may wish to make up your own or have each team make 5 to10 sentences of buried words; then, compile and give the total list to all groups for identification of the buried items. The group to find the most wins.

Building Birds. Start with the name of a bird (or other category) and build horizontally or vertically, as in anagrams. An example follows:

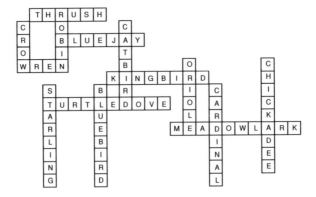

Bird Examples

1. The wolves howled at midnight. (owl)
2. It takes a brave bandit to rob in daylight. (robin)
3. Do doctors always charge so much? (dodo)
4. Do ventilate the new house better. (dove)
5. This pencil is a half-inch longer. (finch)
6. "Hit a fly," catcher Jones shouted from the dugout. (Flycatcher)
7. Fred started up suddenly from his reading. (red start)
8. You can't kill deer without a license. (killdeer)
9. Ralph patted her on the cheek jokingly. (heron)
10. I sent the pastor a Venetian vase. (raven)
11. The boy left the porch with awkward strides. (hawk)
12. The window looks over the garden. (owl)
13. She saw them both rush down the alley. (thrush)
14. Her eyes wandered over the curious crowd. (swan)
15. The crown lay shattered on the granite floor. (crow)
16. Bungalow rents are out of proportion for those of apartments. (wren)
17. The old horse seemed to wheeze worse than usual. (towhee)

Flower Examples

1. After you wash the pans, you may prepare lunch. (pansy)
2. I had to pay several taxes on this car: national tax, state tax, and city tax. (carnation)
3. Did Chopin know Beethoven? (pink)
4. If this car goes any faster I will fall out. (aster)
5. The plane is now dropping food to the marooned people. (snowdrop)
6. Before we knew it, the rhinoceros entered the water. (rose)
7. I believe it is the best plane money can buy. (anemone)
8. That scow slips through the water like a rowboat. (cowslip)
9. I understand that the panda is your favorite animal. (daisy)
10. Is your porch identical to ours? (orchid)

Tree Examples
1. Bring me a long strap, please. (apple)
2. The pin extended under the skin. (pine)
3. A bumblebee chased him about the lawn. (beech)
4. The wind came up so a kite was flown. (oak)
5. The map led us to a lonely swamp. (maple)
6. Does the chapel make you sleepy, too? (elm)
7. The ball bounced artistically down the field. (cedar)
8. The plumes waved in the air. (plum)
9. I will owe you a balance. (willow)
10. We found the owl in the dense swamp brush. (linden)
11. Nancy pressed Randolph's suit neatly. (cypress)
12. The airplane appeared out of the clouds. (pear)
13. Beautiful arches adorned the walls. (larch)
14. He must leap each hurdle in turn. (peach)
15. She went as hurriedly as possible. (ash)
16. The teacher held erasers to throw at the ruffian. (elder)

Categories, Guggenheim, Nature Squares, Versatility. This game can be played as individuals or in teams or groups. Draw a chart as below: (You can change the letters at the top by replacing A-B-C-D-E with T-R-A-I-L or another outdoor-related example. The categories on the left also may be changed.)

	A	B	C	D	E
Trees					
Birds					
Animals					
Flowers					

Example: Fill in spaces as indicated. For example, first line (trees)—apple, birch, cedar, dogwood,and elm. If you change the letters at the top to TRAIL, line two (trees) might be teal, raven, albatross, ibis, and lark. Give one point for each correct answer.

Variation: Single Letter Categories. List all of one category with names beginning with designated letter, e.g., using N and BIRDS-nuthatch, nighthawk, and nutcracker.

Variation: Tail and Head Categories. Any word of the category may be written in the first column; in the second column, though, the word must begin with the last letter of the word in column one; third column word begins with last letter of column—two word, etc. (e.g., nuthatch, hawk, killdeer, robin, and nutcracker).

Other Variations. Players sit in a circle. One player starts by naming a nature category, such as trees, birds, and flowers. Each player going around the circle must then name something in the category, such as trees: oak, maple, or cottonwood. Game can be made more difficult by naming them in alphabetical order: apple, birch, cottonwood, dogwood, etc. A player who cannot name something goes to the "end" of line.

Find the Trees in the Forest. The forest puzzle contains more than 20 species of trees. Can you locate them? The way to find them is to begin with any letter and spell out the trees by moving in any direction without skipping a square. You may go diagonally and repeat a letter if you so desire. Example: Begin with the M in the lower right-hand corner and spell MAPLE. When using with a group, enlarge the square to full-sized sheet.

Variation: Aviary. In the aviary there are 20 different bird names in the "pens." List all you can find. Try to learn something distinctive about each bird you find.

G	F	Y	E	W
I	R	C	H	M
B	A	E	L	O
L	D	B	P	U
I	K	S	A	M

FOREST

D	O	T	Y	N	M	T
U	O	R	A	E	L	O
K	C	U	J	B	U	I
U	A	N	I	A	S	G
L	R	E	T	R	D	A
W	E	C	K	I	P	N
H	O	T	L	A	R	E

AVIARY

A Hiking Romance. In the following story, each player fills in blank spaces with names of trees and flowers. One point for each correct answer.

> This romance began on a hike one day. It is true that he had met her once before down at the (beech), where he was a lifeguard, but they had not been formally introduced until the day of the hike.
>
> Her name was (rose) Budd, while his name was (red, cotton, or dog) Wood. She was very (poplar) with all the boys. In fact, (phlox) of them hung around her home. Her (poppy) was afraid she would wed some ne'er-do-well. He wanted her to (marigold) so that she could have all of the comforts and luxuries she wanted. She had always said, however, that anyone was (plum) crazy who married her for anything but love.
>
> Red Wood thought that she was a (peach) and he fell in love with her at first sight. The hike gave him his opportunity to tell her about it. "(Yew) are a real American beauty. (Yew) are the (apple) of my eye." Thereupon he (aster) to marry him.
>
> She loved him but she pretended to doubt his faithfulness. "What (lady's slipper) did I see in your possession the other day?" she parried. "Oh, that belonged to my brother, (Sweet) William. It was his wife's," he replied earnestly. "Oh, (rosemary) me or I'll have a (bleeding heart.) It is near to breaking now. If you only knew how I (pine) for you."
>
> Just then her little brother Johnny fell down. He continued to lie where he had fallen and sure did (balsam.) His big sister called to him: "(Johnny-jump-up) you're not hurt." "Oh, sis," he yelled back at her, "How can you (lilac) that?"
>
> (Red) resumed his courting, and thought a little French that he had learned in his four years at college. "Mon (cherry) (cherie) je t'aime." Since that was all the French he could remember he fell back on perfectly good English. "Let me press you (tulips) to mine." Johnny thought he was a big (prune), but she thought he was wonderful. "You're a (daisy)," she said as she cuddled in his arms. "We will be married at (four-o-clock) tomorrow. So (jack-in-the-pulpit) performed the ceremony, and all of their days were blessed.

Name These Trees. Give players sheets of paper with pictures of leaves from trees common in your locale. Players identify the trees from the leaves. Sixteen common leaves from the Midwest are pictured here. You may reproduce these or substitute others more indigenous to your location. (The names are put on for convenience. Remove them when preparing for actual use.)

COTTONWOOD   TULIP   MAPLE   WHITE OAK

BLACK WALNUT   BLACK CHERRY   RED OAK   SHAGBARK HICKORY

BASSWOOD   BURR OAK   ELM   ASPEN

DOGWOOD   HONEY LOCUST   STAGHORN SUMAC   BLACK LOCUST

Nature Riddles

Bird Riddles. Each individual or team writes down answers as leader reads the riddle. Person or team with highest correct total wins.

A brightly colored bird, whose first name is a city. (Baltimore oriole.)

To peddle (not pedal). (hawk)

Less than the whole and a long line of hills. (partridge)

The period of darkness, the reverse of out, and a high wind. (night-in-gale)

An instrument for driving horses, having no money, and a boy's name. (whip-poor-will)

A monarch and an angler. (king-fisher)

A boy's nickname, an exclamation, and a part of a chain. (bob-o-link)

The bird of imitations. (mocking bird)

A good-smelling tree, something found in ears, and part of a bird. (cedar-waxwing)

A young fowl and two letters of the alphabet. (chick-a-dee)

Tree Riddles

What tree always sighs and longs for things gone? (pine)

What tree is made of stone? (lime)

What tree grows nearest the sea? (beech)

What tree always has a partner? (pear)

What tree is pulled from the water with a hook? (bass)

What tree is often found in bottles? (cork)

What is the straightest tree that grows? (plum)

What tree is older than most other trees? (elder)

What tree is always found after a fire? (ash)

What tree do some animals wear that keeps them warm? (fir)

What tree wages a war on crops? (locust)

What tree is the neatest tree that grows? (spruce)

What tree is often found in people's mouth? (gum)

What tree runs over the meadows and pastures? (yew)

What tree does everyone carry in his hand? (palm)

What tree is an awful grouch? (crab)

What tree is part of the name of a common office supply? (rubber)

What tree grieves more than any other? (weeping willow)

What tree is worn at the beach? (sandal)

What tree describes a pretty girl? (peach)

What tree is used in kissing? (tulip)

Flower Riddles

What flower do ladies wear at bedtime? (lady's slipper)

What flower is used by cooks? (buttercup)

What flower tells how a person may get rich quick? (marigold)

What flower indicates late afternoon? (four-o'clock)

What flower tells what father says when he wants an errand run? (Johnny-jump-up)

A parting remark to a friend? (forget-me-not)

What flower do people get up early to enjoy? (morning glory)

What flower do young men place rings on? (lady finger)

What flower often hangs on the laundry line? (Dutchman's breeches)

What flower reminds one of church? (jack-in-the-pulpit)

What flower describes a beautiful specimen of an animal? (dandelion)

What flower is both pleasant and distasteful to the palate? (bittersweet)

What flower reminds one of winter weather? (snowdrops)

What flower is another name for dad? (poppy)

What flower reminds one of birds in a group? (phlox)

What flower suggests neat lines? (primrose)

What flower suggests a feline bite? (catnip)

What flower does a child like to throw in winter? (snowball)

Nature Symbolism Race. Name the nature objects often symbolized by the words below. For variation the form may be changed, for example: slyness fox or sly as a fox.

Animals

slyness—fox	fidelity (or faithful)—dog
fleetness (or swift)—deer	majesty—lion, moose
industry (or busy)—beaver	strength—ox
hunger—wolf	coolness—polar bear
gentleness—sheep or lamb	spring—woodchuck
Easter—rabbit	thirsty—camel
stillness—mouse	fierce—tiger
stealthiest—panther	big—elephant

Birds

happiness—lark	wisdom—owl
spring—bluebird	courage—eagle
cheer—robin	craziness—loon
summer—swallow	trumpeter—wild goose
persistence—woodpecker	

Flowers

purity—lily	Easter—lily
modesty—violet	remembrance—forget-me-not
spring—pussy willow	he loves me, he loves me not—daisy
love—rose	innocence—daisy, pansy
Mother's day—carnation	virtue—lily
peace—poppy	contentment—morning glory
cheerfulness—chrysanthemum	Christmas—holly, poinsettia
sympathy—rose	courage—carnation
sweet—rose	

Scrambles. Rearrange the letters to form the name of a bird or tree.

Birds

1. obbthiew (bobwhite)
2. diigrbnk (kingbird)
3. eebhop (phoebe)
4. accefhirty (flycatcher)
5. cdfhignlo (goldfinch)
6. ahkwtihgn (nighthawk)
7. acegklr (grackle)
8. achhnttu (nuthatch)
9. arpswo (sparrow)
10. eiorv (vireo)
11. abelrrw (warbler)
12. ceedkooprw (woodpecker)
13. hhrstu (thrush)
14. adenpprsi (sandpiper)
15. aecukpssr (sapsucker)
16. bidgikmnroc (mockingbird)
17. cjnou (junco)
18. abbcdiklr (blackbird)
19. abcdirt (catbird)
20. accdiheek (chickadee)

Trees

1. north (thorn)
2. panes (aspen)
3. clouts (locust)
4. ample (maple)
5. has (ash)
6. cared (cedar)
7. mug (gum)
8. lpaact (catalpa)
9. amcus (sumac)
10. redreylerb (elderberry)
11. reegvneer (evergreen)
12. usthcten (chestnut)
13. rayecoms (sycamore)
14. gernaipve (grapevine)

RESOURCES

Selected resources have been provided following certain sections; however, the following list includes general nature resources. These resources have ideas and projects relating to all of the sections in this chapter.

Copies of most all of the books cited have been reviewed, as have all of the Internet sites recommended. Brief annotations are provided for some of the resources.

Some references that are older and out of print have been purposely included when they provide excellent information. Frequently these resources can be found in public/school libraries or on the Internet. County extension agents frequently have a variety of helpful resources including pamphlets, software, and booklets.

The resources and information available on the Internet is ever expanding. A few sites have been suggested and although we have tried to select sites from well-established organizations or agencies (public, private, and governmental) that are likely to remain over time, there are always changes. We have provided suggestions for search words that we have used with some success when looking for information about specific topics

Lists of ever-evolving, new materials can be found in periodicals and publication catalogs. Nature centers, conventions and workshops, and bookstores are also good places to check out the latest resources. Caution: be sure to check that crafts, games, and other activities are nature-oriented; too many suggestions in popular resources misuse nature materials or do not involve environmental education.

Some of the resources in Chapter 4: Outdoor Living Skills will also include campcraft games, as do the general nature books included at the end of Chapter 1. Of course there are other areas that will overlap.

General Books on Nature Games

See master publicatons list for cities of Publishers.

Hamilton, Leslie. (1998). *Child's Play in Nature*. Perigee Books: NY.

Hillcourt, William. (1978). *The New Field Book of Nature Activities and Hobbies*. G. P. Putnam's Sons: NY. (out of print, limited availability)

Kavanaugh, James. (2002). *Birds Nature Activity Book: Educational games & activities for kids of all ages*. Waterford Press: Chandler, AZ

— (2002). *Mammals Nature Activity Book: Educational games & activities for kids of all ages*. Waterford Press: Chandler, AZ. (2002).

— *Pond LifeNature Activity Book: Educational games & activities for kids of all ages*. Waterford Press.

— (1999). *Nature Activity Book 1: Games, Puzzles & Activities for Kids of All Ages*, Waterford Press: Chandler, AZ.

Lingelbach, Jenepher, Purcell, Lisa. (2000). *Hands-On Nature: Information and Activities for Exploring the Environment with Children*. University Press of New England.

Miles Kelly Publishing Staff. (editors) (2003). *Nature: Ask Me a Question: A Picture Flip Quiz for 5-7 Year Olds*. Miles Kelly Publishing: Essex, England.

Musselman, Virginia W. (1967). *Learning About Nature through Games*. Stackpole Books, Harrisburg, PA. (out of print, limited availability)

Ripley, Catherine. (2001). *Why?: The Best Ever Question and Answer Book About Nature, Science and the World Around You*. Owl Communications.

Rogovin, Anne, Asner, Edward. (1999). *1,001 Activities for Children: Simple Games to Help a Child Explore the Wonders of Nature, the Imagination, the Senses, Art, Crafts, Music, and Much More*. Gramercy: NY.

OUTDOOR LIVING SKILLS

To "live" in the outdoors and feel at home in nature can be a magical and enriching human experience, As John Muir said: *"Everybody needs beauty as well as bread, places to play in and pray in, where Nature may heal and cheer and give strength to body and soul alike."* Although it is difficult, if not impossible, to explain the incredible experiences that can be attained in the outdoors, Muir came near to it: *"Keep close to nature's heart. . .break clear away once in a while, climb a mountain or spend a week in the woods. Wash your spirit clean. . .Go to the mountains and get their glad tidings. Nature's peace will flow into you as sunshine flows into trees. The winds will blow their own freshness into you, and the storms their energy, while cares will drop off like autumn leaves."*

CAMP NEBAGAMON, LAKE NEBAGAMON, WI

Henry David Thoreau went to the woods because he *"wished to live deliberately, to front only the essential facts of life, and see if I could not learn what it had to teach, and not, when I came to die, discover that I had not lived."* So we go to the woods to enjoy a meal the same way pioneers cooked, to sleep under stars shared by unknown galaxies, to experience camaraderie with friends around the glowing embers of a campfire.

However, magical adventures can turn out to be cold, miserable nightmares if people are unprepared or unskilled. Partially cooked or burnt food; hard, lumpy, slanted sleeping surfaces; cold, wind, and rain chilling to the bone to near hypothermia will most likely rule out a return to the outdoors, Therefore, the role of the leader is extraordinarily important to ensure that enjoyment rather than disaster ensues in the outdoors. Outdoor living skills (OLS) are based on an understanding of nature that can lead to amazing experiences rather than catastrophe. That is why outdoor living skills are fundamental to enjoying experiences in nature.

There has been some controversy regarding the practice of many outdoor living skills based on the current environmental status on planet earth and some groups have chosen to not teach certain skills. We have chosen purposefully to include outdoor skills, because we believe that in specific settings, these skills can and are being practiced in an environmentally responsible manner and they provide a unique opportunity to teach children and adults to care for and to respect, as well as to feel at ease in and to come to love, the natural world.

Because there are many excellent, in-depth resources that address skills and technical aspects of outdoor living, the treatment of these areas is not comprehensive, Instead we have provided information regarding training, a general overview of skills, descriptions of some interesting activities, and a list of carefully reviewed resources that will serve you well. Firecraft, ropecraft, toolcraft, campsites, shelter, and gear are most frequently associated with outdoor living skills and are included in this chapter while outdoor cookery is discussed in Chapter 5. As with other nature-oriented program activities, outdoor living skills may be stand-alone activities or integrated into other events such as club or group activities and instructional situations.

ORGANIZATIONS THAT OFFER PROGRAMS TEACHING OUTDOOR LIVING SKILLS

There are several organizations that offer camping and outdoor living skills instructional programs. The American Camp Association's (ACA) Outdoor Living Skills (OLS) program provides content, instructional materials, and organizational strategies. The program is an achievement program with recognition for completing increasingly challenging program levels. The ACA also trains instructors to conduct the program, however, anyone may use the *Outdoor Living Skills Program Manual* and the *Outdoor Skills Field Guide* that are available from the American Camp Association.

The Girl Scouts, Boy Scouts, and Camp Fire USA have incorporated outdoor living skills and camping as a central focus of troop activities since their inceptions.

The Girl Scouts have handbooks for the various age levels and badges related to outdoor skills. The Boy Scouts publish a *Field Book* that includes many outdoor activities and maintain a website (http://www.scoutstuff.org/cgi/catalog) that includes a section where publications, camping equipment and supplies can be purchased. Camp Fire, like the Girl Scouts and Boy Scouts, has resident camps across the country that emphasize environmental education.

The National Outdoor Leadership School (NOLS) and Outward Bound offer a variety of outdoor expeditions, for all ages, that include intensive instruction in outdoor living skills. NOLS (http://www.nols.edu/) states that their program "focuses on outdoor skills, leadership and environmental studies exclusively." The mission of Outward Bound (http://www.outwardbound.org/) is: "To conduct safe adventure-based programs structured to inspire self-esteem, self-reliance, concern for others and care for the environment."

ENVIRONMENTALLY RESPONSIBLE USE OF THE OUTDOORS

We should seek to inspire a reverence for all living things and, whenever possible, point out the interrelationships in the natural world. Whenever we travel through the woods, forests, deserts, canyon lands and across the mountains, there should be little or no evidence of our passing.

With the increasingly high rates of participation in outdoor recreational pursuits, responsible environmental practices are essential to preserve our natural resources for future generations. There are many environmentally responsible mottos to guide people who enjoy the outdoors such as: "Let living things live!;" "Take nothing but pictures, leave nothing but footprints;" "Give a hoot, don't pollute!", and "Leave no trace." The outdoors, and its beauty, does not belong to any one individual and is not there for us to destroy or use in a way that will deny use to future generations. Most of the plant life, animal life, and other materials found in the outdoors can be observed and studied in their natural environments and remain there to be enjoyed by others. Plant life, particularly wildflowers, must be preserved in its natural state. Every flower that is picked disturbs the reproductive cycle of the plant and it is no wonder that many of the beautiful wildflowers are disappearing. It takes years for a tree to grow and mature, but only one careless stroke of an axe or a hatchet to destroy or mar it for the rest of its life.

The guiding principles for all outdoor living, whether wilderness or local parklands, must be "minimum impact" on the environment. Some refer to this as "low impact camping" or "leave no trace." Instead of using trees in natural areas for firewood, it may be necessary to purchase wood or use charcoal or fossil fuel-based stoves for cooking. (This practice is required in many areas to help prevent forest fires that ravage millions of acres each year.)

There are outdoor areas that practice environmental sustainability, where natural materials still can be used responsibly without permanently damaging the environment. Persons using the outdoors should know the regulations for each area and, even when allowed to use natural materials, they should follow the best environmental practices and ethics. Building roaring bonfires for evening gatherings or cooking is wasteful and unnecessary. Use natural resources respectfully regardless of the regulations.

The American Camp Association's (http://www.ACAcamps.org) Outdoor Living Skills program emphasizes "little or no impact on the environment." This organization, along with many others such as Leave No Trace, Outward Bound, the National Outdoor Leadership School, the Boy Scouts and Girl Scouts, and conservation agencies such as the Sierra Club and the Nature Conservancy, all stress environmental ethics.

Leave No Trace

The Leave no Trace Center for Outdoor Ethics (http://www.lnt.org) "is a national non-profit organization dedicated to promoting and inspiring responsible outdoor recreation through education, research and partnerships." Leave No Trace builds awareness, appreciation and respect for our wildlands.

The seven principles of Leave No Trace are: " 1) plan ahead and prepare, 2) travel and camp on durable surfaces, 3) dispose of waste properly, 4) leave what you find, 5) minimize campfire impacts, 6) respect wildlife, and 7) be considerate of other visitors. Leave no Trace training includes 1) Awareness Workshops that may be 30-minute chats about program principles or full-day workshops, 2) Trainer Courses that are two-day trainings in an outdoor setting led by Master Educators, and 3) Master Educator Courses that are five-day training for people who are actively teaching other backcountry skills or providing recreation information to the public."

Leave No Trace publishes some very good books about environmental ethics and skills for specific regions of the country and ecosystems (mountains, deserts, rainforests, etc.), as well as specific outdoor activities (horse use, mountain biking, rock climbing, etc.). These resources can be found at the end of this section.

Natural areas are under a wide variety of jurisdictions from privately owned to local, state, and federal government agency overseers. Many state and local parks do not allow collecting even dead wood and bar the picking or removal of any natural materials. National parks prohibit taking anything natural, living or dead, from its original location.Federal agencies have rules and guidelines, such as the *Code of Federal Regulations, Title 36, Parts 1 to 199 (36CFR)* that "provides for the proper use, management, government, and protection of persons, property, and natural and cultural resources within areas under the jurisdiction of the National Park Service." In addition, each park and outdoor area has rules specific to the site. It is the outdoor user's responsibility to know the rules regarding campsites, fires, and sanitation, and so on, and to follow them carefully.

While people no longer require outdoor living skills to exist or subsist from day to day, they are still valued outdoor activities. No longer are outdoor living skills considered the exclusive domain of the Boy Scouts, Girl Scouts, and children's camp.

They are used in many outdoor recreation pursuits—outdoor adventure activities, ecotourism, family camping, day camping, special clubs, backyard cooking, special events, historical reenactments, and hunting and fishing, to name a few.

 Books on Environmentally Responsible
Use of the Outdoors

See master publicatons list for cities of Publishers.

See also general campcraft resources at the end of this chapter and Chapter 7, Section G: Hiking and Backpacking.

Hampton, B., and D. Cole. (2004). *Soft Paths*. Stackpole Books: Harrisburg, PA.

McGivney, A. (2003). 2nd revised edition. *Leave No Trace: A Guide to the New Wilderness Etiquette*, 2nd revised edition. The Mountaineers Books: Seattle, WA.

Tilton, B. (2004). *Master Educator Handbook*. National Outdoor Leadership School. Instructor's manual for teaching the seven principles of Leave No Trace.

All of the following Leave No Trace resources can be obtained from Leave No Trace: P.O. Box 997, Boulder, CO 80301. www.LNT.org

Leave No Trace Training Cookbook. Compilation of training ideas for teaching Leave No Trace skills and ethics.

Northeast Mountain Skills & Ethics Booklet

Pacific Northwest Skills & Ethics Booklet

Sea Kayaking Skills & Ethics Booklet

Southeast Skills & Ethics Booklet

Tropical Rainforest Skills & Ethics Booklet

Western River Corridors Skills & Ethics Booklet

Deserts and Canyons Skills & Ethics Booklet

Horse Use Skills & Ethics Booklet

Lakes Region Skills & Ethics Booklet

Rocky Mountains Skills & Ethics Booklet

Mountain Biking Skills & Ethics Booklet

Rock Climbing Skills & Ethics Booklet

All of the following Outdoor Living Skills materials can be obtained from American Camp Association, 5000 State Road 67 North, Martinsville, IN 46151. www.ACAcamps.org

OLS Instructor's Manual. Training manual for adults training adults to teach outdoor living skills to groups. Program overview.

OLS Program Manual. Group instructor's manual.

OLS Field Guide. Flip chart design, samples, charts, visuals for teaching.

OLS Patches. Levels one through five

 ## Internet Resourses: Environmentally Responsible Use of the Outdoors

Suggested search words: environmental ethics/wilderness ethics/environmental camping/environmentally responsible use/outdoor regulations/environmentally responsible land use

Leave No Trace
http://www.lnt.org/.

"The Leave No Trace Center for Outdoor Ethics is a national non-profit organization dedicated to promoting and inspiring responsible outdoor recreation through education, research and partnerships. Leave No Trace builds awareness, appreciation and respect for our wildlands."

National Outdoor Leadership School (NOLS)
http://www.nols.edu/

Since 1965 NOLS has led environmentally sensitive expeditions and trips in the outdoors, They have an online store where books and other outdoor related resources can be purchased.

Outward Bound
http://www.outwardbound.org/about.html

Outward Bound has its origin in the U.S. in the 1950s. Outward Bound emphasizes interpersonal relationships and environmental integrity. The site includes a store with merchandise and manuals.

SECTION A

CAMPSITES, SHELTER, AND GEAR

To obtain maximum enjoyment when living outdoors, you must be comfortable. Comfort comes from knowing "how"—how to make a comfortable bed on the ground; how to keep the rain from getting all your belongings wet inside the tent; how to stay warm in your sleeping bag; how to erect your shelter so that it stays up in a wind and rain storm; how to pack everything you need properly in your backpack without being burdened by excessive weight; how to select your site so you're not sleeping downhill or in the middle of a potential wash out; and how to pitch your tent so that the morning sun warms your rising and dries out dew-laden tents and gear. These are just a few of the many skills that can be learned through an outdoor living skills program.

CAMPSITES

There are basically two types of campsites: (1) organized campsites at established sites, usually with water, toilet, and electrical facilities that can be found in public and private campgrounds, resident camps, etc. and (2) temporary sites oftentimes in backcountry locations where no facilities exist. It is the temporary campsite that is discussed in this section.

CHELEY COLORADO CAMPS, CHELEY, CO.

When selecting a campsite, choose locations well back from lakeshores, streams, and trails (200 feet minimum) and away from fragile vegetation or known animal habitats or breeding grounds. Never cut boughs or poles, put nails into trees, or dig trenches around tents. Before you leave, make sure you remove all string, twine, or rope tied to trees. The thoughtless oversight of leaving a piece of twine around a tree can result in the eventual girding and killing of the tree. Always use established campsites and, if they are not available, don't use the same campsite for more than one night. When breaking camp, leave no evidence that you were there. "Pack it in and pack it out," including trash and everything you brought with you.

When making a campsite, it is no longer acceptable to dig deep trench toilets. Instead each person should dig small "catholes" at least 6 inches deep and at least 200 feet from any trail, campsite, or water or drainage source. These holes can be made with the heel of the boot or a trowel, When finished cover the hole over with dirt. One of the worst things to see in the wild is remnants of toilet paper. If toilet paper is used, the best alternative is to carry it out in plastic Ziploc bags and dispose of it in the toilet (not landfill trash). Burning toilet paper doesn't really work and can cause forest fires. Nonpoisonous leaves can be used as toilet paper and properly buried to avoid this problem.

When hiking to the campsite, use marked trails when they exist and stay on them; don't cut across switchbacks or corners. Be careful not to kick rocks loose. Use appropriate footwear. Heavy-soled boots, designed for traction on hard, smooth surfaces take a tremendous toll on soft, wetland environments and in heavily used campsites. Always use the firmest under-foot landscape possible. When hiking cross-country, never blaze trees or leave other signs.

SHELTER

Sleeping out in the open or under a simple tent or a shelter made from native materials can be one of the thrills of youth that continues throughout a lifetime. People who use the outdoors regularly should know how to make emergency shelters. Most tragic outdoor deaths result from exposure and, it is shelter that prevents exposure. There are children's camps that make and use natural shelters for sleeping throughout the summer. They manage their natural resources in a responsible manner with a plan for environmental sustainability.

Tents offered for sale, like most other camping equipment, are high tech, employing a variety of synthetic fabrics specifically designed to prevent condensation and to be cool in the summer and warm in the winter. Tent poles are designed applying space age metallurgy developments to be lightweight, strong, and compactable. You can spend lots of money on the "latest and greatest." On the other hand, a 6' x 8' piece of 5 mil plastic strung on a rope between two trees can keep you quite dry and comfortable and cost very little. To make a more permanent tube that can be rolled and tied with a piece of rope to your pack, use duct tape to seal the overlapping plastic on the bottom both inside and outside. (Of course there is a rather severe condensation problem with the plastic, but if you spread the sides with rocks or other weights, there is no need to come into contact with the sides.)

Although the high-tech outdoor supply stores sell almost everything you might want to use in the outdoors, great satisfaction can be gained and money saved by making your own gear and shelter. After all, this is how Native Americans and early settlers lived. There are many resources to instruct you in how to do this, including organized training programs (such as those programs referred to in the beginning of this chapter), books and manuals, and experienced outdoor enthusiasts with a wealth of practice of tried and true methods.

GEAR

Chapter 7, Section G: Backpacking and Hiking includes some excellent resources for gear... what you need, how to make it or where to get it, how to pack, and so on, Basic equipment will include such things as backpacks, tents, sleeping bag, hiking boots or shoes, water bottles, cooking equipment, and food containers. Outdoor supply stores can provide nearly any outdoor necessity or gadget you might desire. But remember John Muir hiked from the Midwest to Florida with a sack of rice and the wool clothing and shoes made in the later part of 1800s America. So you can make rather than buy things and live both simply and comfortably.

S E C T I O N   B

FIRECRAFT

Firecraft skills are valuable for outdoor cookery, for evening campfires, and to keep warm. An essential part of every firecraft program is instruction in fire safety and environmental protection. This includes proper selection and preparation of the site, appropriate equipment for controlling the fire, proper method of extinguishing the fire, and leaving no evidence of the fire site when done.

In some areas, overuse, dwindling supplies of wood, air quality considerations, and fire dangers cause outdoor campfires to be highly regulated. Sometimes campfires are prohibited entirely and cooking on camp stoves is recommended or required. Always check local regulations and fire danger levels before using open campfires.

FIRE SITES

If fires are allowed, make sure that you have all necessary permits. Use an existing site whenever possible. Fires should be located at least 8 feet from scrubs, dry grass, or other combustible materials. Metal fire pans will prevent scaring the ground and can be purchased at most outdoor supply stores or you can use pans from old home grills. To prevent scorching of the ground, raise the pan off the ground with rocks or line it with mineral soil commonly found near sandy streambeds, uprooted trees, or near boulder areas. To prepare a place for a fire on the ground, scrape the surface clear in an open area, never locate the fire under or against trees or rocks and don't circle with rocks. Rocks from streams are likely to explode, as are flint and some other types of rock. The smoke from a large or continuously burning fire will kill leaves and branches on overhanging trees.

FIRE SAFETY

Never leave a fire unattended and always have water available to put it out. In fact, before you begin to build the fire, you should make sure that water to extinguish it is placed near the fire. To extinguish, sprinkle it with water and stir with a stick until it is cold. Make sure all embers, sticks, and ashes are soaked and completely out. Test this by carefully touching the dead coals with your hand. Conserve wood and leave no trace. When permissible, use small wood from the forest floor only. Do not use axes or saws on living trees and do not break off branches from living or dead trees.

FIRE CONSERVATION

Remember, to conserve wood and the natural environment, only build fires as big as required to accomplish your task. Use only down wood off the forest floor or purchase wood. Do not cut live branches or break dead branches from trees.

TYPES OF FIRES

Suggestions for special fire-building structures, methods of lighting campfires, making colored flames, as well as types of wood to use can be found in the Chapter 8, Section C: Campfire Programs. Different types of outdoor cooking require different fire lays and types of wood. Suggestions for types of fires are provided with the various cooking methods in Chapter 5. It is a real art to build exactly the right fire for proper cooking.

FIRE STARTING

The only things you need to have fire are fuel, oxygen, and heat. The fuel must start small enough and burn long enough to produce enough heat to catch the larger pieces of wood that produce coals. The three sizes of wood are tinder, kindling, and fuel. Tinder, which is less than the size of a matchstick in diameter, is the key to starting the fire—make sure that it is small enough and there is enough of it to start kindling, the next size of wood, which ranges from toothpick size to about thumb size in diameter. Fuel is the remainder of wood, larger than kindling ranging to logs. Because fire needs oxygen to burn, once the fire is started, fanning the fire with a plate or other flat object will make it roar in a short time. Fanning the coals and adding wood will also rekindle a fire even left overnight.

When there is high humidity or wood is damp, fanning becomes more important. Remember, even after days of rain, it is the outer part of the wood that is wet, not the inside. When the tinder or fire starter gets hot enough, fires can be started in any conditions. To obtain dry tinder, make a fuzz stick (Chapter 3, Section B: Campcraft Games) or make shavings from a stick or the inside of a small split log. The key to starting all fires is having enough tinder that is sufficiently small. One of the most common mistakes is not having enough tinder to start the larger wood.

Following are a few interesting ways to start fires often used for campfires and ceremonies:

1. Use fine steel wool as tinder to start a fire with flint and steel. Many people will not believe that steel wool will burn until they see it. Mold the steel wool into the shape of a bird's nest. Strike the flint on the steel, throwing the sparks into the center of the "nest." Once a spark is caught, blow on it and it will become red hot. Place the glowing steel wool in the middle of a pile of very dry, small tinder at the base of your fire. In the right area, you may be able to find your own flint among the rocks, but first check to see that it is environmentally responsible to remove these rocks.

2. Try making fire by friction, using the methods of Native Americans. This is a lot more difficult than it looks and nearly impossible in a very wet or humid environment. However, under the right conditions, success can be achieved. There are two methods—one using a spindle and the other using a bow. These techniques can be found in some of the general campcraft resources in this manual or by searching for "campfires by friction" on the Internet.

3. Using a magnifying glass is a relatively easy way to start a fire and also can be used for wood burning instead of using an electric wood burner. The sun, however, must be bright, hot, and clear.

4. Make fireplace candles and campfire logs. The latter are described in Chapter 8, Section C: Campfire Programs. To make fire starters (particularly useful on damp or rainy days), roll newspaper tightly into a 1-inch diameter roll. Tie with three strings spaced evenly apart. Cut into 3-inch lengths. Soak in paraffin (old melted candles will be fine); place rolls in a #10 can standing on end, and pour melted paraffin over them until completely saturated. Let cool.

5. An easy way to make a fire, even in wet conditions, is to set a candle upright in the base of the fire and let it burn until it starts the tinder and kindling. This can be especially helpful when wood is very wet and in humid conditions.

6. Look in Chapter 3, Section B: Campcraft Games to find additional firecraft activities.

RESOURCES FOR FIRECRAFT

See general campcraft resources at the end of this chapter and Chapter 7, Section G: Hiking and Backpacking.

 **Internet Sites**

Suggested search words: firecraft/campfires/fire starting

Bob's Blackpowder Notebook:

http://members.aye.net/~bspen/index.html

Detailed instructions for making fire with flint and steel

S E C T I O N   C

ROPECRAFT

Ropecraft appears to be a lost art in today's world. A rope can be very handy (and sometimes essential) in many outdoor pursuits, especially when canoeing or sailing, It's impossible to be an accomplished sailor without being proficient in knots. People who fish know how to secure a hook to slippery fishing line. All good outdoors persons know basic knots—what they are used for and, perhaps, some more advanced, specialty knots for specific purposes.

Ropecraft typically includes making rope, tying knots and hitches and lashing. Lashing is used to construct tables, outdoor kitchens, tripods for fires, and other items used primarily in long-term campsites. If it is environmentally acceptable to use wood in nature, lashed items should be made using dead wood only. It is important to remove all rope and twine when breaking camp. After skills and experience are obtained, the more adventurous may wish to undertake pioneering projects such as rope bridges, sometimes referred to as *monkey bridges* or other advanced projects. There are many resources that provide pictures and directions, including animated knot-tying websites. Some of these resources can be found in the following resource section.

ROPE-MAKING

Rope-making is a fun activity for the playground, day camp, and many other outdoor skills situations. Rope can be made by hand braiding or by using a variety of homemade rope-making machines. To make rope, binder's twine or India hemp is best, unless native materials are available and it is environmentally responsible to gather them.

⛷ ACTIVITIES 🎿

Making Rope by Hand. A simple way to make rope that does not require any special equipment is the "twist and cross" method. Using twine or other cordage material, cut four strands approximately 1¼ times the length of rope you wish to make. Secure four ends to a stationary object so that it can be stretched taut when you hold the unsecured ends. Take two strands in each hand approximately one to two feet from the secured ends of the rope. Begin twisting the strands in each hand to the right. As the twine binds, but before it kinks, cross the right hand over the left hand and exchange hands that are holding the twine. Continue twisting and crossing, moving toward the untied end of the twine until the rope is completed. The ends can be secured with the frapping technique used in lashing or each end can be securely knotted. The rope will be stronger than the four strands used together separately.

Rope Making Machine. Here's how to make your own rope machine.

Step 1. Attach two boards at right angles as shown in the diagram. Use screws for more security. Boards should be 9-inch to 12-inch pine, approximately 5 inches in width.

Step 2. Drill ³⁄₁₆ʺ holes in both the upright board and handle as diagrammed, with middle hole slightly above the other two. A forked stick may be used in place of the strand separator board.

Step 3. Make hooks out of rigid ⅛ʺ wire in form shown. These hooks should move freely in the holes. Insert hooks and the machine is ready to be strung for rope making.

Step 4. Attach twine to one hook and take it out around the awl (the length depends upon how long a rope you want to make). Return to second hook, back to awl, and then tie back to third hook.

Step 5. Insert strand separator and put handle on. Turn handle and the strands will begin to twist, both individually and into a single rope. Hold on to the awl and keep the rope somewhat taut. You will be able to feel the pull necessary to get an even rope twist.

Some prefer to substitute a small piece of board (3ʺ square) with a single hook for the awl, but with no handle-insert portion. The rope is attached to the single hook that should be free to move. For stability, the base board can be fastened to a table with a C clamp. Some do not bother to have this base board but just hold the end board with the hooks and the handle by hand.

Knot-tying games and contests can be found in Chapter 3, Section B: Campcraft Games.

 ## Books on Ropecraft

See master publicatons list for cities of Publishers.
See also general campcraft resources at the end of this chapter.

Blandford, Percy W. (1980). *Practical Knots & Rope Work*. TAB Books: NY

Jaconbson, Cliff. (1999). *Basic Essentials: Knots for the Outdoors*. Globe Pequot Press, Guilford, CT. (Basic Essentials(tm) book) Includes top 10 most important knots and hitches, selecting best knot for a task, choosing the right rope, preparing new ropes for outdoor use, and caring for ropes.

 ## Internet Sites on Ropecraft

Suggested search words: ropecraft/knots/cordage/

Animated knot tying:
http://www.mistral.co.uk/42brghtn/knots/index.html

42nd Brighton (Saltdean), Scout Group, East Sussex, UK. (A scout troop in England. I really like this page. It has simple animations for all basic knots, bends, and hitches.)

Knots on the Web:
http://www.earlham.edu/~peters/knotlink.htm

Includes links to numerous sites on the Web dealing with knots; also includes discussion of software, videos, and books about knot tying.

S E C T I O N   D
TOOLCRAFT

Toolcraft usually includes the use of knives, saws, axes, hatchets, and sometimes wood-splitting tools such as sledges and anvils. Typically the pocketknife is a personal tool, while other equipment (saws, hatchets, etc.) are generally group tools.

Responsible environmental behaviors continue to be a primary concern whenever using tools in the natural environment. Many books and manuals have removed sections describing the use of the axe and hatchet; some have eliminated toolcraft all the time, anywhere. The easy thing to do, with those uneducated in specific needs of a particular environment, is to have a hard and fast rule that prohibits the use of tools and natural materials entirely. An additional consideration is that if people use natural materials in one area, they may transfer this behavior to other areas where it is inappropriate.

We believe that children and adults can be taught to distinguish good and bad practices in various ecosystems and under specific environmental conditions; in fact, we believe this information is imperative for deeper understandings and truly responsible use. What must be ingrained through the educational process is that if you are uncertain, to any degree, then don't use natural materials. Therefore, we have elected to include toolcraft, because we believe it can be practiced responsibly and comprises skills that can be enjoyable and are an important part of our heritage. There are a few organized camps that set up semipermanent campsites and fishing or hunting camps that are established for weeks or months at a time that use axes, saws, and knives to construct camp kitchens, tables, and seats, as well as to chop wood for fires.

SAFETY

If tools are used, it is imperative that proper care and use be taught and practiced. Safety procedures cannot be overemphasized. When working with youth, the saw is preferred over the axe as a beginning tool because of safety. Axes and hatchets should not be used with children because of the potential dangers. When selecting an axe for a beginning user, the intermediate size, sometimes referred to as the Hudson Bay style, is recommended. It has a 2 lb.x 2 1/4 lb. head and a 24″ x 28″ handle. This lightweight axe serves very well and effectively performs work of both the hatchet and the regular axe. Again, unless the instructor/leader is highly skilled and experienced in proper use, as well as in group management, it is best to leave the axe and hatchet alone.

POCKETKNIVES

Pocketknives used to be found in the pockets of youth and adults alike. It was often seen as a mark of being grown up to have the responsibility of a knife that had so many utilitarian purposes. Over the years, the use of pocketknives has declined dramatically; few know how to use them safely or have any degree of real skill. Few adults, for that matter, have such skills. With heightened security at schools and airports and many public venues, by necessity, the pocketknife has virtually disappeared from the pocket. Since it is not common to allow youth to carry pocketknives, most leaders keep knives in a secure location until they are teaching knife care and handling or working with outdoor activities or crafts that use knives. If leaders do not have effective behavior management capabilities, then, regardless of their skill, these activities should not be introduced.

Nonetheless, the pocketknife can be the most important single camp tool. A well-maintained pocketknife can last a lifetime. Knife safety must always be stressed and participants must demonstrate proficiency before they are allowed to handle knives. With children it must always be stressed that knives are tools, not toys. Some fundamental knife safety practices include:

- Always cut away from yourself and make sure that all others are out of range of a knife that could slip.

- In most cases, it is best to close or sheath a knife before passing it.

- When passing an open knife, lay it down on a table or solid object and allow the other person to pick it up. This is particularly important in boats or other unstable places.

- Never push the blade with your thumb; instead wrap your fingers around the handle.

- Always keep the blade sharp. A dull blade potentially is dangerous because it is more likely to slip or catch and jump. Most knives can be sharpened at a 23 degree angle.

- Never use a knife on anything that will damage the blade or break it.

- Always store the blade clean and dry.

- Never carry an open knife when walking.

- When not using a knife, close it and put it away.

- Close the blade with the palm of your hand.

Use of the knife can be integrated very well into a crafts program. See Chapter 2: Nature Crafts, Whittling, and Woodcarving. (under Section A).

SAW

If one tool was to be selected for its utility and relative safety for beginners, the saw would most likely be selected. When used correctly, the saw is a relatively easy to use, safe tool. The bow saw is a good all-purpose saw and is available in several sizes. It will cut wood three times faster than a hand axe and is much safer. Buy a good saw since cheap ones are likely to fail with heavy use. String saws and folding saws can be used when backpacking. When sawing, apply even pressure and push the entire length of the blade through the wood, then release pressure and pull the saw easily into position for the next downward stroke. As with all tools, saws should be thoroughly cleaned and dried before storing.

Resources on Toolcraft

See general campcraft resources at the end of this chapter and Chapter 6.

GENERAL OLS RESOURCES

Selected resources have been provided following certain sections; however, the following list includes general nature resources. These resources have ideas and projects relating to all of the sections in this chapter.

Copies of most all of the books cited have been reviewed, as have all of the Internet sites recommended. Brief annotations are provided for some of the resources.

Some references that are older and out of print have been purposely included when they provide excellent information. Frequently these resources can be found in public/school libraries or on the Internet. County extension agents frequently have a variety of helpful resources including pamphlets, software, and booklets.

The resources and information available on the Internet is ever expanding. A few sites have been suggested and although we have tried to select sites from well-established organizations or agencies (public, private, and governmental) that are likely to remain over time, there are always changes. We have provided suggestions for search words that we have used with some success when looking for information about specific topics

Some of the resources in Chapter 7, Section G: Hiking and Backpacking containg information about outdoor living. Of course you will find other areas that overlap

 ## Books on General Outdoor Living Skills

See master publicatons list for cities of Publishers.

Beard, Dan. (2000) reprinted from 2nd edition of 1900. *The Outdoor Handy Book for Playground, Field, and Forest.* University Press of the Pacific, Honolulu, HI. A classic book filled with games, skills and many "how-to's" all used in the early 1900s.

Blankenship, Bart. (1996). *Earth Knack: Stone Age Skills for the 21st Century,* Gibbs Smith: Layton, UT.

Hammett, Catherine. (1981), revised. *The Campcraft Book.* American Camp Association, Bradford Woods, Martinsville, IN. 46151.

Jaeger, Ellsworth. (1945). *Wildwood Wisdom.* Shelter Publications (reprinted in 1992), Bolinas, CA. Written in 1945, it is a classic wilderness living book that includes how to: build a lean-to, find wild food, follow a trail, use an axe, hitch a mule, and survive outdoors. Lots of illustrations

Scheder, Catherine. (2002) *Outdoor Living Skills Field Guide.* American Camp Association, Bradford Woods, Martinsville, IN. Carry-along field guide for American Camp Association's Outdoor Living Skills program.

Scheder, Catherine. (2002) *Outdoor Living Skills Program Manual: An Environmental-Friendly Guide.* American Camp Association, Bradford

Woods, Martinsville, IN. Manual for American Camp Association's Outdoor Living Skills program.

Scheder, Catherine. (2002) *Outdoor Living Skills Instructors Manual.* American Camp Association, Bradford Woods, Martinsville, IN. Instructor's manual for American Camp Association's Outdoor Living Skills program.

Seton, Ernest Thompson. (1997). *The Book of Woodcraft and Indian Lore.* Stevens Publishing: Dallas, TX. Ernest Thompson Seton (1860-1946) was an early camping youth leader who started the Woodcraft Indians in 1902 and helped cofound the Boy Scouts in 1910. First published in 1929.

 ## Internet Sites on General Outdoor Living Skills

Suggested search words: campcraft/outdoor living skills/camping/camp skills

U.S. Scouting Service Project:

http://www.usscouts.org/usscouts/start.asp

The Boy Scouting web portal. Volunteer Scouts serving scouting through information technologies; links to lots of camping and outdoor topics.

Scoutstuff.org.

http://www.scoutstuff.org/cgi/catalog

CHELEY COLORADO CAMPS, CHELEY, CO.

CHAPTER 5

OUTDOOR COOKERY

Half the fun of campin' out
And trampin' here and there
Is buildin' up your appetite
'Til you're hungry as a bear.
Then sittin' down at mess time
With swell victuals all about-
Boy! that's a livin' what is livin'
And you get campin' out!

Cooking is more than a necessity; it is an activity-it is a time for fun, sharing, and adventure. Planning for outdoor cooking is a major part of the activity and an important part of the educational process. Deciding on menus based on portability, packability, preservability, tastiness, and good nutrition involves understanding foods and the requisites of the outdoor environment. Selecting ingredients and packing them efficiently is an important skill, as is selecting the right equipment and following the best sanitation and environmental protection practices.

This chapter comprises three sections: (A) General Environmental and Nutritional Considerations; (B) Guidelines and Supplies; and (C) Cooking Methods. These cooking methods are illustrated with menus and recipes for items included in the menus.

SECTION A
GENERAL ENVIRONMENTAL AND NUTRITIONAL CONSIDERATIONS

ENVIRONMENTAL CONSIDERATIONS

In addition to environmental concerns regarding campfires (Chapter 4, Section B: Firecraft), there are important considerations regarding water and sanitation associated

113

with cooking outdoors. The following section provides a brief overview of best practices for water and sanitation

Water

Bathing, laundry, cooking, and scrubbing pots and pans should be done at least 200 feet from the shores of streams and lakes. If soap is used, biodegradable soap is recommended. You should never drink water from any natural source without treating it first. There are several purification methods including: (1) boiling 12 minutes; (2) treating with approved chemicals, or (3) filtering with commercial filtration and treatment systems or with solar stills. Certain types of organic contamination, *giardia*, for example, require specific types of treatment, so carefully check conditions in the areas in which you camp. Boiling is not successful with chemical or radioactive contamination.

Sanitation

Sanitation includes washing dishes, storing and handling of food, and disposing of garbage. Wash dishes in hot soapy (biodegradable) water at least 200 feet from natural water sources. Put them in loosely knit nylon or mesh bags (easily homemade), rinse and sanitize by dipping in boiling water; and hang up the bag to dry. Using foods that require minimum or no *refrigeration* avoids the problem of keeping things cool. When refrigeration is needed, a stream-cooled or air-cooled homemade "refrigerator" will frequently suffice. A watertight jar can be anchored in a stream. An air-cooled refrigerator can be made by constructing a "tree pantry" wrapped in burlap. Place a 2-gallon can on top with holes that permit water to drip slowly down the burlap. The air will cause evaporation and cooling. An ice chest, of course, can be purchased. Check for the quality of insulation. Although it usually must be purchased directly from an ice company, block ice lasts longer than cubed or crushed ice.

All garbage and refuse should be packed out and properly disposed of in dumpsters or other established disposal sites. This includes grease and biodegradable foods. Pour grease into a small can or other container until it cools and congeals, then repack it into sealable plastic bags or plastic containers or bottles. *Grease pits should never be used,* The smell of grease attracts animals (raccoons, skunks, coyotes, bears, etc.) that will dig it up. Nothing should be buried or burned. Planning menus that minimize the amount of grease produced in cooking will go a long way in properly managing grease. "Pack it in, pack it out!" Pack out ALL garbage, even those things you think are bird or animal food (this is not their natural source of food) and things that you think are biodegradable. Foil will not burn completely. Leftover food, fish heads, entrails, etc., should be packed out (never buried). It is important to secure garbage in airtight, odor-proof plastic bags or containers to avoid attracting insects and animals. In locations where bears or other animals are a problem, food and garbage should be strung between two trees (cached). Oftentimes there are ranger stations that distribute pamphlets that include specific information about how garbage should be handled in bear country.

NUTRITIONAL CONSIDERATIONS

Diet and exercise are key to healthy lifestyles. Since you are getting outside, hopefully you are involved in lots of exercise. When planning menus and types of cooking (e.g., frying, broiling, baking) outdoors, it remains important to have a balanced diet and watch your caloric, cholesterol, and sodium (salt) intake. With the "obesity crisis," we know that this is important for children and youth, as well as adults and seniors. Calories, cholesterol, and sodium increase risk factors for conditions such as heart disease, high blood pressure, diabetes, obesity, hypertension, etc.

The number of calories people need is determined by their individual metabolism and the amount of physical activity they get. Outdoor cooking, properly planned, can regulate caloric intake. Regardless of all the fancy diets, the basic formula remains- to lose weight, caloric output must exceed caloric input.

Sugar frequently is one of the primary culprits in excessive caloric intake. To reduce sugar intake, plan menus low in sugar, use sugar substitutes, and control the amount of sweets consumed at meals and between meal snacks.

Too much salt (sodium) is another potential health risk. Sodium intake can be limited by not adding additional salt to food, by selecting foods low in salt, by reducing the amount of salt used in cooking, and by using salt substitutes. Herbs and spices can add zest to foods and do not have the bad effects of excess sodium.

High cholesterol is a major risk factor for heart disease. Saturated fat and cholesterol in the food elevate blood cholesterol. The *American Heart Association Cookbook* is a good source of information and recipes for tasty, low calorie, low cholesterol, and low sodium dishes. This cookbook is intended to assist individuals to achieve: (1) a caloric intake adjusted to achieve and maintain appropriate body weight; (2) a reduction in total fat calories achieved by a substantial reduction in dietary saturated fatty acids; (3) a substantial reduction in dietary cholesterol to less than 300 mgs daily; (4) dietary carbohydrates primarily derived from vegetables, fruit, whole grain, and enriched breads and cereals; and (5) avoidance of excessive sodium in the diet. *Good Food for Camp and Trail: All-Natural Recipes for Nutritious Meal Outdoors* by Dorcas S. Miller includes a meal planner, nutrition guide, recipe book, instructions on how to dehydrate at home, and rating for commonly available prepared trail foods. Careful shopping and selecting quality low sugar, low fat, and low sodium foods will help achieve these goals. Most food suppliers provide reduced fat and sodium products and more and more of these products are available at grocery stores.

Children, especially, should have a part in menu planning and food purchasing (or bringing items from home), as well as in the packing and preparing of the food. This is an opportunity for them to learn about healthy diet in a meaningful context. Such activities, also, can be challenging and enjoyable and the information learned can serve them well throughout their lives.

Tufts University maintains a website that provides links to nutrition information/education sites that they have reviewed and rated: http://navigator.tufts.edu/. Information regarding nutrition is continually evolving and changing as scientists discovers more and more about diet and nutrition, To keep up, check out reputable websites like the Tufts site and others such as the American Dietetic Association (http://www.eatright.org/Public/) and the U.S. Department of Health and Human Service's National Institute of Health (http://www.nih.gov/).

Following are suggestions for a number of different types of cooking. These are meant only as *starters*, you will want to try many variations and new ideas of your own or check the many resources found at the end of this chapter. At the beginning are some general pointers regarding equipment, sanitation, fire sites, etc.

There are lots of books on outdoor cooking. Some specialize in lightweight backpacking fare and others in group-camping recipes. The resources at the end of this section include several outdoor cooking books that we have reviewed and recommend.

SECTION B
GUIDELINES AND SUPPLIES

GROUP COOKING GUIDELINES

Youth groups, organized camp groups, family campers, and many other groups of children and adults camp and cook in the out-of-doors. It is always best to keep groups to minimum size both to promote participation and to diminish environmental impact. In most circumstances, groups should be limited to a maximum of 8 to12 participants in established sites. (Backcountry groups should remain much smaller with a maximum of 4 to 6 people and oftentimes less.) This chapter is aimed at groups of 8 to12 who usually cook in established sites designed for group camping in the outdoors.

SUPPLIES

Basic Equipment

Basic equipment for all groups doing outdoor cookery on a wood fire includes:

- Heavy cotton work gloves or potholders
- Pail and folding trench shovel, trowel, or other equipment useful in extinguishing a fire
- First aid kit (can be hung on tree for easy accessibility)
- Twine or other small rope can come in handy when you least expect it!
- Biodegradable soap (liquid is much easier to use, although bar soap or detergent made into a paste can also be used) to soap outside of kettles to make dishwashing easier

- Steel wool pads for scrubbing pots
- Dishwashing equipment (see Sanitation)
- Mesh silverware holder-can be used to rinse dishes in boiling water after washing
- Hand towels, neckerchief, or paper toweling-helps keep things clean, including your hands
- Charcoal may be substituted whenever wood is not available or cooking requires coals. Also, white gas or propane stoves can be used. These come in a wide variety of sizes from those for backpacking to large, multi-burner units.
- Dutch oven if not traveling light
- Reflector oven (see section on Reflector Cooking) or portable stove, both of which fold compactly and can be used for baking
- Kitchen fly (large plastic sheet at least 10' x 10') this serves like a "porch" - big enough to cook, eat, and sit under when it rains!
- Refrigeration (see Sanitation)
- Saw and/or Hudson Bay style axe if you have wood that needs to be split
- Pots and dishes. Compact commercial cook kits, called "nesting kits," are available from most outdoor supply stores. They come in various sizes_those for 4, 6, 8, and 12 people are most common. A heavy aluminum set is a good buy. It will last longer and cook better. Most kits contain two frying pans (one is the lid), one or two pots besides the large container for everything, a coffee pot, and cups and plates. Some have plastic cups, while others are aluminum. There are advantages and disadvantages to both. The aluminum cup does not melt when placed next to the fire and can be used to heat water for instant oatmeal packets.
- If packing space is not a problem, a miscellaneous assortment of old pots, pans, and other utensils can be gathered and carried in cook box or a backpack. Usually a coffee pot, two pots, a mixing bowl, and a frying pan are taken, besides cups and plates.
- It is also helpful to have these utensils:can opener or a utility knife with this feature, paring knife or pocketknife, spatula, mixing spoon. Plastic bags also are convenient to have around for such things as mixing Bisquick dough for bread twists, storing things, and carrying out garbage.
- Packs. A backpack may be useful for carrying equipment and food. Both frame (internal and external) and knapsacks are available. When using pack baskets, backpacks or knapsacks, or kettles to carry food for outdoor meals, pack heaviest things in the bottom. Pack so that there is no room for shifting around. Each item should be in its own container, in proper quantity needed, and well labeled on side and top.

- Containers for dry goods are also necessary, Today that problem is largely solved by plastic bags and other plastic containers. To carry foods efficiently put dry goods into plastic bags and label with a permanent marker. (Be sure to cut directions off box or package and include in the bag.) Note that plastic bags are petroleum-based products and petroleum is a nonrenewable resource, so reuse them as much as possible. There was a time when plastic bags did not exist-a very long time. Early settlers used cloth bags of assorted sizes. You may want to experiment with making such bags from sailcloth, waterproofed with paraffin, and double-stitched at all seams with a wide hem and a drawstring at the top long enough to tie with a half hitch and use as a handle. When cloth bags are used for fine materials like flour, they should be double thickness or double bagged. The inside bag might be a plastic one. Make bags short and broad, with round bottoms, so they will stand upright with minimum danger of tipping over. Label contents with wax crayon that will wash out, or permanent ink for repeated use.

- Liquids should be carried in metal (aluminum) or plastic containers rather than in glass. Semiliquid materials, such as jam and peanut butter can be purchased in plastic containers (some of them squeeze containers) and outdoor supply stores sell special plastic containers if you wish to buy a particular size or shape.

- Breakable items, such as eggs, can be carried inside flour bags. Plastic egg carriers can also be purchased from outdoor supply stores.

Dehydrated and Freeze Dried Foods

There has been a steadily increasing amount of dried, dehydrated, and specially preserved foods on grocery store shelves. Also, packaging has changed-using much less glass and metals and much more lightweight plastics and paper, making food much more convenient to transport and store. Some examples are instant oatmeal (available in individual packages), cake mixes, Bisquick, powdered milk, Minute Rice, instant potatoes, and loads of presweetened powdered drinks. For economy, many things can be purchased in larger boxes and repackaged in plastic bags in the serving size needed for use in camp.

There are many camp outfitters that sell dehydrated foods both as complete meals and as single dishes packed for two, four, or six people, per meal, or for an entire day. Although the quality of flavor is constantly being improved, some brands and dishes are tastier than others. The Internet offers a number of sites that provide reviews of individual meals. Use search words like "camp foods" and "dehydrated camp foods." Field meals produced by the military, commonly known as MREs (meals ready to eat) have continually improved in quality. They can also be purchased at military surplus stores and on the Internet. Prepackaged trail foods can be very expensive and there are many cheaper alternatives that can also reduce bulk and weight. Dehydrated meals require water for preparation and some require presoaking before cooking,

Jerky

Jerky is a method of preserving meats that goes back to early cave dwellers and was a standard part of the diet for Native Americans who lived on the Great Plains. There are many ways to prepare jerky, including hanging it to dry in direct sun covered with cheesecloth and taking it inside each night to avoid the accumulation of dew in the mornings. Following is a recipe to make beef jerky in the oven.

 ACTIVITY

Making Jerky. Use three pounds of lean, firm meat such as beef (brisket, London broil, or flank), turkey breast, salmon, etc. Three pounds will dehydrate down to about 16 to18 ounces.

Step 1. Slice meat thin (about ⅛ ″) with the grain. (Partially freezing meats will make them easier to slice, especially fish.)

Step 2. Mix the following marinating ingredients in a gallon size Ziploc bag: ⅔ cup Worcestershire sauce, ⅔ cup soy sauce, 1 tsp. black pepper, 1 tsp garlic powder, 1 tsp onion powder. (Optional: 1 tsp liquid smoke, 2-3 tsp. hot sauce, 2-3 tsp. crushed red peppers, 2-3 tsp sesame seeds),

Step 3. Add sliced meat to the marinade, turning and mixing every two hours. Beef should be marinated overnight; fish and turkey only require approximately 3-4 hours.

Step 4. After marinating, drain meat in colander and pat as dry as possible with paper towels. Place a cookie sheet or sheet of aluminum foil in bottom of oven to catch dripping. Carefully place meat slices directly onto oven racks. Set oven to 140° and leave door partially open. It will take six to eight hours to cure. Drying times will vary due to differences in ovens and size of meat. Done right, jerky is firm and dry, but not spongy, If it is so dry it breaks too easily, it is probably overdone.

SECTION C
METHODS OF COOKING

The key to all cooking, both indoor and outdoor is heat control. It is, of course, more difficult to regulate heat over an open fire than on a kitchen stove or in an oven.

With experience, outdoor cooks can become very adept at regulating the heat of the fire by the type of wood used, distance of pans from the heat, and the size of the fire. This is a skill that Native Americans and early pioneers mastered.

The following types of cookery are discussed in this chapter: (1) baking with coals (direct coals cookery, hole cookery, and foil cookery); (2) baking with ovens (Dutch and reflector ovens); and (3) frying and boiling over open fires (using a hunter trapper fire, one-pot meals, stick cookery, tin can cookery). A menu is provided with each type of cooking. You would not necessarily cook an entire meal by the same method, although it can be done. For example, you could make a foil dinner that included potatoes, meat, and beans and have a banana boat for dessert. In addition to the menus and recipes, cooking hints and equipment and food quantities are provided for six to eight people.

BAKING WITH COALS

When using wood to cook directly over coals, it is important to select only hard woods that burn for a long time. Only conduct this activity when it is environmentally responsible to use wood in this quantity either by purchasing or splitting it. Fires must be prepared in advance (usually requires 2 to 4 hours) and wood should be added all at once to produce even heat from coals with no part of the wood aflame. Since the fire is exceedingly hot, it is important to observe many safety precautions. Wearing nylon clothing or plastic glasses near this fire may result in their melting. Always have a hose or pail of water and shovel on hand to extinguish the fire.

MENU
"Buffalo" steak
Corn on the cob
Tossed salad
Banana boats

Food items and quantities (6-8 persons):

2-3 large pieces steak
(cut later into 8 pieces)
8 ears corn (16 if want 2 apiece)
1 head lettuce
2 carrots
½ stalk of celery (small)
4 tomatoes
8 bananas
4 Hershey bars, 16 marshmallows
salad dressing
¼ lb. butter or margarine
1 loaf solid, day-old bread (or buns, or other solid bread)

Equipment:

2 small containers (condensed milk)
1 mixing pot (salad)
knife to fix vegetables and cut meat
can opener
shovel and pail (fire control)
2 gloves or pot holders
paper towels and napkins
8 forks, knives, plates, cups
fork to turn meat (long handled)
dishwashing equipment

RECIPES

"Buffalo" Steak. Make an ample bed of hardwood coals. (These must be hardwood coals-pine and other types of wood have resins that taste like turpentine and burn up too quickly.) It will take several hours to burn the hardwood to a bed of glowing coals with no fire remaining.

Step 1. Marinate meat, a large piece of thick (1½ "-2″) boneless steak, 3-4 hours in mixture of oil, salt, pepper, steak sauce as desired, a little catsup, garlic salt, and thyme-and marjoram if desired. Use a two-pronged fork and poke holes in the meat every time you turn it over in the marinating sauce.

Step 2. Cut the fat edge of the steak about every 1½″ so the steak will not curl on the coals.

Step 3. Place steak *directly* on hardwood coals. After 10 to15 minutes (if steak is 1½″ thick), turn once onto a spot of fresh coals where meat has not been cooking. Approximately 10 minutes more will produce medium rare steak. Leave on slightly longer for other degrees of doneness.

When done, tap off coals that cling to meat with a stick and blow off white ashes. Cut into individual pieces. Dip in melted butter and slice into strips.

Corn on the Cob.

Step 1. For freshness, take corn directly from field if possible, leaving cornhusks intact.

Step 2. Soak for 10 to15 minutes in a bucket of water and place directly on hot coals.

Step 3. Rotate to each of the four sides. If coals appear to dry out husks too much, just dip in water again; however, do not be alarmed if *outer* husk leaves burn or get black. Steam cooks the corn. Once the corn is heated through (leave on first side longest so steam can generate), it will take only a few minutes (5 or less) on each side if corn is tender.

Step 4. To keep ready to use, set off to the side of the fire, but still near heat. The corn cannot get overcooked, but make sure the corn husks are damp enough to generate steam. If coals are quite hot you may get "Indian corn," a parched corn some people like very much.

Step 5. When corn is done, strip off husks. With experience, you will be able to strip down husks with all the silks! Butter and eat.

To avoid the messiness of buttering ears with a knife, take a deep pot or tin can, fill it with hot water, and melt butter in it. The butter will come to the surface. Use a stick of butter or more if needed to produce a generous layer of butter! Dip the ear of corn into the can. As the corn is pulled out, it will be completely buttered; add salt if desired and eat. When the water has cooled, the hardened butter can easily be lifted off the top and saved for later use.

Banana Boats

Step 1. Lay banana on a smooth surface with the two ends pointing up toward the sky. Slit the banana skin down the middle from end to end, but not over the ends. Open carefully and, holding back the peel, scoop out a strip of banana on each side with a spoon.

Step 2. Fill the cavity with cut-up or miniature marshmallows and chocolate chips or pieces of chocolate bar.

Step 3. Place like a little boat alongside the fire or in the coals. If using a fire, you must turn the boat around after the side facing the fire has all melted. When nice and gooey, eat.

Be sure to get chocolate and marshmallows spread clear to the ends. If the banana is very ripe or does not have a firm peeling, you may need to tie the banana boat together or put in foil to keep things from spilling out (tie with top partially open).

Additional Menu Suggestions

Potatoes. See Foil Cookery.

Fish in Newspaper. Use fresh fish or *completely* thawed frozen fish. Add lemon, salt and pepper, onion, and other spices you like to add flavor to bland fish. Wrap fish in wax paper. Wrap fish in several layers of newspaper. (May wrap in dry newspaper and soak in water or wrap in wet newspaper.) Place on coals. Cooks by steam. Does not take long-after steam has started, perhaps 10 to15 minutes or less. You need a good bed of very hot coals.

Cake in an Orange

Step 1. Cut 6 large oranges in half and scoop out the fruit with a spoon, being careful to leave the rinds intact.

Step 2. Mix a small box of instant cake mix that only requires adding water. Fill the bottom half of each orange rind with cake mix.

Step 3. Put the top back on the orange and set in coals or wrap in foil. If using foil, leave the top exposed so that the cake can rise above lid if necessary. Bake in hot coals about 20 minutes, turning often.

When done you have a delicious orange flavored cake that you can eat right out of the rind.

HOLE COOKERY

Note: There are some who say that this type of cooking should never be used because it disturbs the environment too much. However, there are those who understand the sustainability of the ecosystems in which they live and use this method without lasting damage. As always, when in doubt, don't do it. But if you know the short- and long-term impacts, there may be places when this is acceptable practice when done properly.

MENU

Baked beans & ham
Dill pickles
Ice cream

Food items and quantities (for 6-8)
2 cups navy beans
salt and pepper
½ t. dry or prepared mustard
½ cup brown sugar
½ cup molasses
2 small onions
1 lb. ham
crushed ice
½ cup white sugar
ice cream salt
1 pt. cream
2 eggs
2 t. vanilla
approx. 1 qt. milk
jar dill pickles

Equipment
pot with tight cover for beans
hay or straw to line one hole
bricks or stones to line other hole
30 lb. frozen food or lard can
cylindrical fruit juice can or
2 lb. coffee can
2 pot holders or padded gloves
matches
shovel and pail (fire control)
8 forks, cups, plates
soap (for dishes, and for soaping pots)

RECIPES

Baked Beans and Ham. Dig a hole that is twice the size of the bean pot in both depth and width. Line with rocks or bricks. Build a fire in the hole, crisscrossing logs on top. Let coals fall into the hole and keep the fire going until the hole is about two-thirds full of coals. Hardwood is best for coals. Shovel out part of the coals; insert the bean pot. Cover the pot with coals on all sides and on top. Seal in heat by covering the coals with dirt. The bean pot should be a kettle with a tight-fitting lid. Leave the beans in the hole for about six hours. Fix them after breakfast and have them for supper on return from an all-day hike.

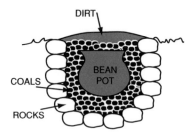

Beans

Step 1: Soak 2 cups of beans overnight. Pour off water.

Step 2. Mix: ½ tsp. salt, ½ tsp. dry mustard (more if wet mustard), pepper, ½ cup brown sugar, and ½ cup molasses. Pour onto the beans in the pot.

Step 3. Put in the ham (½ lb. salt pork may be substituted) and 2 small onions, diced. Cover with water to about 1″ above the beans; put the pot in the hole to cook. You can save cooking time by hanging the pot of beans on a crane over the fire while you are waiting for the fire to burn down to coals.

If you forget to soak the beans overnight, before putting them in the hole, bring them to a boil in the pot over the fire; cover and remove from the heat; and allow to sit one hour.

Ice Cream. Dig a hole large enough to pack 6 inches of hay or straw below and around a 30-lb. can. Put ice cream mixture in a juice can or 2-lb. coffee tin. Place a smaller can containing the mixture inside the larger can and surround with crushed ice and plenty of salt underneath and all around. Put a few nail holes in the larger can just below the top of the mixture can so that the salt water will drain to the outside, not into the mixture! Cover hole with dirt to insulate. Allow 3 to 4 hours for freezing. May stir once if desired. Be generous with the salt on the ice. (Be careful when disposing of the salt. If it is thrown on the ground, it will kill most plant life. It is also caustic on finished surfaces and may eat holes in many surfaces.)

Mixture (for 2 quarts): ¾ cup white sugar, 1 pint. cream, 2 eggs, 1 t. vanilla. Add milk to fill the container (approximately 1 qt.) Half and half cream may be used instead of cream and milk.

FOIL COOKERY

MENU
Baked barbecued chicken
Potatoes
Cabbage salad
Pineapple upside-down cake

Food items and quantities (for 6-8)	*Equipment*
3 chickens (cut up)	1 roll heavy-duty aluminum foil
1 jar barbecue sauce, if desired	2 knives to cut cabbage, peel potatoes
8 medium-sized baking potatoes	2 mixing spoons
½ lb. butter	2 medium-sized mixing pots for
salt	salad and cake
pepper	can opener
1 cabbage	axe or saw
1 jar salad dressing	2 pot holders or gloves
1 #2 can pineapple, crushed	matches
½ cup brown sugar	shovel and pail, (fire control)
1 cup flour	8 forks, 8 cups, 8 plates
1 t. baking powder	soap (dishes, soap pots)
1 egg	paper towels and napkins (a few
1 t. vanilla	towels are handy to keep things
½ cup white granulated sugar	from getting too messy and add a
½ cup milk	little to carry)
	dishwashing equipment (either dip
	bags or dish cloths & dish towels)
	make cake pan from foil

(See recipe for additional items if you wish to "dress up" or modify items.)

RECIPES

Baked Barbecued Chicken. Sprinkle salt and pepper on cut-up chicken. Place in the middle of the foil and add a little grease or butter. Add barbecue sauce, if desired. Fold aluminum properly (see hints), leaving air space for steam expansion, particularly if you are adding sauce. Place package on hot coals (not flame) for 10 to 15 minutes, depending on the size of the chicken, turn over for another 10 to15 minutes. Spread the chicken pieces out, making a flat package, if you wish them to get done more quickly.

Baked Potatoes. Peel or not at your option. Add salt and pepper as desired and a few sprinkles of water, then wrap properly in foil. Rub unpeeled potatoes with grease to keep skins from drying out and poke skin with fork to avoid exploding potatoes. Allow 40 to 50 minutes to bake slowly over coals, turning often. Make sure you are using hard wood coals. If there is fire, the potatoes will burn and not cook through.

Shoestring Baked Potatoes. Peel or not peel at your option. Cut into shoestrings about ¼ inch across. Put salt, pepper, and butter in the package. Wrap and place on the coals, turning often. When the potatoes are about done, if you wish crispy browned potatoes, put them on hotter coals for a very short time. Allow 30 to 40 minutes.

Scalloped Baked Potatoes. Slice peeled potatoes thinly. (The thinner the slices, the faster they will bake.) Add salt, pepper, and butter to the package. Wrap and bake. Turn often. These take the least time, particularly if a flat package is made 20-30 minutes. You can usually tell if the potatoes are done without opening the package by feeling how soft they are.

Potatoes in Salt. Take a #10 can and clean rock salt or ice cream salt. Pack clean small-to-medium-sized potatoes into the can. Surround each potato with salt. In packing, be sure to have ½ inch of salt insulation around the perimeter of the can; *do not let any of the potatoes touch each other or the can.* The potatoes will have a good salty flavor on the outside skin and it may penetrate a little into the potato. (It won't be too salty, though.) Place the can near blazing fire or, better yet, in hot coals. To lower sodium intake, use clean, damp sand instead of salt. The same salt may be used over and over again.

Potatoes take approximately an hour to bake if not sliced; therefore it is important to turn them to make sure they don't burn. They also work best if the coals are not too hot.

Cabbage Salad. Shred (cut) cabbage into bowl or pot. Mix in mayonnaise. Serve. To dress it up, add 1 cup miniature marshmallows and a small can of crushed pineapple. You may desire a dash of salt.

Pineapple Upside-Down Cake

3 T. butter	1 egg
½ cup brown sugar	1/2 cup sugar
2 ½ cups (#2 can) crushed pineapple	2 T. melted shortening or
1 cup flour	butter
1 t. baking powder	⅓ cup milk
¼ t. salt	1 t. vanilla

Make a pan out of foil to hold the cake. Two small pans are better than one big pan, Do not seal top, but make a dome-shaped lid from foil, Some of the foil should extend over edges of pan. Heat in the top part of the oven can be controlled by the amount of coals on the outside of the pan.

Step 1. Melt butter in the pan. Add brown sugar and remove from heat. Sprinkle pineapple over sugar mixture. Sift flour, baking powder, and salt into bowl (this can be mixed before going outdoors). Add the rest of the ingredients and beat until blended. Pour batter over fruit and bake over moderate coals 30 to 35 minutes. Loosen cake from sides and invert on plate or spoon it out.

Variation. Although many youngsters do not have the opportunity to mix a cake from "scratch" (that's why it is done above), white or yellow cake mix can be used instead of making the batter. Other fruits may be used. To cut calories, you may wish to use a sugar substitute. You can also make cobbler (see recipe under Reflectors).

ADDITIONAL
MENU SUGGESTIONS

Ham and Sweet Potatoes. (See reflector baking recipes). Bake all ingredients together in foil.

Hamburgers. Instead of just a plain hamburger in foil, why not try it with a cabbage leaf on the outside and a slice of cheese making a cheeseburger? Cheese and cabbage go well together; cabbage makes a nice moist sandwich lower in calories and nutritious. If you wish to lower carbohydrates, you can forgo the bun and use fresh leaf of cabbage as a holder. A very flavorful variation is to mix a pound of raw hamburger with a package of dry onion soup mix and then cook. You can decrease the amount of onion soup mix to taste.

Casserole (foil dinners). Thinly slice or shred potatoes, dice or cut carrots in thin strips, crumble up hamburger (¼ lb. per person), and add onion, salt, pepper, and a few sprinkles of water. You may also add baked beans depending on your taste. Put in foil package. If you pat it out to make a thin baking package, it cooks more quickly and evenly. This results in a tasty, steamed dish that is a complete meal in itself. It gives better flavor (according to some) than putting each in separately without mixing in casserole fashion.

Rolatun. Take a large piece of round steak, smear it with mustard, and garnish with thinly sliced dill pickles. Roll or fold steak. Place in foil and cook. Some prefer to roll and tie and barbecue over coals until nicely brown. You also can use mushrooms added to a package of Lipton's dry onion-mushroom soup. It tastes better than it sounds- be brave and try something different!

Biscuits, fish, and many other things can be cooked in foil. Be adventuresome. Use spices to "spice" it up and try different things.

Hints

One of the easiest and most successful methods of cookery is with aluminum foil. Cooking is based on the principle of steaming. For that reason, add some sprinkles of water to "dry" foods such as hamburger to add moisture for steam. Potatoes and most vegetables have a great deal of water in them, so you don't need to do this with food that has high water content.

For better protection, heavy-duty aluminum should be used; if not available, double the lightweight aluminum. Wrap foil with shiny side to the inside leaving the dull side facing the fire. *The package MUST be sealed well so no steam or juices can escape.* Use the "drugstore" wrap: Place food in the center of the foil; bring both sides up and fold down together for two or three wraps. Flatten foil package; fold each end several times toward the center of the package. You should be able to place the package in any position without leaking! Allow a little space when flattening the package for steam expansion. When turning the package over in the coals, *do not use a stick* as it is likely to puncture the foil, letting steam escape. Use gloves or tongs to turn. If puncture occurs, reseal by putting another layer of foil around the package. For food items you wish to brown on top and not have soggy, such as cake, use a dome lid as described in the upside-down cake recipe.

Foil cookery takes time and should be done on coals; therefore, make a hardwood fire if possible, since these coals stay hot longer and give a more even heat. *Be sure the foil package is not placed in flame;* be sure the wood has burned to coals. Cooking time varies with degree of heat, type of wood, and thickness of the package. Except for upside-down cakes and similar foods, turn over frequently or, if coals are not too hot, when you estimate food is half done. With apples, do not turn the package over-just rotate the sides toward the fire or simply surround with coals and so no turning is necessary. When practical, packages should be long and flat with a small pocket for steam expansion to cook more quickly. That means plenty of foil should be used so that food can be spread more thinly along the center of the wrap, rather than having a thick portion in the middle.

Be careful when opening foil, because the steam can cause painful burns. If foil is opened carefully, it may be laid back and used for a plate. Various utensils can be made from heavy-duty aluminum foil, for instance, frying pans, pots, and cups. *Let the foil cool and put it in the garbage to be carried out for proper disposal.*

One advantage of foil cookery is that everyone can be actively involved, if each person makes a foil dinner (including seasonings and contents to personal taste) and cooks it. Children can be instructed in the safe use of knives when cutting up vegetables for their own dinners. While dinners are baking in the fire, campers can enjoy "rabbit food"-the leftover celery and carrots, to tide them over. Everyone can also prepare their own baked apple for dessert. By the time the apple is prepared, the foil meal is ready to eat and the apple can be put in the coals; by the time the meal is eaten, dessert is ready.

BAKING WITH CAMP OVENS

Dutch Oven Cookery

MENU
Roast
Apple salad
Carrots
Potatoes
Cake

Food items and quantities (serves 6-8)	*Equipment*
2½"-3 lb. roast	2 Dutch ovens
2-3 small onions	bowl to mix apple salad (mix cake in
salt and pepper	bowl first)
8 medium potatoes	pocketknife to pare vegetables
8 medium carrots	& apples
¼-½ lb. butter	mixing spoon
4 medium apples	axe or saw (if need to split wood)
⅓ lb. dates	matches
½ cup mayonnaise	shovel and pail (fire control)
1 cup miniature marshmallows	dishwashing equipment
½ cup chopped nuts	paper towels and napkins
1 large box cake mix or	8 forks, cups, plates
ingredients for cake	
of your choice	

RECIPES

Roast with Carrots in Dutch Oven. Sear roast in hot Dutch oven to seal in the juices. Add salt and pepper and small onions. Place pared potatoes and carrots around the roast. Add 1 to 1¼ cups water. Heat. Cover with lid and place coals on top of lid. Bake until done.

Apple Salad. Cut up 4 medium-sized apples, together with dates or raisins and marshmallows. Add nuts. Mix with mayonnaise.

Cake. Mix the cake as indicated on the package. Place in greased cake tin. Put the cake pan in the Dutch oven either on an inverted pie tin or on small rocks, so that it is not directly on the bottom of the oven. Close the oven, place hot coals on the lid, and bake. For variation, put applesauce on the bottom of the cake pan and pour gingerbread batter over it, then bake.

Hints

The Dutch oven has been in use in outdoor cooking longer than almost any other piece of equipment except the green stick. It was the main cooking utensil of early pioneers, prospectors, sheepherders, and cowboys. The chuck wagon was incomplete without a Dutch oven for roasting and baking as well as for frying and stewing. For all but those wishing to travel light, this piece of equipment will allow much more variety and interest in the outdoor meals. Veteran cooks would use no other method of baking, because with a little experience, it is almost foolproof.

The best Dutch oven is cast iron. Aluminum ovens are possibly two pounds lighter but lack the qualities of the cast iron model that make it ideal for baking and roasting. The oven is from 3 to 4 inches deep and has a flat snug-fitting lid with a turned-up rim that serves to retain coals placed on top. Three stubby legs support the oven allowing air to circulate underneath to keep coals hot.

The most common sizes are 12 inches in diameter (7 quarts) and 10 inches in diameter (3 quarts). The 8 inch Dutch oven, used by most homemakers, is usually too small for camp use and has a rounded lid that makes it impossible to put coals on top. The oven is equipped with a handle or bail and the lid has a cast iron handle. The cook can use a forked stick to take the lid off to stir or check the progress of the food.

If the Dutch oven is to be used for frying or boiling, a fire with flames should be used to obtain the higher heat needed to fry and boil. However, for roasting and baking, some care must be taken to avoid direct flame on the oven; all of the heat should be provided by coals. It is important that the oven be hot enough but not too hot; the exact amount of heat can only be determined by experimentation and practice. The most common error is to have too much heat rather than not enough. Place the oven on hardwood coals raked out from the fire. Top heat is provided by placing coals on the lid. Heat can be adjusted by adding or taking away coals both above and underneath the oven. Particularly for baking, both the oven and the lid should be preheated.

For all cooking purposes except baking, the food is placed directly in the Dutch oven. Baking, too, can be done this way, but many prefer to put the item to be baked in a separate pan. This makes it much easier to clean the Dutch oven afterwards. When a pan is used, it must not touch the bottom of the oven. It can be placed on an inverted pan or several nonexplodable stones to lift it away from the bottom surface. This allows hot air circulation under the pan that bakes rather than burns the contents of the pan. When baking pies or cakes, be sure the pan is level so that the cake or pie is not lopsided or does not spill out of the pan. Also, there must be sufficient space on top for the cake to rise. If it touches the lid, it will burn on top, so don't overfill the cake pan.

When using the oven for moist foods, grease the oven lightly the first several times to prevent rusting. Do this until a film forms inside the pot, which means the pot is "seasoned." Unsalted grease is best. After use, wash the oven in soapy water, rinse in near-boiling water, and set out to dry. Avoid scouring with cleanser or steel wool because this removes the protective film (seasoning). For prolonged storage in humid climates, a light greasing inside and out is recommended.

A Dutch oven can be used for any food you wish to bake. The ready mixes are ideal. Follow the directions on the packages for preparation and baking time. Check frequently, since a common error is to use too many coals, resulting in the food cooking too quickly, burning on the outside and undone on the inside. Potatoes and apples can be baked in the Dutch oven and it is ideal for pot roast, Swiss steak, and vegetables. A deep-dish pie is easily made by lining the oven with dough, baking for about 10 minutes, filling the shell with two cans of prepared pie filling, topping with crust, and baking until the crust is brown and the filling is hot. Fruit cobbler can be made quickly by using prepared pie filling and topping with biscuit dough.

REFLECTOR OVEN BAKING

MENU
Sliced ham baked with
   sweet potatoes and pineapple slices
Cabbage salad
Cherry pie

Food items and quantities (serves 6-8)

2½ lb. canned ham
   or equivalent
#3can sweet potatoes or fresh
12 slices pineapple
1 small cabbage
1 cup brown sugar
½ cup or jar of salad dressing
2 cans pie cherries (red, sour),
2 T. tapioca, and ½-⅔ cup
   sugar or 1 can sweetened
   pie filling (cherry)
½ lb. butter
salt
pepper
2 cups Bisquick (or make pie
   dough from flour, shortening,
   salt)

Equipment

2 reflector cake pans (for ham)
   or one oblong (but then be sure
   it will fit in reflector)
2 pie tins
2 bowls or pots for mixing
2 mixing spoons
pocketknives for paring and cutting
2 reflector ovens
can opener
matches
shovel & pail (fire control)
2 pot holders or gloves
8 plates, cups, forks, knives
paper napkins & toweling
dishwashing equipment

 RECIPES

Ham and Sweet Potatoes. Lay ¼″ slices of boiled or canned sweet potatoes in a greased pan. Alternate with ham and Spam. Sprinkle with brown sugar and butter chunks. Add pineapple slices. Bake on a moderate fire until thoroughly heated and brown sugar begins to make a syrup. You may reduce quantity of pineapple or omit altogether.

Cabbage Salad. See Foil Cookery menu.

Cherry Pie. The quickest way to make a pie is to use Bisquick or pie crust mix for the crust. Moisten with water or milk and put in a pie tin (greased). You can make pie dough from flour, shortening, salt, and water (see special recipe). For filling use canned cherry (or any other flavor you prefer) pie filling or sour red cherries to which must be added 2 tablespoons of tapioca for thickening and ½-⅓ cup sugar to sweeten.

Instead of making pie, you can make cobbler by putting filling in the bottom of the cake pan and putting Bisquick mix on top-add a little sugar to it. Bake pie "open face," or make sufficient dough to make a top. If a top is used, it can be sprinkled with melted butter and sugar.

Pie Crust Recipe. Use at least ⅓ cup shortening per cup of sifted flour. Cut shortening into flour using two knives until shortening is approximately pea sized. Blend shortening and flour mixture with water, being careful not to overmix. It should just hold together and is usually a little lumpy. For a 9″ pie tin, use: 1⅓ cup sifted flour, ½ teaspoon salt, ½ cup shortening, 3 tablespoons water.

> ADDITIONAL
> MENU SUGGESTIONS

Anything that can be baked in the oven at home can be made in a reflector oven.

Hints

For reflector baking you need a fire bank, fire, and a reflector oven. The fire bank can be constructed on a semipermanent basis by using flat stones supported by a dirt bank or logs. A temporary fire bank can be made by placing another reflector oven across from the first (they reflect back to each other) or use a sliding-saucer sled. A reflector of heavy foil also works. The fire bank should face the wind so that flames and ashes will not be blown into the food in the reflector oven.

The fire should be on the same level as the reflector oven. Build the fire as high and wide as the reflector oven you are using. If the fire is too low, the bottom of the food in the oven will burn before the top is cooked; if too high, the bottom does not cook properly. Keep the fire even and steady. The fire should be constantly tended. The big disadvantage of a reflector fire is that it consumes a great deal of fuel since a flame must be maintained at all times.

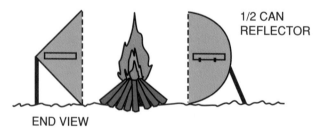

1/2 CAN
REFLECTOR

END VIEW

There are many types of reflector ovens. The ovens must be level so food inside will not tilt, which results in spilled contents or lopsided food, especially for cakes and pies! Sturdy reflector ovens may be purchased or made from sheet metal or cookie tins (large rectangular ones). A temporary oven can be made by lining a box with foil, the shiny side away from the box and inserting a foil-lined shelf. Another method is to set a pan on a grate or sticks 6″ to 8″ off the ground and placing foil at angular positions. A 30-lb lard or frozen-food can be cut in half lengthwise. Insert two long rods on which pans may be placed. Individual reflector ovens can be made by using frying pans set up before the fire, pie tins, etc.

FRYING AND BOILING OVER OPEN FIRES

Using a Hunter-Trapper Fire

MENU

Sausage
Apple pancakes
Celery and carrot sticks
Chocolate tapioca pudding
Coffee

Food items and quantities (serves 6-8)

Food items and quantities (serves 6-8)	*Equipment*

1 sq. Baker's chocolate
  or cocoa equiv.
24 sausages or 2 lb. bulk sausage
1½ cups flour
3 t. baking powder
salt to taste
⅔ cup sugar
3 eggs
1 qt. milk
1 cup shortening
½ t. nutmeg
6 medium apples
¼ lb. butter
1 stalk celery (small)
6 carrots
1 pt. syrup
3 T. tapioca
1 t. vanilla

Equipment
1 medium-sized frying pan
  (pancakes)
pail and shovel (fire control)
2 pot holders or gloves
axe or saw (if need to split
  or size wood)
2 medium kettles or pots
knives to pare apples, cut celery
  and carrot
2 mixing spoons
1 spatula
1 cooking fork
matches
8 forks, spoons, cups, plate
paper napkins and a few
  paper towels
dishwashing equipment
soap, to soap pots

RECIPES

Sausage. Fry sausages in pan over flame. Be sure they are done.

Apple pancakes

1½ cup flour	1 cup milk
3 t. baking powder	3 T. shortening (melted)
½ t. salt	2 eggs
5 T. sugar	6 medium apples (cut finely)
½ t. nutmeg	

Mix dry ingredients (preferably before you go out). Combine with liquid (milk), shortening, and beaten egg. Add apples chopped quite fine. Cooked apples will also work. Fry in frying pan over moderate-heat. Coals must not be too hot or it will not get done in the middle. Serve with butter and syrup.

Variation. Other fruits such as blueberries may be added instead of apples. Bisquick may be used instead of making mixture from scratch. Mix Bisquick with milk, add one egg for better flavor; add 3-4 T. sugar depending on tartness of apples. Add nutmeg.

Chocolate Tapioca Pudding

1 egg beaten	⅛ t. salt
3 T. tapioca	1 t. vanilla
2¾ cup milk	1 chocolate square
⅓ cup sugar	

Mix all ingredients except chocolate square (mix in cocoa if used to replace chocolate square) **and bring to a boil. Cook 6-8 minutes stirring in chocolate square.** Cool 15-20 minutes. Serve either warm or cold. For fluffier pudding, separate yolk and white of egg. Beat whites and add last. Use yolk as before.

Coffee Making. There are many ways to make good coffee on an open fire and each outdoor cook has a favorite method. The prime concern in all methods is how to settle the grounds. Here are a few suggestions to try at your own risk! Use a level tablespoonful of coffee for each cup of water.

Step 1. Put coffee grounds into boiling water. Stir; put in an eggshell or dash of cold water; let sit in warm place 5 minutes.

Step 2. Put coffee grounds in cheesecloth bag and place in cold water. Bring to a brisk boil.

Step 3. Put coffee grounds in cheesecloth bag with a few grains of salt. Pour boiling water on it and allow coffee to come again to a full boil. Let stand 20 minutes on low heat. To clear, add some cold water.

Step 4. Mix coffee with one egg and just enough water to moisten. Add cold water; cover and slowly bring to boil, stirring occasionally. Remove from fire; let stand in warm place 3-5 minutes; add ¼ cup cold water to settle grounds.

Step 5. Make in any manner and settle grounds by swinging pot with a full arm arc! Be CAREFUL that you don't throw scalding coffee water on yourself or anyone else!

Hints

The hunter-trapper fire is really a type of fireplace, rather than a type of cooking. This fireplace is constructed from logs about 3 feet long and 6 inches thick. Logs are placed close enough together to support cooking pots; they may be placed in a V shape as in the diagram. The open end is toward the wind. If more draft is needed, a "damper stick" might be placed under one of the support logs. Variations: if logs are not big enough, dig out dirt in a semi-trench to give more depth. Stones may be used in place of logs. The trench fireplace is also basically the same; however, the end toward the wind should be slanted to allow more draft (see diagram).

Set pots on the dirt sides of a trench (trench may have nonexploding rocks lining the edge if desired). Build fire between logs, beginning with teepee style. If you wish to bake, burn down to coals and push coals into the V of the logs; then, you can have another small teepee fire towards the open end for frying and preparing other foods in a pot. This dual purpose fire is excellent for conserving fire space. Also, a small fire can cook a lot of food and the fire is protected somewhat. Anything that can be baked, fried, or boiled can be done on a hunter-trapper fire.

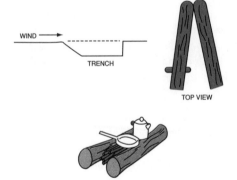

ONE-POT MEALS

MENU
Slumgullion
Celery and carrot sticks
Dill pickles
Plank bread
Baked Apples

Food items and quantities (for 8)

2 lbs. hamburger
½ lb. bacon
2 large onions
4 cans tomatoes
½ lb. American cheese
6 carrots
1 stalk celery
  (½ is all that's needed)
1 small box Bisquick
8 apples
1 cup brown sugar
salt
pepper

Equipment

large cooking pot
1 small mixing pot or plastic bag
  for bread dough
1 wooden cooking spoon
can opener
2 ft. of heavy-duty
  aluminum foil
2 pot holders or gloves
shovel and pail (fire control)
8 plates, cups, knives, forks, spoons
knife for fixing vegetables,
  cutting bacon
matches
paper towels and napkins
dishwashing equipment
soap, especially for soaping pot

RECIPES

Slumgullion. Cover the outside of cooking pot thoroughly with a thin layer of liquid soap or lather made from a bar of soap. Dice ½ lb. bacon; fry in the bottom of cooking pot until crisp. Chop onion and add to bacon along with the 2 lbs. of hamburger. When the meat is done, add tomatoes and simmer about 15 minutes. Add cubed cheese last and let melt. When cheese is just melted, serve. Salt and pepper to taste.

Plank Bread. Mix Bisquick and water until you have a semi-sticky dough. Cover split log (plank) with foil. Drop the dough onto the plank with a spoon, or if your dough is stiffer, you can make molded biscuits. Prop up plank so biscuits bake in the heat of reflected fire. A frying pan may also be used.

Baked Apples. One of the easiest and surest desserts is the baked apple. Core apple and fill the center with brown sugar, wrap it in foil and bake in coals. Fancier versions include butter, sugar, cinnamon. You may also add marshmallows, currants, raisins, or other desired filling. Takes only 5 minutes on a side. Be especially careful to seal foil well.

Additional Menu Suggestions

Almost any kind of one-pot meal can be made by using bacon, onion, and hamburger as the base. Add character to the one-pot meal by including additional ingredients. Some suggestions:

American Chop Suey. Add 2 cans of spaghetti with tomato sauce and green pepper. For a little different flavor, add a bit of sausage to the hamburger and some cooked celery.

Chili. Add to the bacon, onion, hamburger base 2 cans of diced tomatoes and 2 cans of kidney beans; season with chili powder.

Campfire Stew. Add 2 cans of concentrated vegetable soup and enough liquid to prevent sticking. A fresher alternative is to start from scratch with fresh vegetables sliced relatively small and add a dry vegetable soup mix for flavoring, Boil/heat until vegetables are tender.

Ring-Turn-Diddy. To 1 lb. of hamburger, add 2 cans of tomatoes, 3 cans of corn, green pepper, and ½ lb. cheese. *Variation:* Omit hamburger and add 1 to 1½ lb. of bacon.

Bags-of-gold. Heat tomato soup almost to a boil. Drop in small balls of Bisquick dough that have been wrapped around cubes of cheese. Simmer until dumplings are done.

Hints

Make a substantial crane on which to hang the pot. The diagrams below illustrate three ways to do this. When placing the kettle over teepee type fire, do *not* lower it down into flame, but keep it above the flame. The hottest portion of the flame is *at* the tip, not *in* it.

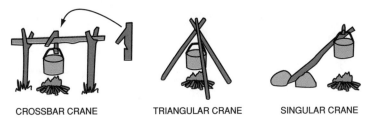

CROSSBAR CRANE   TRIANGULAR CRANE   SINGULAR CRANE

Soap pot well on the outside with liquid soap or use a bar of soap with water. By doing this you will make dishwashing much easier. Be generous with the soap and cover every spot on the outside, of course be careful not to get soap inside the pot.

Fry the bacon first, to grease the pot and keep other foods from sticking. Meat must be cooked almost done before already cooked items are added. If you are adding raw vegetables, allow sufficient cooking time (approximately 20-30 minutes).

For some fun. Place an egg in a paper cup full of water and place right in the fire. It will not burn as long as water remains in the cup. As the water boils away, the top edge will also burn. Boil as long as you like to make hard or soft-boiled eggs. You can also take a brown paper sack and line the bottom with bacon and crack an egg over the bacon, roll the top closed, poke a stick through the top under the rolled portion to hold the bag, and hold over the fire or coals to cook. Most people won't believe it-you'll have to show them!

STICK COOKERY

MENU

Pioneer drumsticks
Bread twists
Apple salad
Macaroons

Food items and quantities (serves 6-8)
2 lbs. ground beef
1 cup cornflakes, crumbled fine
2 eggs
pepper, onion, salt
1 med. size box Bisquick
4 medium apples
½ lb. grapes
1 cup miniature marshmallows
1 jar mayonnaise
6 "old" buns (not too fresh)
1 can sweetened condensed milk
1 pkg. shredded coconut
¼ lb. butter
1 jar jelly

Equipment
8 green sticks (thumb size
   diameter)
2 mixing pots for salad
   and drumsticks
4-8 plastic bags (see bread twist
   recipe)
pocketknife to cut apples and bread
small bowl (see macaroon recipe)
8 forks, cups, plates
2 mixing spoons
can opener
matches
shovel and pail (fire control)
dishwashing equipment
paper towels and napkins
3 ft. aluminum foil
   (may be lightweight)

Pioneer Drumsticks
    2 lbs. hamburger (ground beef)
    1 cup cornflakes
    2 eggs
    onion, salt, pepper
    For a good flavor, add a little pork sausage to ground beef.
       Be sure to cook well.

Mix beef, seasonings, eggs, and cornflakes thoroughly. Divide into 8 portions. Wrap a portion around a green stick (thumb size diameter) that has been "skinned" (bark peeled off) on one end. If the skinned part is short, make two rather than one thick one. Mold onto stick thinly. Cook slowly over coals, turning frequently so all sides are evenly cooked. Twist slightly to take off the stick. Can be served with bread.

You can also put foil around stick before putting hamburger on and it will conduct heat from the inside. Be careful that meat doesn't slide off-the meat must not be too greasy!

Bread Twists. This is probably the most common stick-cookery food (besides hotdogs!). If the end of the stick is covered with foil, the heat is conducted inside the dough and the bread twist gets done more quickly and the dough raises better, hence a more delicious bread twist. Bisquick is the simplest ingredient to use-just mix it with milk or water. It may be mixed easily and with less mess in a plastic bag. Everyone can mix their own (or two can share a bag), using about ½ cup Bisquick for each bread twist. If the dough is a little sticky, the stick may be put into the bag, and the dough twisted around it, making a thin coating of dough on the foil-covered stick. If you wish, add more Bisquick (or less water) to get a less sticky dough. You can also take the dough out of the bag with your hand and roll into a "snake." Then spiral or twist dough around the stick or just mold onto the stick. Always be sure the dough is in a *thin layer*. Cover the end of the stick so filling will not come out later! Bake slowly by holding it about 6" above the coals at first, so the inside will bake. Turn around gradually so that it will brown evenly on all sides. When bread twist is done, it will be easy to loosen from the stick. If it is tight, it is not done. Stuff hole with your choice of bacon, jam, jelly, cheese, butter, honey, etc. Also delicious is a mixture of butter (melted), cinnamon, and sugar. A cooked (roasted) hotdog or small sausage can also be inserted into hole. You can mix grated cheese or orange rind in the dough before baking to get a cheese or orange bread twist. Be sure sticks are at least thumb-size diameter.

Apple Salad. Cut up 4 medium-sized apples together with grapes and marshmallows. Nuts may be added. Mix in mayonnaise.

Macaroons (also called angels on horseback). Cut "old" buns or bread, preferably solid-loaf Italian or Vienna, into 1" cubes; dip in sweetened condensed milk; roll in shredded coconut. Place on stick and brown slowly so milk caramelizes, making a macaroon. Better than a round stick, a pronged or flat sharp-pointed stick will help keep the macaroon from turning around and around on the stick. *Do not hurry* cooking time or milk will *not* caramelize. The coals should be quite hot, but not flaming. You may add a bit of almond extract to the milk, if desired. Macaroons can also be made by mixing two bags of shredded coconut and ½ teaspoon of almond extract with sweetened condensed milk to a gummy consistency. Drop on foil and bake on coals or in reflector oven. If on foil, coals must not be very hot. Bread cubes spread with white syrup and toasted are good, too.

ADDITIONAL
MENU SUGGESTIONS

Kabobs. On a thin peeled stick, alternate pieces of steak or chicken about 2″, square, onion, ¼ ″ sliced potatoes (preferably parboiled), tomato, zucchini slices and green pepper pieces if desired. Cook *slowly* over coals, turning frequently. For well-done meat, place pieces about ½″ apart and for rare, place fairly close together. This can be basted by interweaving bacon strips to provide a very fine flavor.

S'mores. A simple, old favorite standby for many. Cook marshmallows slowly until hot and gooey. Place between graham crackers with one-half of a chocolate bar. The hot marshmallows will melt chocolate making a delicious, but sweet and messy, dessert or snack!

Variations: To cut sweetness and add flavor, add a slice of apple to the "sandwich," or use mint chocolate wafers instead of plain chocolate. Use dried apricots and toasted marshmallows between soda crackers for a variation.

Hints

Stick cooking requires *much patience.* It is a slow way to get things *done.* It is not advised for the impatient or for young children, not only because of the time required but also because difficulties frequently occur in keeping food on the stick. To assist "patience," racks may be easily made.

Select sticks that are straight and not too long (approximately 24″). Crooked sticks make even turning difficult, while sticks that are too long are unwieldy and dangerous. Use one fire for each group of eight people to avoid overcrowding.

INDIVIDUAL PROP

GROUP PROP
WATCHED BY ONE
PERSON WHO TURNS ALL

   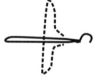

Often it is not possible to find sticks nearby or it is not appropriate to take wood from the environment. This is no reason to be denied the delicacies that can be prepared on a stick. Coat hangers have long been a standby for roasting wieners and marshmallows. Cut off the hook part of the hanger and bend the remainder so that it forms a handle and a two-pronged point that serves to keep food from turning or falling off.

For stick cookery that requires a solid, large core (e.g. pioneer drumsticks and bread twists), a ¾" to 1" dowel rod about 18" long may be used. Wrap the end used for cooking with aluminum foil to prevent burning.

TIN CAN COOKERY

MENU
Fried ham and potatoes
Tossed salad
Peach cobbler

Food items and quantities (serves 6-8)	*Equipment*
2½ lb. ham	10 #10 cans
8 medium-sized potatoes	5 tuna fish cans or cans of similar size;
1 head lettuce	tin cups can be used
2 carrots	5 one-lb. coffee tins
3 tomatoes	8 knives, forks, spoons, cups, plates
little celery, if available	can opener
½ cup French or other dressing	2 pot holders or gloves
1 #2 can sliced peaches	tin snips
½ cup brown sugar, if desired,	knife for cutting potatoes and ham
otherwise white	2 mixing spoons
1 T. butter (for cobbler)	2 mixing pots (tossed salad and
1 cup Bisquick	cobbler dough, plastic bag may be
½ cup shortening	substituted for latter
salt	matches
	shovel and pail (fire control)
	dishwashing equipment
	paper towels and napkins

 RECIPES

Fried Ham and Potatoes. Nothing special here. Be sure you have sufficient grease on the tin can top. Do not put too much food on top or it will spill over and waste. (See Hints-Hobo Stove.)

Tossed Salad Clean lettuce, carrots, tomatoes, and celery. Cut up into pot together. Add dressing. Ingredients may be anything you like to put into a salad-green pepper, cucumber, etc.

Peach Cobbler. Use a tuna can for a baking tin. Grease it. Put some peach slices, a little juice, some sugar, a shake of cinnamon if desired, and a dot of butter into the can. Mix up some Bisquick and water to form dough. Put thin layer of dough on top of peaches. Sprinkle with sugar and cinnamon. Bake. See *Hints* for how to bake in a #10 tin can (hobo stove).

ADDITIONAL
MENU SUGGESTIONS

Anything that normally is fried can be made on the top of a hobo stove. Particularly good are French toast, apple pancakes, bacon and eggs, and hash brown potatoes. For a special sandwich, fry a thick slice of ham, put a slice of cheese on top, add a pineapple ring, and if desired, a little brown sugar. Serve between slices of bread. This sandwich is called "pi-che-am."

Hints

Hobo Stove. A #10 tin can be used for cooking and is called a "hobo stove." Tin cans can be easily obtained in quantity from school cafeterias, restaurants, or institutions that cook in quantity. If you have a choice, select cans with smooth ends rather than those with circular grooves. If you have a grooved can, you may wish to hammer the grooves smooth for a more easily cleaned and better-cooking surface. (The closed end of the can is the cooking surface.) Using tin snips, cut a 3″ doorway in the bottom as shown. You may wish to leave the door attached in order to adjust the amount of air, or it may be cut off and inserted into the end of a stick and used as a spatula. For safety, it is desirable to turn the cut edges back with pliers and hammer down until smooth. Punch holes near the top for a chimney. If you burn twigs, you will need more holes for a draft. Cut the holes on the side opposite the door. Three to five holes usually are sufficient. For greater draft on the bottom, raise the can on rocks or make a tunnel to give a cross draft. Two types of fuel can be used with hobo stoves: natural fuel and buddy burners.

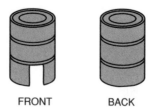

FRONT   BACK

Buddy Burners. A quick hot fire good for wet weather is provided by the buddy burner. To make a buddy burner, use a tuna fish can, roll a piece of corrugated cardboard the same height as the can, and place inside. Pour paraffin into can. The top of the cardboard becomes the wick. Usually a buddy burner takes less air than natural fuels. This makes a good project to complete before going on the cookout.

If the buddy burner is not employed, use dry twigs for fuel, inserting in the door of the hobo stove. Hard woods are preferable. You may wish to get your *small* teepee fire going and have some coals before placing your hobo stove on the fire. Put sticks in criss-cross fashion to provide better air. For the "lazy guy or gal," a length of ¼" rubber tubing can be used to direct more air into stove. Fuel must be fed into a hobo stove almost continuously.

Be sure the hobo stove is level. This is both for safety (grease will spill over and blaze up) and to avoid frustration, when frying eggs particularly. Once white begins to spill over, the yolk follows *rapidly*. When frying, *do not* fry all the bacon at once; it is hard to save the grease (next to impossible!) and it may cause a big fire blaze. Rather, fry only enough bacon to make sufficient grease for the next thing you are frying. A good way to fry an egg is to put two pieces of bacon around the outside of the can top and an egg in the middle. Another way to fry eggs is to cut a hole out of the middle of a slice of bread and fry the egg inside the hole. Then you have eggs and toast ready at the same time and the egg does not spill out as easily. If using natural fuel, have one person cook and one person feed the fire.

To bake, put three small stones on top of the stove. For a more permanent can, insert three stove bolts on top of the hobo stove. This lifts the baking tin (tuna can) off the stove top, permitting circulation of warm air beneath the can. For a baking tin use a tuna can, tin cup, small pie tin, or similar container that will fit. Invert a one-pound coffee tin over the baking tin to complete the oven.

For tin can cooking, do not forget the ordinary coffee can stew. Just place small pieces of meat and vegetables in the water in a coffee can with a well-fitting lid. Bring to a boil in coals and then simmer until done. Season with spices or an envelop of dry vegetable soup mix.

Blizzard Bucket (also called vagabond stove) and Safari Grill. To make a blizzard bucket, take an old bucket, cut slits in both sides and the bottom for air. Use as a charcoal burner or build a wood fire inside. Place a frying pan on top or cut down a #10 tin can for a frying pan. Anything that can be prepared in a skillet can be cooked. This type of fire has a great safety advantage in windy weather or when there is no suitable place to build a fire. Remains also can easily be cleaned up and there is no fire scar left.

A safari grill is very similar. It is made from a metal container about twice the size of a regular bucket. Holes are punched in the bottom for air, as well as about one-third the distance up the side. A hinged grill is placed over the top. Use newspapers for fuel. Crumple four newspaper double sheets (not in tight wad) and light in the bottom of the grill. The flame will sear the meat in the grill on top. Be sure to turn meat over while the flame is still high so both sides are seared to seal in the juices. When newspapers are nearly burnt up, raise the grill and add more crumpled newspaper. It takes about 12 newspapers and 15 to 20 minutes to roast two half chickens. The safari grill works best when there is a slight wind outside to cause a draft and when the grill on top is covered pretty well with food.

 Books on Outdoor Cooking

See master publicatons list for cities of Publishers.

American Heart Association. (1998). *American Heart Association Cookbook*, 6th edition. Clarkson Potter. Although not directed at outdoor cooking, the recipes emphasize good nutrition and can be prepared using the various methods described in this section.

Conners, Tim, and Christine Conners. (2000). *Lipsmackin Backpackin*, Falcon Publishing Co.: Helena, MT. Lightweight, trail-tested recipes for back-country trips.

Fahr, Jean. (1989). *Pocket Stew: The Expanded Collection of Favorite Girl Scout Outdoor Recipes*. Girl Scout Council of Southeastern Louisiana, New Orleans LA

Holm, Don, (1976). *The Old Fashion Dutch Oven Cookbook*, 8th printing. Caxton Printers: Caldwell, ID. Authentic sour dough cookery and old-time arts of smoking and jerking fish and game.

Jacobson, Cliff. (1999). *Cooking in the Outdoors*. Globe Pequot Press, Guilford, CT. (Basic Essentials(tm) book.) Includes cooking for large groups, plan and pack meals, cooking in rain, wind, and snow, and safe drinking water and disposal of waste.

Kraus, Barbara. (1985). *The Barbara Kraus Cholesterol Counter*. Perigee Books, The Putnam Publishing Group: NY.

Longacre, Doris Janzen. (1980). *More-with-Less Cookbook*. Herald Press: Scottdale, PA.

Miller, Dorcas S. (1996). *Good Food for Camp and Trail: All-Natural Recipes for Nutritious Meal Outdoors*, Back Country Press: Grangeville, OH. Complete meal planner nutrition guide and recipe book. Includes dehydrating food at home and ratings of commonly available prepared trail food.

Pearson, Claudia (ed.). (2004) *NOLS Cookery*, 5th edition. Stackpole Books: Mechanicsburg, PA. (National Outdoor Leadership School). Excellent cookbook for backcountry travelers. Some great recipes, plus menu and ration planning, packaging, fire preparation, stove and open-fire cooking and site maintenance.

Prater, Yvonne, and Ruth Dyar Mendenhall. (1982). *Gorp, Glop, & Glue Stew*. The Mountaineers: Seattle.

Internet Sites on Outdoor Cooking

Suggested search words: dutch oven, campfire baking
Dutch Oven Cooking:
> http://www.ceedubs.com/

The International Dutch Oven Society, Logan UT:
> http://www.idos.com/

Ol' Buffalo Outdoor Cooking Page.
> http://www.three-peaks.net/cooking.htm

Lots and lots of recipes, detailed information, plus pictures/diagrams on Dutch ovens, starting fires, temperature control, box oven cooking, etc.

Military Meals Ready to Eat (MREs)
> http://www.marrich.com/mre/mremaster.htm

MREs have improved substantially in quality since WWII and Vietnam. Often they can be purchased from Military Surplus stores. They are more widely available than in the past.

Dehydrated and Freeze-dried Food Suppliers:

Adventure Foods, 481 Banjo Lane, Whittier, North Carolina 28789
http://www.adventurefoods.com/afsearch.asp

Cache Lake Camping Foods:
http://www.cachelake.com/index.html

A division of NPO Foods, 506 Beltrami Avenue, Bemidji, Minnesota 56601

Mountain House. Survival Enterprises, 4368 W. Seltice Way, Coeur d'Alene, Idaho 83814
http://www.survival.com.mx/food/mountain-house/

C H A P T E R

PROJECTS AND HOBBIES

MANY PEOPLE FIND that their greatest enjoyment and satisfactions are achieved through projects and hobbies based on outdoor experiences and materials. These satisfactions and enjoyments ("pursuits of happiness") are the inherent right of all people including generations to come. It is of utmost importance, therefore, that good conservation policies and practices be followed during participation in projects and hobbies such as those described in this chapter.

People learn to respect and appreciate the natural environment as they become familiar with the characteristics of natural processes. Keen interest and basic understandings are important factors in the development of attitudes and appreciations. One thing that distinguishes hobbies and projects from other activities such as outings and picnics is the level of commitment in the activity that often involves a considerable investment of time and sustained effort. For many people these activities become lifelong avocations and, in some instances, vocations and, therefore, provide excellent opportunities for the development of proper attitudes toward the conservation of natural resources.

Just because people are in the outdoors or participating in a nature-oriented activity does not mean they are necessarily forming desirable attitudes. If changes are to take place, leaders of outdoor activities will need to develop specific objectives that plan for and evaluate this change. Everyone interested in the outdoors should assume the responsibility to help others develop appreciation for the natural environment. One approach to ecological involvement that leads to lifelong interests in the outdoors is sensory, based in the affective, or "feelings," domain. What is the meaning of the outdoors? How do you foster awareness of a personal relationship with the natural environment? One approach, developed by Steve van Matre and others is *acclimatization.* Van Matre's *Institute for Earth Education* (http://www.eartheducation.org/default.asp has the following objectives:

- Creating adventuresome, magical learning experiences
- Building complete educational programs with integrated components for the head, the heart and hands

147

- Focusing on the "big picture" ecological processes
- Fostering good feelings for the natural world
- Crafting more ecologically harmonious lifestyles
- Participating with others in lessening our collective impact on the planet
- Incorporating "ecological feelings" in the daily routines of living and learning
- Paying attention to the details and adding natural touches in learning situations
- Developing deep personal relationships with the earth and its natural systems and community*

Central to this approach is helping people understand how the world functions. This kind of awareness program may be used for all types of groups of various ages to introduce them to more meaningful relationships with the environment. (See references at the end of this chapter for ideas related to this area.)

The vast variety of materials found in the outdoors can serve as a basis for hobbies and projects for all people, regardless of age, activity, or interest. For the physically active there are many challenging terrains to explore along with the vigorous activities related to hiking and camping. For those who are physically challenged passive and less active alternatives abound. The outdoors provides a constantly changing scene of natural beauty that invites everyone to observe and enjoy. Nature in winter is as fascinating as in the summer. (See Winter Activities in Chapter 8, Section B.) The serious student of the out-of-doors is challenged by a never-ending supply of new materials and processes that remain to be discovered, studied, and recorded.

Nature hobbies can be inexpensive and few require extensive equipment. For field hobbies, most people will want a field guidebook and a small notebook to make notations and sketches of what they have observed while in the field. The rest is up to the individual. Genuine curiosity, alertness, and a lot of patience are required of the amateur naturalist. You must be ready to develop your senses to become keenly alert and aware of what is going on around you. To fulfill these requirements, you will need to make an honest effort to improve yourself and to find answers to your questions.

The wide range of possible outdoor hobbies and projects makes it impossible to discuss them adequately in this manual. This section includes a few of the representative areas that have become meaningful to many people who are interested in the outdoors. Additional activities can be found in the resources listed at the end of each section.

Videos (CDs, DVDs, video streaming, films, etc.) for interpretation, education, and stimulation are also helpful in developing a nature-oriented program. Check the Internet and contact the local state conservation commission and nearby colleges and universities for pertinent videos. Many have excellent films for nominal rental fees. Because of the many excellent videos (across many formats) now available, no effort is made here to give a listing. For titles, search the Internet and watch nature-related and program-oriented periodicals for reviews of video resources and for new films.

Ecology/Environmental Quality

Ecology and environmental quality are essential foundations for any nature-oriented program. The two are integrally entwined with one another and with human behavior. The natural environment is composed of animals, plants, soil, and minerals, all tied together in an intricate, balanced network of dependence and support. This sometimes is referred to as *the web of life or the balance of nature*. Knowledge regarding the various elements of nature is very important to understanding ecological concepts. Most of the activities in this chapter provide a base for better understanding these interrelationships. (In addition to activities in this chapter, see Community Resources in Chapter 1, as well as the resources at the end of each section in the chapter.)

Human beings, by their lifestyles, have seriously threatened and, in fact, disrupted the balance of nature. There have been terrible human impacts, sometimes irreversible, on the entire planet. Developed societies' attempts to satisfy their insatiable drive for higher standards of living, with corresponding demands on non-renewable resources and high consumption of energy, have left in their wake waste products that detrimentally affect both the natural environment and human beings. There is a real need to help people: become a) more aware of the environmental problems that have an impact not only locally but also nationally and globally; b) more knowledgeable about what we know and don't know about environmental problems and potential solutions; and c) motivated to take action, both on a personal level and to support efforts to enhance environmental quality.

Participation in group observation-discovery, as well as educational trips, often lead people into new awareness of some of the community's problems relating to the environment. Another useful group activity is watching the newspaper for a month, noting (clipping) items about environmental concerns locally, regionally, and statewide, and those of national and international relevance. Individuals may also choose to affiliate with groups such as the Sierra Club, the Nature Conservancy, the World Wildlife Fund, and the Environmental Defense Fund, to name just a few of the environmentally concerned organizations, that advocate for better environmental practices locally, nationally, and internationally.

Pollution

Water Pollution. Water is essential to life; human beings cannot survive more than three or four days without it. Freshwater is in limited supply and is rationed whenever an extreme drought occurs. Yet, people treat water as if there is an unlimited supply. Pollutants are dumped directly into rivers and lakes, requiring water purification to make it safe for drinking and swimming. Water testing for both drinking and swimming is done by the local health department—visit a pool or municipal water supply to see how purification is done and talk with the personnel there as well as with public health officials.

Pesticides and fertilizers used in agriculture also are finding their way into natural water sources and into the food chain for fish, birds, animals, and humans. The advent of corporate farming including intensive hog operations cause ongoing concern related to public health including direct impact on the environment (ground water pollution, etc.) and human health (respiratory problems, etc.) You might want to visit a farmer and talk about the pesticides and fertilizers used and question whether there is runoff into the streams or absorption into the underground water system.

You, can do your own checking by gathering some water samples from nearby creeks, rivers, ponds, or lakes and test for pollutants. Your high school science teacher or county extension agent will be able to provide information on how to test the water. Many county extension offices have testing kits that you can borrow or you can check with the local public health office. If you find pollutants, where do they come from? Should you express your concern to county, state or federal officials? Why don't you serve as a catalyst to spur your group into action? There are many projects you can undertake...see the section on water.

Air pollution. Relating to both air and water pollution is acid rain. Acid rain is emissions (usually from industry) of sulfur dioxide and nitrogen oxides that are carried in the atmosphere and deposited often many, many miles from point of origin into lakes and streams, causing acidification that alters the aquatic system and also affects forests and soils. Acid rain is a global concern because of the conveyance of pollutants via the atmosphere/weather, namely, wind currents, convection, and turbulence. Another global concern involving the atmosphere is the disappearing ozone layer that protects the earth from the sun's ultraviolet rays. Despite denials from some groups, the Union of Concerned Scientists maintains that evidence of Global Warming is clear and compelling. The "greenhouse effect" that results in Global Warming will increasingly impact life as we know it affecting human health, as well as the quality of vegetation and animals. Some related activities are suggested in Section G: Weather/Atmosphere in this chapter.

Two additional aspects of air quality at the local level are toxic air pollution such as smog and indoor air pollution. Awareness of air quality inside houses and buildings is growing, as is research related to it.. Great strides have been made in America, as well as in many other parts of the world in limiting cigarette smoking and banning this activity entirely indoors.

A different type of air pollution is noise pollution, both continuous noise and extremely loud noise. There are harmful effects both to human beings and to animals. This includes noise from snowmobiles, helicopters, etc. in outdoor or wilderness areas. Much technical and educational information on air pollution is readily available on various websites and through government and environmental protection agencies and organizations.

Soil pollution/impaction. Environmental quality related to soil includes soil pollution, soil impaction, and litter. Almost everyone agrees that litter is ugly and unsightly. Unfortunately this remains a serious problem in today's society. Litter can be found on every playground, park, roadway, as well as in remote wilderness areas, and even in such pristine environments as Mt. Everest and remote ocean and beach locations. Preventing litter is something that should be emphasized in any group of responsible citizens concerned with environmental quality and aesthetics. What evidence of litter do you find in your community? What can you do about it?

Soil quality includes awareness of impaction and overuse of certain recreational areas by people, especially when using horses and off-road vehicles. Have you wondered why big trees sometimes begin to die where there has been heavy picnicking? It may be due to impaction, if the conditions under which the tree first grew have changed. Check in your park picnic areas. Overuse of an area or trail also may result in extensive erosion. As you bike, see if the trail has evidence of overuse. Poor conservation practices and irresponsible use of herbicides and fertilizers are polluting and depleting the very soil that many people depend upon for food. There also may be water runoff that carries soil residues removing valuable top soil and polluting streams and ground water.

ACTIVITIES

Measuring Water Infiltration There are a couple of simple ways you can measure water infiltration: (1) filling a measured hole with water and (2) completely filling a can of water placed on the surface. The comparative measure is the amount of time the water takes to soak completely into the soil.

MATERIALS NEEDED:

shovel
spade or trowel
Measuring tape
Bucket
Watch
Gallon can
2 x 4 or 2 x 6 about 2 feet long
Site map

Test 1 requires digging a hole that is measurable, such as a 4-inch cylinder or square, 4 to 6 inches deep at several locations and comparing them. Each hole tested must be the same size. Once you've dug the hole, fill it with water to the top. Record the time it takes the water to completely soak into the soil.

Test 2 is a bit more difficult, but provides a more accurate measure. Fill a gallon can with both ends removed that has been laced on the surface. The tricky part is keeping the water within the body of the can rather than leaking out from under it, into the soil horizon beneath. When finished, replace the soil in its original location. Here are some additional tips:

- You can find gallon cans in restaurants where they are standard bulk size for tomato sauces, etc.

- If you stand on the top of the can while your partner pours in the water you will keep the water from leaking out. This is where the 2 x 4 or 2 x 6, about 2 feet long comes in handy. Put it on the top of the can and stand on it. Be prepared to stand there for a while. It may take 20 minutes or more for the water to drain into the soil on compacted sites.

- You may want to use less water. Place a mark that is easily seen halfway up the inside of the can and fill to that level each time (about ½ gallon)

- Pick sites that have some flat surfaces where the can will sit level

Record the test locations on a map of the area. Note the time in minutes and seconds for each observation. Record any significant visual observations at the test site such as ground cover, shrubs, a trail, a parking area, etc. Compare times between samples from different areas.

Making a Soil Profile.

> **MATERIALS NEEDED:**
> *Shovel*
> *Spade or trowel*
> *Measuring tape or ruler*
> *Camera*
> *Site map*

This assessment requires digging and removing cross sections of soil profile and measuring (1) its overall depth (to mineral soil) and (2) the depth of various horizons. Take samples to compare at several locations. Samples may be collected adjacent to water filtration tests. Record the depth of the profiles and horizons. It may be useful to take photos of the removed cross sections with a scale or ruler next to them, so that they can be compared when not in the field. Assess the profile cross sections for compaction, truncation, presence, or absence of litter and humus. Compare these organic profiles where recreation activity is heavy and where use is light. Record your findings and the implication of those findings regarding recreational use and soil impacts. Tip: remove the profile cross-sections carefully, keeping the litter layer intact. When finished, return the cross sections to their original locations.

Solid waste. Deterioration of environmental quality has been evidenced extensively by the pollution of the air, water, and soil. Society has left in its wake waste products that it doesn't know how to dispose of. Polluted air and water threaten much of existing life, both of human beings and of the natural environment. In the 21st century, the "throw away" society continues to grow, making disposal of solid waste products a critical problem in terms of both location and quantity. Although some progress has been made in certain areas, the outlook is still grim. Much waste is non-biodegradable, such as the fossil fuel-based styrofoam, plastics, and yes, the convenient disposable diaper. Space for landfills is at a premium. However, disposal is not only a matter of decomposition, but also of harmful substances leaching into the soil and finding their way into surface water bodies and underground water systems.

How are solid waste materials (garbage) disposed of in your community? Why not go to a "dump" or a sanitary landfill? Talk to the staff about the processing of waste, the quantity of waste, and the staff's concerns. Recycling paper, plastics, and glass is one way to show commitment to trying to alleviate to a small degree, the solid waste problem. Visit a recycling center. If your community does not have such a center, why not? While community-wide waste disposal is a major project, you can practice good waste disposal practices when on camping trips or outings. What do you do with your waste? Do you purchase foods and use containers that can be recycled or are biodegradable, practicing good stewardship of natural resources? (See Chapter 4).

Summary

Yes, environmental quality is multifaceted. The quality of environment is dependent upon an understanding of the laws of nature, the capabilities of technology, and the behaviors/lifestyles of people. Responsibility must be assumed by individuals for both their own acts and for those of the wider society, as well as the interaction of nations. There are many resources available relating to environment quality, and thus the focus of this manual does not encompass projects and activities relating to environmental quality, but is suggestive of the scope.

 Books on Sensory Awareness and Ecology/Environmental Quality

See master publicatons list for cities of Publishers.

Brown, Vinson. (1982). *Reading the Outdoors at Night.* Mechanicsburg, PA: Stackpole Books. Sounds, sights, smells after dark. (out of print, limited availability)

Cornell, Joseph, Michael, Deranja,. (1995). *Journey to the Heart of Nature: A Guided Exploration.* Dawn Publications.

Cornell, Joseph. (1995). *Listening to Nature: How to Deepen Your Awareness of Nature.* Dawn Publications.

Cornell, Joseph. (2000). *With Beauty before Me: An Inspirational Guide for Nature Walks.* Dawn Publications.

Cornell, Joseph B. (1998). *Sharing Nature with Children*, 2nd edition. Dawn Publications.

Duensing, Edward. (1997). *Talking to Fireflies, Shrinking the Moon: Nature Activities for All Ages.* Fulcrum Publishing.

Horsfall, Jacqueline. (1997). Play *Lightly on the Earth.* Dawn Publications.

Leslie, Clare Walker, and Charles E. Roth. (2000). *Keeping a Nature Journal: Discover a Whole New Way of Seeing the World around You.* Storey Books.

Low, Mary, and Connie Coutellier.. (2003). *Creek Stompin' and Getting' into Nature: Environmental Activities that Foster Youth Development.* American Camp Association. Full of activities that include objectives, age range, number of participants and equipment needed.

Petrash, Carol, and Donald Cook. (1992). *Earthways: Simple Environmental Activities for Young Children.* Gryphon House. Organized by seasons includes nature crafts and natural toys.

Raven, Peter, Linda, Berg, and John Aliff (2003). *Environment*, 4th edition. Wiley Text Books.

Roa, Michael L. (2002). *Environmental Science Activities Kit: Ready-to-Use Lessons, Labs, and Worksheets for Grades 7-12.* Jossey-Bass.

Rockwell, Robert E., Elizabeth A. Sherwood, and A., Williams, Robert A. Williams. (1990). *Hug a Tree and Other Things to Do Outdoors with Young Children.* Gryphon House: Mt. Rainier. MD.

Schwartz, Linda. (1990). *Earth Book for Kids: Activities to Help Heal the Environment.* Learning Works, Inc. All activities aimed at learning about the environment and having fun.

Shaffer, Carolyn, and Erica Fielder. (1987). *City Safaris.* (Sierra Club Books). Sierra Club: San Francisco. (out of print, limited availability)

Sheehan, Kathryn, and Mary Waidner. (1994). *Earth Child: Games, Stories, Activities, Experiments, and Ideas About Living Lightly on Planet Earth.* Council Oak Books. Loads of projects.

Smith, Roger. (2001). *Strands in the Web.* New Society Publishing. 200+ environmental activities.

Van Matre, Steve. (1974). *Acclimatization.* American Camp Association: Martinsville, IN.

Van Matre, Steve. (1979). *Sunship Earth.* American Camp Association: Martinsville, IN.

Van Matre, Steve, and Bill Weiler. (1985). *Earth Speaks.* Institute for Earth Education.

Van Matre, Steve. *Earthkeepers: Four Keys for Helping Young People Live in Harmony with the Earth.* Institute for Earth Education.

Van Matre, Steve. (1990). *Earth Education: A New Beginning.* Institute for Earth Education. Steve Van Matre has a long history with caring for the earth through his acclimatization series. In this book he discusses how he believes environmental education has failed and puts forth "earth education" as an alternative made up of "magical learning adventures."

Internet Sites on Sensory Awareness and Ecology/Environmental Quality

Suggested search words: environment/ecology/protecting the environment/ environmental activities/ environmental awareness/environmental education/nature appreciation

Earth 911: http://www.earth911.org/ Motto: "Making every day earth day!" Can enter your zip code and view local environmental information.

EarthVision: http://www.earthvision.net/ Collection of environmental news stories arranged by topic following topics: business/technology; sustainability; education; advocacy/policy; and recreation.

EcoWorld: http://www.ecoworld.com Information on the status of earth's species and ecosystems. Dedicated to preservation and restoration.

EE-Link: http://eelink.net/ North American Association for Environmental Education provides resources for students, teachers, and professionals that support K-12 environmental education. Includes projects, activities, facts, data, and many useful links.

EnviroTech: http://www.envirotech-list.com Directory to environmental education websites.

Environmental Education Station: http://web.centre.edu/enviro/ Maintained at Centre College with funding from Rasmussen Foundation and the Association Colleges of the South. For students and teachers.

Institute for Earth Education: http://www.eartheducation.org/default.asp Organization associated with Steve Van Matre

Natureconservancy.com: http://www.natureconservancy.com/ Touts the "best science links on the web"

Reading *A Sand County Almanac* **resources:** http://ecoethics.net/hsev/9910-res.htm

Sierra Club: http://www.sierraclub.org/ Their motto is: "explore, enjoy and protect the planet."

US Environmental Protection Agency: http://www.epa.gov/ Lots of resources including data, educational resources, laws and regulations, programs, etc.

US Geological Survey, Environment page: http://www.usgs.gov/themes/environ.html This government agency studies natural, physical, chemical and biological processes.

SECTION A

ANIMALS

The meadows and forests provide homes for many different forms of animal life. Through their daily activities, these animals (particularly smaller mammals, reptiles and amphibians, and birds) provide the observant student of nature with one of the most interesting pastimes. As part of the animal kingdom, human beings should respect other forms of animal life, avoiding indiscriminate killing, habitat disruption, or any manner of interference.

Since many forest animals are nocturnal, the best time to observe them in their natural environment is in the early morning, late afternoon, or twilight hours. (See Chapter 8, Section A: Nighttime Activities.) Even at these times you may need a great deal of patience and the ability to remain quietly in one place for long periods of time. Quietly waiting for wildlife is sometimes called *Seton Watching* after the Canadian naturalist Ernest Thompson Seton who founded the Woodcraft Indians, an outdoor youth group that later merged with other groups to become the Boy Scouts in America. Seton practiced sitting quietly for many hours essentially becoming part of nature. In the *Handbook of the Canadian Rockies* it is reported that *Seton Watching* can produce "astounding results," including mice running over your shoes, birds landing on your head. They even report one incident of a beaver climbing out of a pond and curling up in a woman's lap. The rewards attained through extreme patience allowing you to observe animals in their natural habitats as they follow their daily routines are so great that you will consider your time and effort well spent.

TRACKS AND TRACKING

Tracking and track casting are enjoyable activities related to animals. You should not forget that tracking can be done in the snow during winter. Tracking can lead you to animals to observe or provide the satisfaction of accomplishment in being able to follow tracks over a considerable distance. (For information about how to make casts of tracks, see Chapter 2: Nature Crafts, Section D: Crafts that are Reproductions.)

ENDANGERED SPECIES

Federal and state game and migratory bird laws prevent owning or possessing endangered and threatened animals, as well as any part of the animals (feathers, furs, etc.) The fines for breaking these laws can be very high. Further, there are many local and state regulations prohibiting owning animals or keeping animals in urban or other locations. Wild animals never truly become "tamed," so it is best to protect the animals', natural habitats and let them exist free and naturally

CHELEY COLORADO CAMPS, CHELEY, CO.

HABITAT DESTRUCTION

The biggest threat to animals in general is the continuing destruction of natural habitats. With modern farming techniques, most fence rows, once havens rich in wildlife, have disappeared and our insatiable appetite for more and bigger houses continually turns wildlands into housing developments.

Destruction of habitat and encroachment also has resulted in the appearance of many wild animals in suburbs (deer, raccoon, skunks, etc.) and urban areas (falcons nesting in Chicago and New York City high-rises for example). When wild animals clash with human beings, the animals ultimately lose.

ENCOUNTERING ANIMALS

Whenever you encounter animals during activities in the field, it is important not to approach them. Wild animals that can be approached are likely sick or injured, and thus potentially very dangerous. Unless you are knowledgeable about the care of injured animals, assistance should be sought from people who are trained in dealing with wildlife, such as the US Fish & Wildlife Service, state conservation agents, nature center specialists, animal control officers, or veterinarians.

 **Books on Animals**

See master publicatons list for cities of Publishers.

Burns, Diane. (1995). *Snakes, Salamanders and Lizards.* NorthWood Press: Chanhassen, MN. Includes tips to find for all animals and hands-on activities. Good color illustrations. Very attractive book for children, with many ideas for leaders.

Holley, Dennis. (1997). *Animals Alive!: An Ecological Guide to Animal Activities.* Roberts Rinehart Publishers. Covers animals from lower invertebrates (sponges, etc.) to mammals.

Kavanagh, James. (2002). *Mammals: Educational Games & Activities for Kids of all Ages.* Waterford Press. Entire 8½ x 11 paperbound booklet is games and activities that can be done in the car or sitting inside.

Whitaker, John. (1996). *National Audubon Society Field Guide to Mammals, North America.* Knopf: NY. High quality color photographs and illustrations.

Animal Tracking:

Jaeger, Ellsworth. (2001). *Tracks and Trailcraft: A Fully Illustrated Guide to the Identification of Animal Tracks in Forest and Field, Barnyard, and Backyard.* Lyons Press: NY. Excellent illustrations and wide variety of animals, plus some plants. Also includes how to make plaster casts and tracking games.

Miller, Dorcas. (1981). *Track Finder: A Guide to Mammal Tracks of Eastern North America.* Nature Study Guild Publishers: Rochester, NY. Pocket-sized book, well done.

Murie, Olaus. (1974). *Animal Tracks,* 2nd edition: Houghton-Mifflin. (A Peterson Field Guide)

Nail, Jim. (1994). *Whose Tracks Are These? A Clue Book of Familiar Forest Animals.* Roberts Rinehart. Publishers: Niwot, CO. Children's story, early elementary.

Rezendes, Paul. (1999).. *Tracking and the Art of Seeing: How to Read Animal Tracks and Sign,* 2nd edition. HarperCollins: NY. Uses photographs (many in color) rather than illustrations.

Internet Sites on Animals

Suggested search words: animals/mammals/animals in nature/endangered species/ animals in nature/animal tracking/wildlife.

Enature.com: http://www.enature.com Nonprofit site partnered with National Wildlife Federation.

EndangeredSpecie.com: http://www.endangeredspecie.com/ "EndangeredSpecie.com is dedicated to providing all the best endangered species information, links, books, and publications regarding rare and endangered species. This site also includes information about conservation efforts and endangered species organizations that are dedicated to saving and preserving the world's most endangered wildlife and plant life."

Endangered Species Program: http://endangered.fws.gov/ US Fish and Wildlife Service site. Includes laws and lots of information on endangered species.

National Wildlife Federation: http://www.nwf.org/ Membership organization founded in 1936 is dedicated to: "educating and empowering people from all walks of life to protect wildlife and habitat for future generations." Excellent site for information about wildlife and up-to-date news items. Includes wonderful sites for kids, as well as general wildlife programs and activities.

World Wildlife Fund: http://www.worldwildlife.org The WWF leads international efforts to protect endangered species and their habitats.

SECTION B

BIRDS

There are numerous activities associated with birds in nature. Bird watching is probably the most popular activity of bird lovers. Many people like to follow through with a bird feeding program, making a bird house or bird sanctuary, or joining in the research part of bird study that includes bird banding.

BIRD WATCHING

One of the most interesting and exciting hobbies available to people who enjoy and appreciate the outdoors is bird watching. Birds are interesting little creatures clothed in a variety of colors ranging from drab gray to brilliant reds. Their songs have added cheer to many dreary days. Their ability in homemaking and nest building has amazed even the most advanced naturalists and held them spellbound as they watched parents prepare for raising their young.

As with other animals, the best time to look for birds is in the early morning or late afternoon when they are most active. Walk away from the sun because it is difficult to see the colors when you are looking into the sun. The best places to go in search of birds are along the edge of the forest, edges of fields and pastures, marshes, and other areas where feed and water are abundant.

You do not need expensive equipment to begin bird watching. In fact, you do not need anything except your eyes and an interest in birds. There are a few aids that will make bird watching more enjoyable and will help you to learn about birds more rapidly. The first of these is a pocket guide such as Peterson's *Field Guide to the Birds*. (This guide also has a companion CD of bird calls and songs.) This book is arranged so that it not only helps you identify the bird, but quickly points out its distinguishing characteristics—size, shape, song, surroundings, sweep (flight), and shade (color) sometimes referred to as the *Six S's*. Soon you will want to take a small notebook with you to jot down observations of your explorations.

A good pair of binoculars is a big help, as they bring the birds close enough for detailed study. Binoculars should be selected with care. Good binoculars are expensive, but since this is a lifetime investment, it will pay you to get a durable pair with good lenses. The best sizes for bird-watching are 7 x 35 or 7 x 50, preferably with central focusing (focusing both lenses simultaneously). There are binoculars that also take digital pictures. Like much technology, the quality is likely to improve rapidly.

BIRD FEEDING

As your interest grows in bird watching, you may want to expand your efforts to include planting gardens with vegetation and trees that attract specific types of birds. Feeding birds in the winter is the way to bring the birds to you. Simple bird feeders can be easily constructed. Once you begin feeding birds, they will come to your area regularly and you may be able to observe them from your window all winter. You should continue feeding all winter since the birds come to rely on your supply of food. Suggested food for birds include suet, sunflower seeds, and a variety of small grains and seeds. You can mix your own or, of course, many stores sell bird feed.

BUILDING BIRD HOUSES

Building birdhouses and setting out nesting materials are projects that groups can undertake. Directions for birdhouse construction can be found on the Internet and are included in several of the references at the end of this section. Different species of birds have their own preferences for size and shape of house, so you should decide what kind of bird you want to attract before beginning to make birdhouses.

BIRD BANDING

Much of what is known about birds has come through the information gathered by amateur bird watchers. Bird enthusiasts can participate in annual bird counts or in bird banding programs. Banding programs capture birds, band them, and release them; the bander does the identification and record keeping. You must have a permit to participate in this program. Contact the Audubon Society or the U.S. Geological Survey for information regarding bird counts and bird banding opportunities.

BIRD CALLS AND OTHER RESOURCES

Anyone can go to the Internet and find loads of information on birds including audios of bird calls. In addition to books, there are numerous videos (in many formats—CDs, DVDs, and VCRs), as well as live video-streaming on the Internet that provides information about bird calls, bird identification, birding trips, nest building and much more. There are also portable electronic gadgets that have pictures, bird calls, and other bird identification information.

 Books on Birds

See master publicatons list for cities of Publishers.

Able, Kenneth. (1999). *Gathering of Angels: Migrating Birds and Their Ecology.* Comstock Books: Ithaca, NY. Color and black and white photographs. Identifies locations that must be preserved if birds are to have secure resting spots.

Haus, Robyn, and Stan Jaskiel. (2001). *Make Your Own Birdhouses and Feeders (Quick Starts for Kids!)* . Williamson Publishing: VT.

Kerlinger, Paul. (1995). *How Birds Migrate.* Stackpole Books: Mechanicsburg, PA. Researcher Paul Kerlinger unravels intricacies and wonders of bird migration.

Klutz. (1999). *Backyard Birds: A Coast-to-Coast Guide to the Birds You're Already Supposed to Know.* Klutz Press. (Klutz Guide)

Peterson, Roger. (2002). *Birds of Eastern and Central North America,* 5th edition. Houghton-Mifflin: Boston. (Peterson Field Guide)

Roth, Sally. (2000). *The Backyard Bird Feeder's Bible: The A to Z Guide to Feeders, Seed Mixes, Projects, and Treats.* Rodale: Emmaus, PA. Literally starts with the letter A and progresses to Z using words associated with bird feeding. Lots of color photographs and illustrations.

Roth, Sally. (1998). *Attracting Birds to Your Backyard: 536 Ways to Turn Your Yard and Garden onto a Haven for Your Favorite Birds.* Rodale: Emmaus, PA. Uses each letter of the alphabet to head chapters that are keyed by words beginning with the chapter letter. Lots of color illustrations.

Walton, Richard, and Robert Lawson. (1989). *Birding by Ear: A Guide to Bird-Song Identification. Eastern/Central.* (2 compact discs). Houghton Mifflin: Boston. Audio recordings of over 170 birds. Learn to recognize birds by their songs and calls.

 Internet Sites on Birds

Suggested search words: birds/attracting birds/bird gardening/birds in nature/bird watching/bird banding/ornithology/bird songs

American Birding Association: http://www.americanbirding.org/ "Aims to inspire all people to enjoy and protect wild birds."

Birding.com: http://www.birding.com/ Extensive and detailed information on almost all topics related to birding including beginning birding, bird identification, attracting birds, etc.

Birdwatching.com: http://www.birdwatching.com/ It is about wild birds and the sport of birding. It's for everyone who's interested in birdwatching and enjoying nature

Hummingbirds.net: http://www.hummingbirds.net/ Excellent site; information on attracting, watching, feeding, and studying North American hummingbirds

National Audubon Society: http://www.audubon.org/

North American Blue Bird Society: http://nabluebirdsociety.org/ Includes specifications and directions for making bluebird nest boxes and bluebird trails.

O.W.L.: http://aves.net/the-owl/ The ornithological web library. Links to over 1850 sites devoted to wild birds and their study.

U.S. Geological Service, Patuxent Wildlife Research Center: http://www.pwrc.usgs.gov/ BBL/homepage/ Detailed information on bird banding

SECTION C

INSECTS

Everybody has had some experience with insects and no wonder, for more than half of all the known animals in the world are insects. Too frequently associations with insects have not been under favorable conditions and many people have a negative reaction at the mention of the word. They immediately think of mosquitoes they have slapped, flies that molested their naps, or ants that were the uninvited guests at their picnics.

Actually, a very small percentage of insects are nuisances and all perform essential roles in the cycle of life. Fortunately, nature has provided a system of checks and balances so that natural enemies have kept most undesirable species under control. There is a real fascination in the study of these small, six-legged creatures. The brilliant colors of many of the insects, such as the butterfly and beetle, beckon us to take a closer look—and soon we are thrilled with the beauty that we had never before seen. The highly developed social systems of ants, termites, wasps, and bees continue to amaze even the most ardent students of insects, for they are to the insect world what human beings are to the world of mammals.

The purpose behind watching these little creatures is to learn as much about them and their living habits as possible. There is a real advantage for a beginner to work with someone who has experience working with insects. Frequently the science teachers in the local school can give you some help or suggest others in the community who share your interest. There are a wealth of Internet sites with information, pictures, video streaming and much more about insects. Many of these sites are associated with entomology departments at universities. Several of these sites are listed at the end of this section.

FINDING INSECTS

Insects can be found almost everywhere. The problem is finding the kind that you want. Many different kinds can be found in grassy areas, in gardens, and on trees. Many insects have a desire for sweet food, so it is possible to place some food out for them and wait for the insects to come to you. Light also attracts insects and it is possible to make insect traps using lights. Insects may be found during any time of the year, even in midwinter, but are most active in the late summer and fall.

OBSERVING INSECTS

There are many other projects related to insect study that are of interest to adults as well as children. Because of their relatively short life span, it is possible to capture insects and watch them go through their entire life cycle in as little as a four-week period. A large jar with holes in the lid containing some leaves makes an excellent cage for a caterpillar. You can then observe it go through the process called metamorphosis, emerging as a butterfly. Making observation hives for bees or an ant house for a colony of ants is always fascinating. Also, a number of nature centers are developing live butterfly areas where people can enjoy the beauty of butterflies and also study their characteristics.

ACTIVITY

Ant House (formicary). Take two pieces of window glass, 10″ x 14″, 12″ x 18″, or whatever size you have available, and insert 1″ apart into a frame grooved to hold the glass. The top of the frame should be removable so that the ants can be put in. Two or three holes should be made through which the ants are fed and watered. Close holes with corks or small strips of wood that turn on a nail or screw. The house can be put together with strong tape. If desired, place house on wooden blocks. It is desirable to seal around the glass fitting with paraffin—ants have a way of getting out the smallest crack!

To fill with ants, locate an ant hill and scoop out a couple of handfuls or trowelfuls of ant-dirt mixture. Try to get eggs, larvae, pupae, and a queen. The queen is especially important as the ants frequently will not work well without her. She is a larger and fatter ant. Pour ant-dirt mixture between glass panes. Fill to about 2″ from the top. Before fastening top, hang two small sponges under the two openings. Keep one moist with water and the other moist with sugar water or honey water. Occasionally throw in a few flies or other insects. Cover with heavy paper or cardboard to keep dark except when viewing. You will then be able to observe the ants' tunnel-digging prowess and how they move things.

COLLECTING INSECTS

A good book to help identify and classify insects is almost a must. In addition to this, a few simple homemade materials such as a collecting net, killing jar, mounting boards, and display boxes will be sufficient to get you started.

Killing Jar

A homemade killing jar can be made by placing blotter paper or newspaper cut into discs that fit snugly in the bottom of the jar. A stack of disks ½ inch high is sufficient. Pour fingernail polish remover or rubbing alcohol onto paper disks. Pour off any fluid that is not absorbed. When using the jar, place a few strips of tissue paper in the jar to absorb moisture and give insects a place to hide. Wrap the bottom 1-1½ " of the jar with masking tape or adhesive tape to prevent shattering in case the jar happens to drop or hit against something. Even though fingernail polish remover is relatively harmless, killing jars should be marked as "poison" and kept away from young children.

Collecting Net

A serviceable collecting net can be made by bending a coat hanger into a circle, attaching a length of broom handle to the hanger-hook part that has been straightened, attaching cheesecloth (to form a net) to the circular form, and sewing up the side and bottom to make a sack.

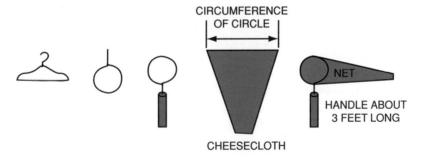

CIRCUMFERENCE OF CIRCLE

NET

HANDLE ABOUT 3 FEET LONG

CHEESECLOTH

Displaying Insects

Mounting or Spreading Boards. Insects such as butterflies and moths should be placed on a spreading board to dry so that the wings will remain in an attractive open position. You can make a spreading board from a paper plate by cutting out a thin strip in the center for the insect's body, and using strips of paper to hold the wings in place. A more permanent spreading board can be made from soft wood, with a strip of balsa wood below the groove to hold the inset pins. Lightweight cardboard strips can be attached to the top to hold the wings in place.

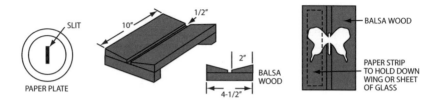

Display Boxes Cigar boxes or cardboard school supply boxes sold at many dollar stores make nice display cases. It is best to use thin dressmaker's pins for insect mounting rather than regular straight pins because the latter are too thick. Use #1 pins for most insects, #2 for butterflies, and #3 and #4 for large moths and butterflies. When mounting, the pin should be put through the thorax of most insects, slightly to the right of center. Bugs, however, are pinned through the small triangle in the center of the back, while beetles are pinned through the right wing covering. Grasshoppers and crickets are pinned through the saddle.

Insects are difficult to identify since there are over 650,000 known species with new species still being discovered. These are divided into 25 major orders, some of which are known by common names such as beetles, moths, butterflies, flies, termites, etc. Once identification is made, the insect should be properly mounted, labeled, and displayed. Labels should be attached to the mounting pins as shown in the diagram and include the name of the insect, the location where found, date, and name of finder if desired.

 **Books on Insects**

See master publicatons list for cities of Publishers.

Brock, Jim, and Kenn Kaufman. (2003). *Butterflies of North America.* (A Kaufman Focus Guide) Houghton Mifflin: NY. Has a very nice pictorial table of contents. High quality color illustrations.

Johnson, Jinny. (1997). *Simon & Schuster Children's Guide to Insects and Spiders.* Simon & Schuster Children's Publishing. Aimed at grades 4–6.

Klutz. (2000). *Spotter's Guide to the Nastiest Bugs in the Backyard.* Klutz Press. (Klutz Guide)

Leahy, Christopher, and R. Peterson. (editor). (1998). *Peterson's First Guide to Insects of North America.* (Peterson Field Guide). Houghton Mifflin.

Lovejoy, Sharon. (1999). *Roots, Shoots, Buckets, and Boots: Gardening Together with Children.* Workman Publishing: NY. Connecting children to nature through gardening. Twelve easy-to-do ideas for theme gardens, includes activities and crafts.

Milne, Lorus, and Lorus J. Milne. (1980). *National Audubon Society Field Guide to North American Insects and Spiders.* (Audubon Society Field Guide). Alfred A. Knopf.

Mitchell, Robert, and Herbert Zim. (2002) revised and updated. *Butterflies and Moths: A Guide to the More Common American Species.* St. Martin's Press: NY. (A Golden Guide) A pocket book with high quality color illustrations.

Rosenblatt, Lynn. (1998). *Monarch Magic!: Butterfly Activities and Nature Discoveries.* Williamson Publishing: Charlotte, VT. Not a pocket book (8½ x 11). Chock-full of activities.

Roth, Sally. (2001). *Attracting Butterflies and Hummingbirds to Your Backyard.* Rodale: Emmaus, PA. Detailed information and high-quality photographs.

Schneck, Marcus. (1993) *Creating a Butterfly Garden: A Guide to Attracting and Identifying Butterfly Visitors.* Simon & Schuster: NY. A pocket book with high quality color photographs and illustrations.

Tekulsky, Matthew. (1985). *The Butterfly Garden: Turning Your Garden, Window Box or Backyard into a Beautiful Home for Butterflies.* The Harvard Common Press: Boston. Step-by-step guide to gardening for butterflies.

Waldbauer, Gilbert. (2003). *What Good Are Bugs: Insects in the Web of Life.* Harvard University Press.

Wilsdon, Christina. (1998). *Insects.* (National Audubon Society First Field Guides). Scholastic.

Zim, H., C. Cottam, J. Latimer, D. Wagner, J. Irving, S. Simon, and H.S. Zim. (2001). Revised and updated. *Insects: A Guide to Familiar American Insects.* (Golden Guide). A pocket book with lots of high quality color pictures St. Martin's Press, NY.

 Internet Sites on Insects

Suggested search words: insects/entomology/butterflies/bugs

Many university entomology departments host excellent sites relating to insect identification and descriptions. A few are listed below.

Ant Colony Developers Association: http://www.antcolony.org/ An international nonprofit organization founded in 1998 whose mission includes "to provide the most complete web resource regarding ants online."

Bugbios: http://www.insects.org/

Butterfly Website: http://butterflywebsite.com/

North American Butterfly Association: http://www.naba.org/

Texas A&M Entomology: http://insects.tamu.edu/extension/insctans/ identification/ Includes an easy to use field guide.

University of Kentucky Entomology:
http://www.uky.edu/Agriculture/Entomology/ entfacts/efmisc.htm

US Geologic Service Children's Butterfly Site:
http://www.mesc.usgs.gov/resources/ education/butterfly/bfly_start.asp

Virginia Tech, Insect Identification Laboratory:
http://everest.ento.vt.edu/Facilities/ OnCampus/IDInfo.html

Virginia Tech, 3D Insects: http://www.ento.vt.edu/~sharov/3d/3dinsect.html
Fascinating web sit that included how to build virtual insects including moving pictures.

Young Entomologists' Society:
http://members.aol.com/YESbugs/bugclub.html

SECTION D
PLANTS, INCLUDING GARDENING

Plant life covers most of the planet from fragile flowers near the tops of mountains to lush valleys and deserts. Many nature-oriented activities can revolve around plants. Wildlife gardening and gardening with children lead off this section, followed by terrariums; field plot studies; seeds; edible plants and weeds; and trees. In addition to growing plants in a garden and forest areas, the program might also include activities in conservation, garden therapy, horticulture, nature study, civic beautification, flower arranging, food preparation. Other activities that can expand knowledge and resources are visits to greenhouses, florists, vegetable markets, nurseries, flower and vegetable shows and exhibits, and fairs; performing of experiments; tours of the town and visits to private vegetable and flower gardens. (For preservation of flowers, leaf prints, and other crafts from native materials, see Chapter 2: Nature Crafts.)

GARDENING FOR WILDLIFE

In addition to gardening for vegetables and flowers, gardening for wildlife is an enjoyable, educational activity. Gardening can be done in a public park or other public area where plantings can be made, on school grounds, in neighborhood lots, and in family backyards. Most gardening with wildlife focuses either on birds or animals, although both can be incorporated into one plot. Youngsters and senior citizens alike gain enjoyment from this nature activity, both in the gardening and in the observing of the birds and animals attracted to the plot. Gardening for wildlife involves design and layout of the area followed by planting and care of the plot—it is a project for all seasons. Water adds a special dimension to the area. The National Wildlife Federation sponsors the Schoolyard Habitats(r) certification program, as well as Backyard Wildlife Habitat certifications (http://www.nwf.org/education/). (See Internet sites following this section.)

CHILDREN'S GARDENING

Although this section focuses on children gardening is an activity for all ages and is particularly suited to families and senior citizens. Children's gardens are areas where children help plan and maintain the land and the vegetation that is grown. Many children's gardens are school sponsored, but because the growing season extends into summer, frequently this may be in conjunction with a municipal recreation department that can assume supervision after school is out. Some private organizations, such as garden clubs and botanic gardens, also sponsor children's gardens.

Junior Gardener's Pledge

I promise to help protect birds, plants, trees, and flowers everywhere; to help make my community healthful and beautiful and not throw candy wrappers, fruit peels, or paper on streets, sidewalks, or lawns, no matter whether I am walking or riding in a car. I will be careful of other's people's places and things as I would like them to be of mine; and I will do my best to sow seeds or plant flowers or a tree at least once a year.

You Can Almost Tell

Folks who make a garden,
Who love to weed and hoe,
Always seem less worried
Than other folks I know.

They also seem more gentle,
Their hearts with love abound.
You can almost tell such people
By the look they carry around.
Can it be that gardening
Plays a double role,
Fulfills creative longing
And cultivates the soul?
    -RUTH R. HEUTER

The values of gardening experience for children are many. Here are a few:

1. For many children this is their first experience with growing plants.

2. They will gain a better understanding of a plant's life cycle by observing its seed sprout, grow, mature, bear fruit, and die.

3. It provides an opportunity to accept responsibility, for they will soon learn that they "reap what they sow" and they must take care of their plants if they want them to grow and produce.

4. They will develop new appreciation for the work that goes into the production of the world's food.

5. They will be learning by actually doing, through working with their hands. Safe use of tools can also be learned.

6. Their understanding of the need for conservation will grow - the role of fire, insects, disease, and water.

7. The opportunity for work experience in the natural environment is particularly important for city children.

8. The chance to work on a group project teaches cooperation on boundaries, paths, equipment, and sharing of joy in the achievement of others.

9. It creates a love and appreciation for beautiful things. This will encourage them to make things beautiful and give them a feeling of joy in the care and propagation of plants.

10. They will develop interests that may grow into valuable lifetime hobbies and wise use of leisure time.

There are various types of gardens. Both vegetables and flowers should be planned in a children's garden program. Specialty gardens are valuable. Gardens also differ in location and design. The home garden is very common, but when gardening in the community recreation program, specific guidance and visitation should be provided. The most common type (sponsored by municipalities and schools) is the tract garden where each child has a small plot in a large garden area and children take care of their own plots. A third type of garden is the farm, camp, or forest garden that may have individual gardens, but is usually cared for by a group. This garden is usually away from the city so that transportation must be provided. There are a variety of specialty gardens—dish gardens, indoor terrariums, flats, miniature gardening on a button in a bowl, window boxes, rock gardens, wildflower collections, and the like. In all gardening activities children should help in designing or landscaping the area. They should help prepare the land, plant the seeds, care for the garden during the growing season, reap the harvest, use the crop, and then clear the area. They should also learn what tools to use, when and why to use them, and how to care for them. Here are some guiding principles for supervising children's gardens:

1. Children should be mature enough to handle tools and follow through with the activity to start a gardening program.

2. Involve the children in all phases of gardening, including planning, purchase of seeds, preparing the ground, planting, hoeing, and reaping. Using the harvest—flower arrangements, cooking, etc.—can further enrich the entire experience.

3. Discuss the items that should be considered in the selection of a garden site—good soil, proper drainage, shade, and sunlight.

4. Plan your garden on paper, including a diagram of the area and a list of the seeds that will be needed. (Many county extension agencies now have computerized programs for garden design that they make available to the public. Quite a bit of commercial gardening software is also available.)

5. Gardens do not need to be large (8' x 10' minimum). Rectangular plots with well-defined paths around them are preferred to square ones.

6. Include a variety of flowers and vegetables in your plans. Choose those that mature rapidly and are hardy so that beginners will be assured of success.

7. Children should learn how to start plants and know which ones need to be started indoors.

8. Work the soil when it is dry enough so that it does not form mud balls.

9. Plant the seeds at the proper time and depth.

10. The following equipment will be needed in your gardening program:
    - spading fork
    - iron rake
    - sticks or pot labels (for marking end of rows)
    - yardstick
    - heavy string
    - trowel
    - hand cultivator
    - hoe

TERRARIUMS

Another popular and interesting project to show environmental interrelationships is the terrarium. Terrariums are miniature habitats. Simple, inexpensive containers may be constructed from large-mouthed gallon jars or old aquariums. The primary types of terrariums are desert, woodland, bog, and semi-aquatic. Each has different kinds of plants and requires different planting and care.

Preserving Herbarium Specimens

Collecting, preparing, and preserving plants is a popular and rewarding activity. The following is an easy, cheap, and efficient method for preserving herbarium specimens of vascular plants. (Based upon material prepared by the Department of Botany, State University of Iowa.)

1. Carefully select the specimen in the field. Care should be taken not to take specimens when there is danger of disrupting the ecology of the area; always make sure that it is environmentally responsible to collect each specimen. Check with experts who know local ecology and plant life before collecting. It is preferable that the specimen be in flower or fruit. Underground parts of herbaceous plants should be included and carefully dug with a strong trowel, collecting pick, or small shovel. For woody plants, where it is not feasible to take the root portion, a branch showing leaf, bud twig or flower or fruit characteristics can be obtained.

2. Immediately upon taking each specimen, a record should be made in a notebook indicating habitat, location, and date. Notation should be made of petal color, glaucescence (covered with a grayish, bluish, or whitish waxy coating or bloom that is easily rubbed off), and other characteristics often lost in drying. The height of the plant and the diameter (at about 4½ feet—chest height) should also be noted for woody plants.

3. Pressing plants should take place as soon as possible in order to preserve them in their best condition. If a field press is not used, the tagged specimen should be placed in a metal collecting can (vasculum) or plastic bag with moist newspaper to keep the specimen fresh. Pressing can be delayed overnight in cool climates if the specimen is stored in a cool place.

4. To prepare the specimen for pressing, remove the soil and excess moisture from roots and judiciously prune superfluous leaves, being careful not to destroy parts necessary to identify the plant. Place in a folded newspaper. Plants that are longer than a folded half newspaper sheet should be bent accordion-style. (V or N-shaped) with roots at lower left corner of the sheet. Some leaves should be turned over so that both upper and lower surfaces are displayed in the dried specimen. Extra flowers and fruits of the specimen should be included if possible. Collection date should be

written directly on the sheets, at least in abbreviated form, in order to avoid confusion of specimens or data later.

5. After the plant is placed in the folded newspaper, place the newspaper between blotters or felt driers (12"x18") that are in turn separated from each other by corrugated cardboard or aluminum corrugates that serve as ventilators. The resulting pile of newspapers with plants, blotters, and corrugates is pressed between press frames 12" x 18", usually ash or hickory slats riveted together. The material is put under pressure by tightly tying straps or sash cord around the frames. After the ventilated press is tightly bound, it is placed over a source of dry, heated air. Usually 24 hours of drying suffices for all but the most succulent plants when corrugates and an artificial heat source are used. A good source of dry heat is a series of light bulbs in a wooden frame on top of which the pressing frames are placed with open corrugates down so that the heat will flow up and through the corrugates. If corrugates are not used, blotters should be alternated with the folded newspaper with specimens inside and must be changed for warm, dry ones every day until the specimens are dry. These moist blotters should be placed in the sun to dry more quickly.

6. After drying, the specimens may be stored permanently in the labeled newspaper sheets in which they were dried or they may be prepared for mounting. In either case, specimens should be labeled with neatly written (using waterproof ink), typed, or printed labels bearing the name of the plant with authorities for the name (as *Buchloe Dactyloides*. (Nutt.) Engelm. Or *Quercus ruba* L.), the habitat, location, date of collection, and other pertinent information, and the collector'name and collection number. The label should be 100 percent rag paper 4"x 2½ " or larger. One label should be placed with each specimen sheet.

7. If mounting specimens, they should be attached to 100 percent rag paper, standard size herbarium sheet (11½ " x 16½ ") that can be obtained from local printer or stationery shop or a biological supply house or a variety of suppliers can be found on the Internet. Carefully paste label in one corner, preferably lower right-hand. The specimen may be attached to sheet by use of bands of quick-drying liquid plastic, gummed cloth strips, thread, special herbarium paste or glue, or combinations of these methods. If glue or paste is used, spread it in a thin layer over a sheet of glass (14" x 20" or larger) with a small paint brush. The specimen, face upward, is placed firmly (without smearing) on the glue, lifted with tweezers or forceps, and dropped carefully in the desired position on the mounting paper. Excess drops of glue should be removed with a damp cloth. The sheet is then placed between clean, unprinted newspaper sheets (newsprint) in a pile under a light weight. When the glue is dry, the twigs and other heavy parts of the specimen are taped or sewn to the sheet for added reinforcement.

8. The finished sheets are now ready to be inserted with other sheets in stan-
    dard manila envelopes, each holding a genus, and placed in insect proof
    and dustproof herbarium cases. Protection for insects and mold can be
    provided by storing in dry places with Paradow (mothballs) or occasional
    fumigation. Large herbaria often use alcohol solutions of bichloride of
    mercury for dipping specimens before mounting, or paint specimens after
    mounting for more permanent protection.

FIELD PLOT STUDIES

Field plot study is one of the most interesting methods of integrating observations of
plants, animals, and soils. Such studies encompass those investigative activities that
can be carried on with a small, defined land area on or near school grounds, in park
areas, or in the backyard. The plot chosen should have a wide variety of features and
be away from heavy traffic (people trampling). Several plots with contrasting features
might be selected for comparative purposes. Plots may be as small as one square yard.
The features of the plot are studied in some depth. Usually a plot is approached from
three views: (1) where it is located in relation to its surroundings—relief, topographic, and contour maps can be used; (2) biological aspects involving the requirements of living organisms, both plant and animal, to sustain life, the
interdependencies and interrelationships of plants and animals, and the characteristics of the organisms under study; and (3) the biotic influences or physical properties, including the effects of rocks, land forms, soil, water, and climate upon the plot
ecology and its inhabitants. Look through nature activity books, especially those
with scientific orientation for more ideas and resources for this activity.

JOYCE KOEPER, MARTINSVILLE, IN.

SEEDS, EDIBLE PLANTS, AND WEEDS

Of particular interest to youngsters, especially those gardening, are activities with
seeds: how seeds travel (shot from pods, hitchhikers that steal rides, seeds that fly);
seeds used for pixies and pictures; food for birds (set up a bird cafeteria); germina-
tion experiments; raising trees from seeds (miniature tree garden); growing seeds in
water to eat sprouts. Collecting and preparing edible wild foods make interesting
activities, but these activities must be led by persons who are experts in edible plants

to avoid harmful or dangerous plants. One can learn many fascinating things while studying plants normally called "weeds." Wildflower inventories can become as popular a hobby as keeping a bird list.

TREES

There are also a host of activities associated with trees, some of which have already been mentioned. Tree stump explorations; study of dendrology and making a tree calendar; leaf skeletons; identification boards and leaf exhibits, seeds, winter twigs, wood specimens; and making leaf keys, as well as nature crafts and other activities, are just a few that can be included in the nature-oriented community recreation program.

 Books on Plants & Gardening

See master publicatons list for cities of Publishers.

Briggs, Josie. (2001). *Creating Small Habitats for Wildlife in Your Garden.* Guild of Master Craftsman.

Broekel, Ray. (1982). *Aquariums and Terrariums.* Children's, Children's Book Press, Chicago. (limited availability)

Conrad, Jim. (1996). *Discover Nature in the Garden: Things to Know and Things to Do.* Stackpole Books: Mechanicsburg: PA.

Daley, Allen, and Stella Daley. (1986). *Making and Using Terrariums and Planters.* Blandford Press, (out of print, limited availability)

Ernst, Ruth. (1996). *The Naturalist's Garden,* 3rd edition. Globe Pequot:

Knope, Jim, Sally Wasowski, John Kadel Boring, Glenn Keator, Jane Scott, and Erica Glasener. (1996). *Natural Gardening.* (Nature Company Guide). Time-Life Books. Principles of gardening in harmony with nature.

Martin, Deborah. (1999). *1,001 Ingenious Gardening Ideas: New, Fun, and Fabulous that Will Change the Way You Garden Forever!* (Rodale Garden Book). Rodale Books.

Moore, Bibby, and Kendal Brown. (1989). *Growing with Gardening: A Twelve-Month Guide for Therapy, Recreation and Education.* The University of North Carolina Press. Provides information for garden/horticulture therapy including wheelchair accessible gardens.

Ocone, Lynn, and Eve Pranis. (1990). National *Gardening Association Guide to Kids' Gardening: A Complete Guide for Teachers, Parents and Youth Leaders.* (Wiley Science Editions). John Wiley & Sons.

Roth, Sally. (2002). *Attracting Butterflies and Hummingbirds to Your Backyard: Watch Your Garden Come Alive with Beauty on the Wing.* Rodale Books.

Stokes, Donald, and Lillian Stokes. (1998). *Stokes Bird Gardening Book: The Complete Guide to Creating Bird-Friendly Habitat in Your Backyard.* Little, Brown.

Tufts, Craig, and Peter Loewer. (1995). *Gardening for Wildlife: How to Create a Beautiful Backyard Habitat for Birds, Butterflies, and Other Wildlife.* St. Martin"s Press.

Wilson, Charles L. *The World of Terrariums.* Galahad Books, 1977.

Xerces Society, Smithsonian Institution. (1999). *Butterfly Gardening: Creating Summer Magic in Your Garden.* Sierra Club Books.

 Internet Sites on Plants & Gardening

Suggested search words: nature gardening/butterfly gardening/children's gardening /terrariums/wildlife gardening/bird gardening

American Association of Botanical Gardens and Arboreta: http://www.aabga.org/

Butterfly Gardening, The Butterfly House: http://www.butterflyhouse.org/gardening.html Site of the Sophia Sachs Butterfly House & Education Center in Chesterfiled, MO

Butterfly Gardening: http://www.monarchwatch.org/garden/ University of Kansas Entomology Program.

Kid's Gardening: http://www.kidsgardening.com/

National Garden Clubs http://www.gardenclub.org They have a section on youth gardening with activities for children.

National Wildlife Federation Backyard Wildlife Habitat program: http://www.nwf.org/backyardwildlifehabitat/

Stokes Birds, Basic Bird Gardening: http://www.stokesbirdsathome.com/ birding/gardening/

U.S. Department of Agriculture, Home Gardening: http://www.usda.gov/news/ garden.htm

SECTION E
ROCKS AND MINERALS

There are more than 1,500 different species of minerals and well over 100 kinds of rocks. A *mineral* is a chemical element or inorganic compound that occurs naturally, having definite physical properties and chemical composition. A *rock* is an aggregate of two or more minerals. These can be identified in the field by their appearance.

People collecting rock specimens may also want to be on the lookout for fossils. Fossils are prints, remains, or any other evidence of prehistoric life usually found in or among rocks. Fossils are interesting because of their story and age and are a help to the scientist in determining the period in which the rock was formed.

ROCK COLLECTING

Collecting rocks and minerals is a popular hobby and appeals to all age groups. Remember, whenever collecting you must make sure it is environmentally responsible to do so and you have appropriate permissions. Even preschool children like to gather pebbles that are pleasant to the touch and have appealing colors. As you study rocks, you become aware that the entire history of the evolution of our planet is hidden within them. From this realization on, searching for rocks, minerals, and fossils becomes an exciting adventure where one discovery leads to another.

It is not necessary for you to know much about rocks and minerals before you begin your collection. The important thing is to get started, for your knowledge will grow rapidly once you start working with the materials. As you begin your collection, you will want to establish a method of labeling so that you will have a record of the kind of rock and the date and place where it was found.

JUDY BROOKHISER, GREAT SMOKY MOUNTAINS NATIONAL PARK.

Rock Collecting Equipment

You do not need expensive equipment to begin your work with rocks but it will help to have some of the basic equipment with you when you go looking for sample. Basic equipment includes:

- Geologic pick—a hammer will do, but a pick is preferable
- Magnifying glass—a cheaper 8–10 power will be fine
- Container or collecting sack in which to place your samples
- Cold chisel for breaking rocks
- Materials for testing hardness—penny, knife, glass
- Pocketknife
- Notebook and pencil
- Adhesive tape and newspaper for marking and wrapping specimens

Types of Rocks

Rocks are the materials from which the crust of the earth is made and can therefore be found in almost any locality. Rocks usually are divided into three major categories depending upon their origin: igneous, sedimentary, and metamorphic. *Igneous rocks* are those formed at high temperatures from molten materials and include rocks such as lava and granite. Limestone and shale are representative of *sedimentary* rocks that are formed by the settlement of fine rock particles carried by water or wind and later hardened into rock because of pressure. Much of this type of rock is formed at the bottom of the seas. *Metamorphic rocks* are those that have undergone radical change due to high temperatures and extreme pressure, turning limestone into marble and shale into slate.

Finding Rocks

While rocks may be found in almost every area, there are certain places that are better than others for finding specimens. Places that are usually good are old rock quarries, road cuts with rocks exposed on the sides, dried-up stream beds, coarse sand beaches, openings to mines and slag piles, tops of hills and mountains where erosion has taken place, and areas where there has been recent volcanic eruption. As with all natural materials, make sure that it is environmentally responsible to remove samples before taking anything.

Identification and Display

After you have returned from a field trip on which you have collected a variety of rocks you will want to identify them and prepare them for placement in a display case. Rocks and minerals are identified through observation and simple tests. These characteristics include color, luster, hardness, specific gravity, streak, and fracture. Keys and instructions for rock identification can be found in the resources at the end of this section.

Lapidary

Many people like to expand their rock collecting efforts into craft activities. Rocks can be cut and polished and used as semiprecious gems to make jewelry. This craft is known as lapidary.

Books on Rocks & Minerals

See master publicatons list for cities of Publishers.

> Bial, Raymond. (2000). *A Handful of Dirt*. Walker Publishing. Discusses the nature and importance of soil and the many forms of life it supports. Something like a small coffee table book.

Chesterman, Charles. (1989). *National Audubon Society Field Guide to North American Rocks and Minerals.* (Audubon Society Field Guide). Random House.

Pough, Frederick. (1998). *A Field Guide to Rocks and Minerals.* (Peterson Field Guides). Houghton Mifflin.

Rhodes, Frank. (1991). *Geology.* (A Golden Guide) St. Martin's Press. Pocket guide with high quality color illustrations.

Rhodes, Frank, Herbert Zim, and Paul Shaffer. (1990). Fossils: *A Guide to Prehistoric Life.* St. Martin's Press: NY. (A Golden Guide) Pocket book with color illustrations.

Ricciuti, Edward, and Margaret Carruthers. (1998). *Rocks and Minerals.* (National Audubon Society First Field Guides). Scholastic.

Shaffer, Paul R., and Herbert S. Zim. (2001). *Rocks, Gems and Minerals.* (A Golden Guide). St. Martin's Press: NY.

Sorrell, Charles. (2001). *Rocks and Minerals: A Guide to Field Identification.* (Golden Field Guides). St. Martin's Press: NY.

 ## Internet Sites on Rocks & Minerals

Suggested search words: rocks minerals/lapidary/gems/rockhounding/geology/earth science

British Columbia Bureau of Mines, Identification of Common Rocks:
http://www.em.gov.bc.ca/mining/geolsurv/publications/infocirc/ic1987-5/intro.htm

Rock Identification Key:
http://www.rockhounds.com/rockshop/rockkey/index.html

RocksForKids.com: http://www.rocksforkids.com/

U.S. Geological Survey, Collecting Rocks: http://pubs.usgs.gov/gip/collect1/collectgip.html

SECTION F

ASTRONOMY

The heavens with their brilliant stars and roving planets have fascinated people since earliest times. From ancient carvings and tablets it has been determined that the movements of the planets were fairly well understood as early as 3000 B.C. Astronomy is one of the oldest sciences. There were professional astronomers long before there were scientists such as botanists or biologists. Early astronomers were given places of honor and prestige and instructed to chart the courses of the stars and make predictions about future events based upon their observations. Early explorers were able to cross vast oceans using the stars. The Lewis and Clark expedition that traveled from St. Louis to the Pacific Ocean depended on the stars to find their way there and back, as well as to chart their discoveries.

There are many amateur astronomers today who observe and study the skies. From the stars they can determine time, direction, and location on earth. While this information has been helpful to some people like sailors, most of the modern amateur astronomers observe the sky because of their interest and curiosity and the inner satisfaction they receive from the activity. Their attention usually focuses on the study of the stars, planets, meteors, comets, star clusters, and nebulae.

STARGAZING

Between six and seven thousand stars can be observed with the naked eye, so it is not necessary to have expensive equipment to become an active astronomer and enjoy the skies. A star guide book or charts that show the location of the stars at the various times of the year (many can be found on the Internet) is helpful. While many stars can be seen with the naked eye, a pair of binoculars can make stargazing even more exciting. Binoculars are excellent for observing the details on the face of the moon (including craters in the different phases of the moon), watching the moons of Jupiter as they circle the planet, or sweeping across the Milky Way just to see the tremendous number of stars in the galaxy. It is remarkable how distinct individual stars appear and how much brighter the constellations appear through binoculars. Many homes already have binoculars or it may be possible to borrow them from friends, especially those who are bird watchers. A good pair of binoculars for astronomy is 7 x 50. This gives you a 7-fold magnification, large field of vision, and good light.

Later, as your interest grows, you may want to purchase or build a telescope that will make it possible for you to see more stars and many other interesting things that are impossible to see with the naked eye. Making telescopes and other astronomical equipment can become an interesting hobby in itself.

A few stars usually can be seen from any location, but it is advisable to get away from as much light as possible when you are studying the skies. In the 21st century we have more light pollution on the planet than at any other time. Scientific observatories are located far from big cities in remote areas to avoid the pervasive lights from civilization that dim the skies.

As you look up into the night sky, do not hurry; it will take about 15 minutes for your eyes to fully adjust to the darkness. If you are out with a group of people, a flashlight with a bright beam can be used to point out stars and help communicate what you are seeing to others in your party. Set a goal for yourself and try to become familiar enough with the sky so that you can recognize 20 major constellations and 12 of the brighter stars. This knowledge will serve you well as a point of reference in your future study.

Constellations

The ancient star watchers soon located stars that appeared to be grouped in such a way that, with a bit of imagination, they could see in them the shape of an animal like a bear, a horse, or a dog. These groups of stars are constellations, and interesting stories and legends were told about them. The telling of these legends and looking for constellations make interesting evening campfire and recreation programs. Today the sky has been divided into sections that are named after the constellation that they contain that serves as a point of reference.

Sky Phenomena

Unique occurrences such as solar and lunar eclipses have been magical events in most primitive cultures and have always interested astronomers. Today they can be predicted to the exact moment of their appearance. Always follow the instructions for viewing eclipses to protect your eyes from potentially serious damage. Meteor showers with shooting stars thrill sky watchers, as do the "paintings in the sky" made by the Northern and Southern Lights.

ACTIVITIES

Navigating by the Sun and Stars. An aspect of astronomy sometimes overlooked is finding directions using celestial bodies. Location of the North Star, of course, is the most common. Sundials have also been popular. A Virginia Boy Scout developed what is known as the "Shadow Tip Method" for finding direction. It has been field-tested by the U.S. Army and Air Force and found to work very well. Here is how to do it:

1. Drive a stake vertically into the ground, allowing a minimum projection of 3 feet above the ground.
2. Mark the tip of the shadow on the ground.
3. Wait 10 minutes or more.
4. Mark the spot where the tip now is.
5. Draw a line between the two tip marks. This line is always east and west and the second point made is always east.

Even on a dull, cloudy day, it is usually possible to get a shadow if an open field is used and a light-colored cloth is spread to catch the shadow.

Planetarium Visits. Visits to planetariums and observatories are a good way to interest youth groups in astronomy. Shows at planetariums are diverse and varied from show to show. The Hubble space telescope has taken us into farther reaches of the universe. The National Aeronautics and Space Administration (NASA) continues to expand information through human and robotic explorations including missions to the moon, Mars and Saturn. Remarkable pictures are available on the Internet from these amazing missions. Planetarium programs include recent attempts to conquer space as well as programs exploring ancient mythology. Public museums and astronomical societies usually are very happy to assist amateurs.

 ## Books on Astronomy

See master publicatons list for cities of Publishers.

Baker, Robert, and Herbert Zim. (2001). *Stars: A Golden Guide.* St. Martin's Press.

Burnham, Robert, Alan Dyer, Robert Garfinkle, Martin George, Jeff Kanipe, David Levy, and John O'Byrne. (2001). *Backyard Astronomy: Your Guide to Starhopping and Exploring the Universe.* Nature Company Guides.

Chartrand, Mark. (1991). *National Audubon Society Field Guide to the Night Sky.* Alfred A. Knopf.

Chartrand, Mark. (1990). *Night Sky. St. Martin's Press.* (A Golden Field Guide)

Klutz. (1998). Backyard Stars: *A Guide for Home and the Road.* Klutz Press. (Klutz Guide)

Levy, David, and John O'Byrne. (1995). *Skywatching.* (Nature Company Guide). Time-Life Books.

Mayall, R. Newton, Margaret Mayall, and Jerome Wyckoff. (1985). *The Sky Observer's Guide.* St. Martin's Press: NY. (A Golden Guide) A pocket book with high-quality illustrations.

Passachoff, Jay, and Roger Peterson, (editors). (1998). *Peterson First Guide to Astronomy.* (Peterson Field Guide). Houghton Mifflin.

Passachoff, Jay, and Roger Peterson, (editors). (1999). *A Field Guide to Stars and Planets,* 4th edition. Houghton Mifflin. Sky tour for amateurs. Color pictures.

 ## Internet Sites on Astronomy

Suggested search words: astronomy/stars/constellations/night sky/ nature astronomy/astronomy guides/amateur astronomy/universe/space exploration

American Association of Amateur Astronomers: http://www.corvus.com/

American Meteor Society: http://www.amsmeteors.org/ "non-profit scientific organization established to encourage and support the research activities of both amateur and professional astronomers who are interested in the fascinating field of Meteor Astronomy. Our affiliates observe, monitor, collect data on, study, and report on meteors, meteor showers, meteoric fireballs, and related meteoric phenomena."

Astronomical League: http://www.astroleague.org/ Composed of over 240 astronomy clubs across America. "Our basic goal is to encourage an interest in astronomy (and especially amateur astronomy) throughout America."

Astronomy for Kids: http://www.dustbunny.com/afk/ For kids and beginners of all ages. Although a site maintained by an individual enthusiast, there are excellent resources here for the beginner.

Astronomy Magazine: http://www.astronomy.com/

Hubble Space Telescope: http://hubble.stsci.edu/

Kids Astronomy.com: http://www.kidsastronomy.com/ Another outstanding site for kids maintained by an astronomy enthusiast.

NASA: http://www.nasa.gov National Aeronautics and Space Administration, the U.S. space exploration agency. Has special areas for kids, students and educators.

SECTION G

WEATHER/ATMOSPHERE

Everyone who participates in outdoor activities is well aware of the weather and the role that it plays in people's lives. Farmers, sailors, and pilots, for example, are especially dependent upon weather conditions and predictions. Frequently outdoor activities have to be modified or canceled because of a sudden rain or other unexpected change in the weather. Certainly people on camping and hunting trips can benefit greatly from knowing something about how weather works and how weather is predicted. There are a number of different projects related to weather that make interesting hobbies. These include building a weather station, keeping a record of daily weather conditions, and making weather predictions.

WEATHER AND ATMOSPHERE

Weather, however, is but one component of the atmosphere, and to put it in proper perspective, you need to know about the atmosphere. The condition of the atmosphere is of concern to environmentalists because it relates directly to quality of life on the planet. The atmosphere is composed of a number of life-sustaining gases, such as oxygen, carbon dioxide, and nitrogen, and surrounds the earth up to an altitude of about 100,000 feet. The balance of gases and the quality of the atmosphere is vital to the continuation of life as we know it.

Human misuse of natural resources through industrialization (especially coal-burning industries), building large cities and factories, and cutting or destroying of forests has sent pollutants into the atmosphere, altering its composition and threatening our very existence. The haze in the sky and the smog lying over our cities are evidence of these changes. The ozone layer protects all living things from the ultraviolet rays from the sun. It also absorbs the heat from the sun's rays and distributes it evenly throughout the atmosphere, giving it stability. Despite numerous federal and state Clean Air Acts, pollutants today are threatening to alter or destroy the ozone layer and could produce significant changes in the earth's temperature and patterns of weather. Acid rain is an illustration of atmospheric pollutants damaging the natural environment. While one must be concerned with atmospheric quality and endeavor to understand it better and what is required of society to maintain and enhance the quality, this section focuses only upon weather projects and activities.

WHAT IS WEATHER?

Weather is the condition of the earth's atmosphere described in terms of heat, pressure, moisture, and wind. Changes in weather are caused through interplay of the sun, the air, and the rotation of the earth. As the sun warms the air, the air becomes lighter and begins to move upward. Heavier cold air then rushes in to replace it, causing winds. Warm air can take on additional moisture through evaporation. As the warm air rises and cools it loses its ability to hold as much moisture and, therefore, it rains.

BUILDING A WEATHER STATION

Building a weather station is not difficult nor does it require expensive equipment. The box to contain the equipment should be large enough and have enough ventilation so that the weather conditions inside the box will be the same as outside the box.

The weather station should be placed in an open area and have a roof on it so that the sun does not affect the inside temperatures. A weather station should contain a barometer, hygrometer, high-low thermometer, weather vane, and rain gauge. Some of these instruments can be made in a workshop, but it would probably be better to buy commercially made instruments if you want accuracy.

Barometers

At one time there were only two types of barometers—mercury and aneroid. Now choices include digital barometers some of which come packed with other gadgets-for instance, Bushnell product that includes such things as barometer, compass, calendar, clock, thermometer, altimeter, weather forecaster, map light, stopwatch, temperature alarm, altitude alarm, bearing feature, and declination adjustment. The big drawback of digital barometers is that they require an energy source usually in the form of batteries or electricity. Therefore, the aneroid will probably be better because it does not require a power source nor as much room as a mercury barometer.

Hygrometers

A hygrometer can be made out of two thermometers by placing a wet wick around the bulb of one in order to keep it moist. The relative humidity can then be computed through a comparison of the wet and dry bulb readings and interpreted through the using the following chart.

Daily Weather Chart

Date	Time	Barometer		Relative Humidity			Temperature			Rain-fall	Wind		Clouds		Observations or Forcast
		Read	Trend	Dry	Wet	%	High	Low	Pres.		Dir.	Vel.	%	Type	

Reading the Instruments

The weather instruments should be read at about the same time each day. Some weather enthusiasts read their instruments two or three times a day and keep detailed records. A simple chart on which a daily record can be kept is shown on page 000. The information to be recorded is: barometric pressure, clouds, relative humidity, temperature, and wind.

The following information should be recorded:

Barometric Pressure. The barometer indicates air pressure and is calibrated in inches of mercury. A dropping air pressure usually indicates the approach of a low-pressure front that may contain rain or snow. A rise in air pressure suggests the approach of a high-pressure front and fair weather.

Clouds. There are four basic types of clouds: cirrus, cumulus, stratus, and nimbus. Cirrus clouds appear high in the sky (5-10 miles) and are often referred to as "mares' tails." The large white puffy clouds are called *cumulus* and are generally thought of as fair-weather clouds. When the sky becomes overcast so that the entire sky is covered with layers of clouds, these clouds are referred to as *stratus. Nimbus* refers to any cloud from which rain is falling.

Relative Humidity. The hygrometer tells us how much water or moisture is presently contained in the air as compared to the amount that it could hold if saturated. Relative humidity, therefore, is expressed as a percentage. Warm air is able to hold more moisture than cold air. On a warm, muggy day when the relative humidity is high, you may expect showers as the air cools in the evening. A relative humidity table follows.

Relative Humidity Table

No. of Degrees Difference— Wet and Dry Bulb	Dry Bulb Reading —Fahrenheit (Percentage Figures)							
	30°	40°	50°	60°	70°	80°	90°	100°
1	90	92	93	94	95	96	96	97
2	79	84	87	89	90	92	92	93
3	68	76	80	84	86	87	88	90
4	58	68	74	78	81	83	85	86
6	38	52	61	68	72	75	78	80
8	18	37	49	58	64	68	71	74
10		22	37	48	55	61	65	68
12		8	26	39	48	54	59	62
14			16	30	40	47	53	57
16			5	21	33	41	47	51
18				13	26	35	41	47
20				5	19	29	36	42
22					12	23	32	37
24					6	18	26	33

Temperature. The high and low temperatures for the last 24-hour period should be recorded as well as the present temperature at the time of reading. A sudden drop of temperature on a hot humid day could produce thunderstorms.

Wind. Both direction and speed of wind should be recorded. A wind blowing from the east generally indicates approaching rain or snow whereas a wind from the west generally indicates fair weather. The harder the wind blows, the sooner you can expect the change to take place. The Beaufort Scale follows.

Beaufort Scale—Wind Estimation

Beaufort Number	Mph / Knots	Description	Observation	Weather Map Symbols
0	0-1 / 0-1	Calm	Smoke rises vertically	◎
1	1-3 / 1-3	Light Air	Smoke drifts slowly	
2	4-7 / 4-6	Slight Breeze	Leaves rustle	
3	8-12 / 7-10	Gentle Breeze	Leaves and twigs in motion	
4	13-18 / 11-16	Moderate Breeze	Small branches move	
5	19-24 / 17-21	Fresh Breeze	Small trees sway	
6	25-31 / 22-27	Strong Breeze	Large branches sway	
7	32-38 / 28-33	Strong Breeze	Whole trees in motion	
8	39-46 / 34-40	Gale	Twigs break off trees	
9	47-54 / 41-47	Gale	Branches break	
10	55-63 / 48-55	Whole Gale	Trees snap and are blown down	
11	64-75 / 56-55	Storm	Widespread damage	
12	above 75 / above 66	Hurricane	Extreme damage	

Wind Chill

Weather has importance for more than the interesting hobby of prediction. It is essential to understand something about how the elements make you feel, particularly if you wish to go hiking or backpacking or engage in other physically active sports. In winter discomfort is measured on the wind chill index, that is determined by the wind speed and the temperature. The greater the wind speed, the greater the wind chill factor. This is one reason why it is so important to protect against the wind in very cold temperatures—frostbite occurs more quickly when the wind is strong, even if the temperature is not unduly cold. Use the following wind chill chart to figure out just how cold it feels in relation to the wind speed and the thermometer temperature.

Wind Chill Chart

Estimated Wind Speed in mph	Actual Thermometer Reading (°F.)															
	35	30	25	20	15	10	5	0	-5	-10	-15	-20	-25	-30	-35	-40
Calm	35	30	25	20	15	10	5	0	-5	-10	-15	-20	-25	-30	-35	-40
5	33	27	21	16	12	7	1	-6	-11	-15	-20	-26	-31	-35	-41	-47
10	21	16	9	2	-2	-9	-15	-22	-27	-31	-38	-45	-52	-58	-64	-70
15	16	11	1	-6	-11	-18	-25	-33	-40	-45	-51	-60	-65	-70	-78	-85
20	12	3	-4	-9	-17	-24	-32	-40	-46	-52	-60	-68	-76	-81	-88	-96
25	7	0	-7	-15	-22	-29	-37	-45	-52	-58	-67	-75	-83	-89	-96	-104
30	5	-2	-11	-18	-26	-33	-41	-49	-56	-63	-70	-78	-87	-94	-101	-109
35	3	-4	-13	-20	-27	-35	-43	-52	-60	-67	-72	-83	-90	-98	-105	-113
40	1	-4	-15	-22	-29	-36	-45	-54	-62	-69	-76	-87	-94	-101	-107	-116

Wind speeds greater than 40 mph have little additional effect	LITTLE DANGER for properly clothed person (Very to Bitter Cold)	INCREASING DANGER danger from freezing of exposed flesh (Extremely Cold)	GREAT DANGER (Extremely Cold)

Find the temperature on the top line and the wind speed at the extreme left. Where the two intersect, you will find the wind chill factor. For instance, if the temperature is 10 degrees and the wind speed 25mph, the chill factor is minus 29. A blizzard is usually considered winds of at least 35 mph and considerable falling or blowing snow; a severe blizzard is winds of at least 45 mph with falling or blowing snow and temperatures lower than 10 degrees. Note: various charts will differ by a few degrees for the estimated wind chill. The chart will, however, give a good approximation of what happens when wind increases in relation to temperature.

Heat Index

In summer the wind helps to cool, and discomfort comes from humidity and high temperatures. Sometimes this is called an "index of discomfort" or, for short, "heat index." It is really a temperature-humidity index. Areas of the United States that refer to their "dry heat" (and say that is why they do not mind the hot weather) are really talking about low humidity. The point at which people begin to be uncomfortable with humidity varies; however, the temperature-humidity index chart that follows indicates the range of discomfort for most people.

Temperature-Humidity Index

Temperature	Relative Humidity (%)													
(°F.)	20	25	30	35	40	45	50	55	60	65	70	75	80	85
100	81	82	83	84	85	86	88	89	90	92	93	94	95	96
95	78	79	80	81	82	83	84	85	86	88	88	90	90	92
90	76	77	77	78	79	80	81	82	83	84	85	86	87	87
85	73	74	74	75	76	76	77	78	78	79	80	81	82	83
80	70	71	71	72	72	73	73	74	74	75	76	77	78	79
75	68	68	68	69	69	70	70	70	71	71	72	72	73	74

On this "Index of Discomfort" almost everyone is uncomfortable at 79 or more. Compute relative humidity from the chart on page 169.

Conservation of Energy for Heating and Cooling

Another aspect of weather that is particularly interesting and has importance in energy conservation is the amount of fuel saved by maintaining room temperatures lower than 75 or 76 degrees during the summer or above 65 to 70 degrees in the winter. Fuel units needed to maintain a certain room temperature in a building have been calculated for different outside temperatures. The fuel saving chart that follows does not consider the wind chill factor or the impact of the wind or the "tightness" of the building in retaining heat.

Fuel Saving Chart

Outside Temperature	Average Indoor Temperature							
	72 degrees		68 degrees			Fuel units66 degrees		
	Fuel units		Fuel units		Percent Saved	Fuel units		Percent Saved
	Needed	Saved	Needed	Saved		Needed	Saved	
70	2	0	0	0	100	0	0	0
60	12	0	8	4	33	6	6	0
50	22	0	18	4	18	16	6	0
40	32	0	28	4	12	26	6	10
30	42	0	38	4	9	36	6	20
20	52	0	48	4	7	46	6	30
10	62	0	58	4	6	56	6	40
0	72	0	68	4	5	66	6	50
-10	82	0	78	4	4	76	6	60
-20	92	0	88	4	4	86	6	70

Table based on straight line relationship of temperature difference to fuel requirement.
Percent saved based on a comparison between the "usual" room temperature of 72 degrees and that indicated. Chill factor or impact of wind were not considered in calculations.

Predicting Weather

It is interesting to make weather predictions based upon your own observations. Compare your prediction with those of the weather forecaster on TV or in the newspaper. You should be able to predict weather correctly 80 percent of the time.

 ## Books on Weather/Atmosphere

Breen, Mark and Kathleen Friestad. (2000). *The Kids' Book of Weather Forecasting: Build a Weather Station, "Read" the Sky, & Make Predictions.* Williamson Publishing.

Gibbons, Gail. (1993). *Weather Forecasting.* Alladin. For children grades 2-4.

Hardy, Ralph. (1999). Teach Yourself Weather. McGraw-Hill.

Kahl, Jonathan. (1998). *National Audubon Society First Field Guide Weather* (National Audubon First Field Guide). Scholastic.

Lehr, Paul, R. Burnett, and Herbert Zim. (2001). *Weather.* (A Golden Guide). St. Martin's Press.

Schaefer, Vincent J., and John A. Day. (1998). *A Field Guide to the Atmosphere.* (Peterson Field Guide Series) Houghton Mifflin.

 ## Internet Sites on Weather

Search words: weather/weather prediction/weather prediction outdoors/weather prediction activities/meteorology

Miami Museum of Science, Making a Weather Station:
http://www.miamisci.org/ hurricane/weatherstation.html

National Oceanic & Atmospheric Administration, Educational Resources:
http://www.education.noaa.gov/

U.S. Environmental Protection Agency, Kids Site: http://www.epa.gov/ globalwarming/kids/ Covers global warming, climate and weather, greenhouse effect, explanation of climate, history of climate, etc.

Weather Channel: http://www.weather.com/

Weatherprediction.com: http://www.theweatherprediction.com/

SECTION H
WATER, STREAMS, AND PONDS

A nearby pond or stream makes an exciting location for water ecology and water quality activities. (For water sports, see Chapter 7, Section C: Canoeing, Kayaking, and River Running and Section: D: Casting and Fishing.)

WATER ECOLOGY, MAPPING POND ZONES

The study of life in fresh water is called *limnology*. To get an overview, take a boat field trip to study ecological succession of plants in a pond. Select an undisturbed stretch of shoreline in a pond. Go out in a boat to the central, deep, dark, barren bottom zone of the lake. As you go you will probably notice that you pass over a number of plant communities in concentric zones. Then as you come back toward shore study the various plant species making up the community of each zone.

The first zone after the central barren one is *submerged plants*, that is, those plants rooted to the bottom of the lake or pond with leaves completely below the surface. Plants like water milfoil and coontail can tolerate low levels of incident sunlight and grow in this deep area. Next are plants rooted in the bottom but with their leaves floating on the surface; this zone is referred to as surface-leafed or *floating-leaf plants*. Pond weed and water lilies are the best known of these plants. In the shallow water is the *emergent plant* zone where the roots and part of the stems are beneath the surface of the water but the tops protrude above the water. Finally, at the edge of the pond is the first terrestrial zone, the first habitat without any part of the plant actually in the water. Each zone or plant community has its own characteristic plants— the varieties are few and easily identifiable.

OBSERVING POND TRANSITIONS

Given enough time, any pond or lake will fill in completely; gradually the central, barren area gives way to submergent plants, then the floating-leaf plants, and the emergent plants. Succession continues on the land, too. This is apparent in the swamp or bog area, which is really the transition from emergent plants to the first terrestrial zone with its sedge meadow plants such as reed grass, cattail, and sedge. As the soil gets deeper, these plants are followed or replaced by moisture-loving shrubs, like shrub willow and dogwood. The shrubs give way to immature forest and shade tolerant trees and finally the climax forest. Ask an "old timer" to talk about how an old pond that has a swampy area has changed over time.

FINDING POND LIFE HABITATS

Of course, the animal life of a pond as well as plant life is interesting to study. Ponds abound with life ranging from minute organisms to large animals. The question is, where can you expect to find the various types—a bass, a water strider, a crayfish, for example? The easiest way to answer that question is to learn about habitats and characteristics. A good way to begin is by classifying animals according to where they live—in the bottom sediments, on the bottom, on or among vegetation, free swimming, hanging from the surface of the water, or on the water surface. Still other animals live at different levels over the water surface.

The "bottom dwellers" show the greatest diversity of form and lifestyle. If you have access to a microscope, you may want to dredge up a sample from the bottom and look at the various fungi and bacteria, as well as the protozoans that occur in almost every drop of water in a lake or pond. A variety of animals burrow into the bottom sediments, but there are also foragers, scavengers, and predators on the bottom of the pond. Snails are normally found foraging for algae and crayfish are active scavengers. Another group of creatures spend most of their time in the thick growth of aquatic vegetation in the littoral zones. Then there are many, many species of tiny swimming and drifting plants (phytoplankton) and tiny swimming and drifting animals (zooplankton). Of the many larger animals, the next in size are the air-breathing aquatic insects; and, of course, we all think about fish when we think of ponds. So get a good pond book (see resources at end of this section) and, with a collecting net and sediment tube, search a section of the pond bottom—the animals among vegetation, free swimming, and just under, on, and above the water surface.

COLLECTING AQUATIC ORGANISMS

As with any collection activity, you must first determine that it is environmentally responsible to collect samples. There are quite a few devices for collecting aquatic organisms. The fineness of the mesh depends upon the smallest animals you are collecting. A kitchen wire sieve with a handle is probably the most useful because it is of fairly sturdy construction and mud can be washed from the sample simply by moving the sieve back and forth in a bucket of water with the top of the sieve just out of the water.

Window screen can also be used; a piece approximately 1' x 2' stapled to two pieces of wood on each end for handles can be used very nicely to catch animal life coming downstream. If the screen has a woven edge, place it down; if it does not, fold the screen (like a small hem) before attaching the handles. This type of device works best when two people work together. One person holds the screen in the stream current with the bottom of the screen resting on the bottom of the stream, while the other person goes a few feet upstream and turns over rocks, wiping animals off the rocks by hand; the current carries the animals into the screen.

For sampling organisms in the bottom sediment, a large can such as a 3-lb. can may be used. Scoop up a can full of mud and pour into the kitchen sieve, then wash clean of the mud. If the pond is more than an arm's length deep, a smaller can about pint size can be fastened on to the end of a broomstick. Be sure to punch a few small holes in the bottom and side of the can to allow excess water to pass through. To take a core sample of the bottom of the pond in order to identify stratification or layers of sediment, a tube will hold the sample together better than cans. A plastic or metal pipe 2″ in diameter and 2′ to 3′ long works well. Plunge the tube (pipe) closed with the hand to prevent the core (sediment) from being lost in the water when brought up to the surface. Then, the sediment can be carefully pushed out with a broomstick or similar object into a pan. Incidentally, a white enameled tray makes a good examining tray not only for sediment core samples, but also for the animals caught with the sieve as they are easily seen against the white background.

OBSERVING CHARACTERISTICS OF STREAM BEDS

Stream beds also have various types of habitats and are usually considered to be of four types: (1) bedrock, (2) rubble and gravel, (3) sand, and (4) silt and mud. Since bedrock stream beds provide very little food and protection, they contain little life. Life will also be affected by the type of rock, type of vegetation on the banks, source of water, etc. A fast-moving stream is usually found on rubble or gravel bottoms that have ample supplies of food and oxygen carried to animals lying in wait among the nooks and crannies provided by the stony bed. Muddy or silt-bottomed streams are usually high in productivity and with the buildup of mud and silt, plants root and gradually the stream bed begins to fill in. In extremely slow waters, duckweed may grow in stagnant areas and eventually cover the water's surface. Fish found in slow-flowing streams are quite different from those in fast-flowing streams. To become good at fishing, one must learn about the habitats of different fish!

MEASURING WATER QUALITY

Looking at water qualities in terms of physical and chemical properties can provide many very interesting nature-oriented activities. Some of the chemical properties that can be tested include dissolved oxygen, hardness, alkalinity, suspended and dissolved solids, turbidity, and conductivity. While these tests are not difficult, you may want to ask a local science teacher to help. Color, transparency, water pressure, stream volume of flow, temperature, density of water, etc. are physical properties that help us understand better water quality.

MEASURING WATER TEMPERATURES

Environmental temperature is an important regulator of life processes and is an important factor in determining the distribution of organisms. Water temperature is especially important because most aquatic organisms are cold-blooded, that is, their body temperature is about the same as that of their water habitat. Many aquatic organisms can survive only within specific, narrow temperature ranges. Water temperatures change gradually, and water has the capacity to store vast amounts of heat. Water temperature may vary with depth in still ponds or in deep lakes and reservoirs. An interesting activity is to take temperatures of water in different locations and depths and see what type of aquatic life can be found at each temperature. For measuring temperatures near the surface, the thermometer bulb is immersed. Watch that you are not holding the thermometer so that your body heat influences the temperature being recorded. The thermometer bulb remains in the water approximately five minutes for an accurate measure.

A "sampler" bottle can be used to secure water samples from various depths. It is simple and inexpensive to make. Take a 1-quart bottle and put a mesh net around it. The net can be made by knotting cord or it can be a mesh bag. There should be weights of lead or stones on the bottom and a calibrated cord (so you know how deep the bottle is) attached to lower the bottle to given depths. The bottle should have a cork inserted (not too tight!) with cord leading to the top. When the bottle reaches the desired depth, jerk the cord and uncork the bottle; the bottle will then fill with water from that specific depth. Allow a few minutes for the bottle to fill, then bring it to the surface and insert thermometer. The water temperature, of course, must be measured promptly before temperature is lost or gained in the above surface atmosphere. It is desirable to take several readings from the same depth and use an average of the readings. Recording can be made during different times of day, especially under different conditions, such as evening, rainy and sunny days, etc.

MEASURING VOLUME OF STREAM FLOW

Another interesting but easy activity is to measure volume of stream flow. Select a short section of stream that is not too wide, but has fairly straight banks and is mostly free of obstacles protruding above the surface level of the water. Determine

JUDY BROOKHISER, GREAT SMOKY MOUNTAINS NATIONAL PARK.

the length, average width, and average depth of that section of stream. Compute the volume of water in the "test section" by multiplying the length times width times depth. Put a small floatable object (stick) at the upper end of the test section and, using a watch with a second hand, find the time it takes the stick to float from one end of the test section to the other. Divide the volume (which you should convert to liters or gallons) by the number of seconds and you will have the number of liters that flow downstream in one second. Of course, you could also find how much water flows downstream in a day.

 Books on Water, Streams, and Ponds

See master publicatons list for cities of Publishers.

Anderson, Margaret, Nancy Field, and Karen Stephenson. (1998). *Leapfrogging through Wetlands.* Dog-Eared Publications: Middleton, WI. For elementary level students. Helps young people understand the importance of wetlands in the ecosystem of North America.

Caduto, Michael J. (1990). *Pond and Brook.* University Press of New England.

Cushing, Colbert E. and David Allan. (2001). Streams: Their Ecology and Life. Academic Press.

Lawlor, Elizabeth. (2000). *Discover Nature in Water and Wetlands: Things to Know and Things to Do.* Stackpole: Mechanicsburg, PA. Explores the properties, processes, and phases of water and the plant and animal life associated with it.

Mitchell, Mark K. and William B. Stapp. (1996), *Field Manual for Water Quality Monitoring,* 11th edition. William B Stapp. (out of print, limited availability)

Morgan, Ann Haven. (1930). *Field Book of Ponds and Streams.* G. P. Putnam's Sons, NY. Identification manual. (this would be a treasure to find)

National Wildlife Federation. (1989). *Wading into Wetlands.* McGraw-Hill: NY. (Ranger Rick's Nature Scope Series) Kids K-8 hands-on activities aimed at understanding wetlands.

Needham, J. G., and P. R. Needham. (1988). *A Guide to the Study of Freshwater Biology,* 5th edition. McGraw-Hill.

Reid, George. (2001). *Pond Life.* St. Martin's Press: NY. (A Golden Guide) A pocket book with high quality color illustrations.

Reid, George Kell and Herbert S. Zim (editors). (2003). *Pond Life: A Guide to Common Plants and Animals of North American Ponds and Lakes* updated edition. St. Martin's Press.

Ross, Michael E. (2000). *Pond Watching with Ann Morgan* (Naturalist's Apprentice Biographies). Carolrhoda Books.

Zim, Herbert, and Hobart Smith. (2001), revised by Jonathan Latimar, and

Karen Nolting. *Reptiles and Amphibians*. St. Martin's Press: NY. (A Golden Guide) Pocket book including 212 species in color.

Internet Sites on Water, Streams & Ponds

Suggested search words: streams/ponds/wetlands/amphibians/estuaries/limnology/ watersheds

Ducks Unlimited, Greenwings:
http://www.greenwing.org/greenwings/home1.htm Activities for kids.

eNature.com, Habitat Guides:
http://www.enature.com/outdoors/outdoors_home.asp

Izaak Walton League of America, American Wetlands Campaign:
http://www.iwla.org/ sos/awm/

Missouri Botanical Garden, Fresh Water Wetlands:
http://mbgnet.mobot.org/ fresh/wetlands

National Wildlife Federation: http://www.nwf.org/

U.S. Environmental Protection Agency, Wetlands:
http://www.epa.gov/owow/wetlands/

U.S. Environmental Protection Agency, National Estuary Program:
http://www.epa.gov/ OWOW/estuaries/about1.htm

U.S. Fish & Wildlife Service, National Wetland Inventory:
http://wetlands.fws.gov/

U.S. Geological Service, National Wetlands Research Center:
http://www.nwrc.usgs.gov/

US Geological Services Water Resources: http://water.usgs.gov/

SECTION J
NATURE PHOTOGRAPHY

More and more people are becoming interested in nature photography. With the increasing amount of inexpensive photographic equipment and materials available today, many people are beginning to keep pictorial records of their trips into the parks, forests, mountains, and other natural areas. Black and white and color pictures are taken with many different types and sizes of cameras. With the introduction of digital cameras, the entire landscape of photography has changed.

DIGITAL CAMERAS

Digital cameras can be extremely small and lightweight and are often imbedded in other technology such as cell phones. The seemingly endless trend in technology that includes reduction in prices and increase in quality has transformed photography. Digital images can be sent in real time nearly anywhere in the world and software enables photographers to immediately print their images, as well as to edit them in highly sophisticated manners. Where all this technology will end up is anyone's guess, but it's a pretty sure bet that it will be smaller, cheaper, and imbedded into many multiple-use devices. The software available to edit, enhance, print, and transform digital pictures has opened an endless opportunity for creativity and expression through photography. The ability to store, share and make presentations of pictures both printed and electronically is truly amazing.

USING PICTURES FOR DOCUMENTATION, ART, AND SCIENTIFIC PURPOSES

Some people are primarily interested in documenting the things they have seen and the places they have been. Frequently their emphasis will be "artistic" in nature; the photographer will attempt to capture some of the beauty and color to take home so that the experience can be relived at a later date. Many teachers and amateur naturalists are taking pictures for scientific purposes. These pictures can be used for identification purposes or to illustrate some form of nature in its real-life setting. Excellent subjects for this kind of photography are birds, animals, wild-flowers, and insects. Care should be taken to show these animals in their natural habitats and in realistic situations.

PICTURES THAT TELL A STORY

It is important for the beginning photographer to spend some time planning the trip before departure. An attempt should be made to tell a story through a series of pictures, rather than to take pictures at random and then try to build a story around the pictures. "A day in the forest" or "exploring a stream" are themes that might be used. Decide what type of pictures will best help you tell your story and then take them with this purpose in mind. For time exposures, a sturdy tripod is helpful. Strobe lights or flashbulbs help to get good exposures made in deep forest, shaded areas, or in areas with other poor lighting conditions, as well as in "freezing" action shots.

PHOTOGRAPHING BIRDS AND ANIMALS

There are many subjects in nature that will be a challenge to the best of photographers. Birds are extremely colorful and are always available. It is difficult, however, to get close enough for a good shot without a telephoto lens. There are binoculars made with digital cameras built -in, and as with other technology, the quality of these dual-purpose devices is likely to increase. Placing a remotely controlled camera so that it covers a spot where birds frequently come will make it possible to get interesting poses. It is a challenge to construct blinds that will enable the photographer to get close enough to animals to take good pictures. Many wild animals are difficult to photograph because they are active only at night or in the late evening. Most animals are afraid of people and will avoid them or any area that contains their scent. This means that great care must be taken in setting up the camera so that everything appears normal to the animal. Triggering devices attached to food can lead to most interesting pictures. Use natural feeding places. Underwater photography is another aspect that offers challenge and adventure.

FILM DEVELOPING AND EDITING

Although the immediate processing of digital images has altered the entire film development industry, people still gain a great deal of satisfaction from the traditional film processing techniques that require a darkroom to expose film. Seeing the picture of a bird or an animal coming out on the paper while it is still in the solution is a thrill that is difficult to duplicate. A sense of completion results from not only taking the pictures but also carrying the process through to a final product. With digital there is the craft "art" of using photo-editing software. Adobe Photoshop is among the most popular software used for photograph editing. Another activity in photography that most groups enjoy is shooting a sequence of pictures telling the story of their club, of an activity, or of something in nature for publicity and promotion purposes—poster series, computerized presentations for illustrated talks, websites, etc.

 Books on Nature Photography

See master publicatons list for cities of Publishers.

Cox, Jonathan. (2002). *Digital Nature Photography.* Amphoto Books. Amherst Media.

Fitzharris, Tim. (2003). *National Audubon Guide to Nature Photography.* Firefly Books.

Gomersall, Chris. (2001). *Photographing Wild Birds.* Amphoto Books.

Kahn, Cub. (2002). *Beginner's Guide to Nature Photography.*

Rokach, Allen, and Anne Millman. (1995). *The Field Guide to Photographing Flowers.* (Center for Nature Photography Series). Amphoto Books.

Shaw, John. (2000). *John Shaw's Nature Photography Field Guide.* Amphoto Books.

Silliker, Bill Jr., and Bill Silliker. (2003). *The Master Guide for Wildlife Photographers.* Amherst Media.

Tharp, Brenda. (2003). *Creative Nature & Outdoor Photography.* Amphoto Books.

 Internet Sites on Photography

Suggested search words: nature photography
Nature Photographers Online Magazine:
   http://www.naturephotographers.net/
North American Nature Photography Association:
   http://www.nanpa.org/

SECTION J
CREATIVE EXPRESSION

A common need shared by all human beings is to express their inner feelings and interpret their surroundings. In this sense, all of us are artists and have some artistic ability—although the channels through which we give expression may vary greatly among individuals.

People need to learn how to express themselves in a manner that is personally satisfying and acceptable to society. We have a responsibility to teach children constructive ways of expressing themselves creatively. If we fail to do this, we may expect them to develop undesirable habits and to participate in activities that are harmful both to themselves and their community.

The outdoors provides a setting conducive to creative expression. The multi-hued, relaxing scene of the setting sun or the beauty of elegant spring wildflowers creates the desire to capture the beauty of the moment, retain it for future enjoyment, and share the experience with others. In order to do this, we need to be observant so that we see, analyze, and understand what is visible in the natural world. Then we will want to look for the medium through which we can best interpret to others what we see. The following are some forms of creative expression.

SKETCHING

With such simple and inexpensive materials as a soft lead pencil or a piece of charcoal and some paper, it is possible to capture some of the action and beauty of the moment. A gnarled and twisted oak silhouetted against the sky or the sleek form of a deer or other animal make excellent subjects for sketching.

PAINTING

Oil paints enable the aspiring artist to capture rich colors in the scene not possible, of course, in sketching with charcoal. Equipment for oil painting includes an easel, canvas, oil paints, brushes, etc. Many amateur painters have derived hours of pleasure from this rewarding activity. The use of watercolors should not be overlooked.

PROSE AND POETRY

Too many people have the idea that poetry and prose can be written only by a selected few who have a talent in this area. This is not true. If you have never had the opportunity to go into the natural world by yourself and try to express your feelings in words, you have missed the opportunity of a lifetime. Many people are writing poetry and prose today for the satisfaction that comes only through creative expression.

SONG AND MUSIC

Some people find it rewarding to express themselves through music, for truly there is magic in the rhythm and song of the natural world. This can be done either by creating new melodies or by creating new words to known melodies. Children of elementary and middle-school age particularly enjoy this type of activity. A way to combine music and art is to sketch, sculpt, or paint while listening to recordings of music from nature or nature-themed music.

There are many other ways in which people can express their feelings creatively. Some of these include wood carving, basketry, and photography. (See Chapter 2: Nature Crafts.)

 Books on Creative Expression

See master publicatons list for cities of Publishers.

Agnew, John. (2001). *Painting the Secret World of Nature.* North Light Books.

Barlowe, Dorothea, and Sy Barlowe. (1998). *Illustrating Nature: How to Paint and Draw Plants and Animals.* Dover Publications.

Harvey, Gail. (1990). *New Poetry Series: Poems of Nature.* Random House Value Publishing. Collection of nature poems from famous masters—Milton, Longfellow, Emerson, Thoreau, etc. Arranged by seasons—spring, summer, fall winter.

Johnson, Cathy. (2000). *The Sierra Club Guide to Painting in Nature.* Sierra Club Books.

Johnson, Cathy. (1997), new edition. *The Sierra Club Guide to Sketching in Nature.* Sierra Club Books.

Koury, Stephen. (2002). *Painting Nature's Little Creatures.* North Light Books.

Leslie, Clare Walker. (2000). *Nature Journal: A Guided Journal for Illustrating and Recording Your Observations of the Natural World.* Storey Books.

Leslie, Clare Walker, Roth, Charles E. (2003), 2nd edition. *Keeping a Nature Journal: Discover a Whole New Way of Seeing the World Around You.* Storey Publishing.

Rothenberg, David, Ulvaeus, Marta. (2001). *The Book of Music & Nature.* Wesleyan University Press. Book & CD explore the relationship of music and the natural world.

 Internet Sites on Creative Expression

Suggested Search Words: nature sketching/nature painting/nature prose/nature poetry/expression in nature

Many poems, songs, painting, etc. can be found on the Internet... some commercial, some free, as well as places that offer supplies and lessons.

Sketching as an aid to seeing nature: http://www.cmc.org/cmc/tnt/ 956/edsketchingtoseenature.htm Article on Colorado Mountain Club site.

SECTION K

HISTORICAL-CULTURAL ACTIVITIES

The United State's Bicentennial celebration, supplemented by local and state festivities, placed increased emphasis on "heritage activities," and certainly the natural environment provides rich opportunities to engage in them. The Lewis and Clark bicentennial celebration from 2002 through 2006 provided a new impetus for interest in historical heritage. In 1804, Thomas Jefferson saw Meriwether Lewis off to meet William Clark to form the Corps of Discovery that ultimately completed an epic journey from St. Louis to the Pacific coast in Washington State and back to St. Louis through a vast, uncharted wilderness that doubled the size of the United States. The expedition charted the unknown wilderness, carefully documented plants and animals never seen by most of the world, and marveled at Native Americans' ability to thrive in the natural environment. Outdoor living skills enabled the expedition to survive and complete their mission.

Through better understanding of what has transpired between people and nature, and also of the "monuments" that people have left in the natural environment, perhaps greater insights can be gained into the impacts of present day decisions that must be and are being made on the quality of environment. In Chapter 1 under Community Resources, a number of historical places are suggested for field trips. Many of the crafts in Chapter 2 might be considered "pioneer crafts." The survival sports of hunting and fishing are discussed in Chapter 7, and many of the outdoor living skills are included in Chapters 4 and 5. In Chapter 8 there is also a section (Section D) on Native American Life. All of these contribute to historical understandings. "Heritage activities" have a responsibility beyond the fun of participation to be authentic, scientifically researched and accurately portrayed so that participants are educated about outdoor skills and early life.

HOMESTEADING

President Lincoln signed the Homestead Act during the Civil War in 1862. Under this act, any adult citizen or intended citizen, male or female, could "take up" a quarter-section (160 acres) or an eighth-section (80 acres), depending on the quality and location of the land, by paying a $10 recording fee. The homesteaders had to live on the land, cultivate it, and make certain minimum improvements, and at the end of five years, they owned the place. When the pioneers were looking for land, they looked for a place where there was good soil and plenty of water and timber. When they found land that pleased them, they staked their claims. They measured the land by paces; a good-sized step by an adult, or about one yard. Eighty-four paces each way made an acre, and 750 paces each way made 160 acres. The corners of the claim were marked in different ways—with a big rock, a stake with a sign, or a mound of dirt. A stream or a row of trees might be used to mark the boundary of a claim, or as rocks were removed form a field, they might be formed into a boundary. In the Midwest, the government had given the railroads a considerable amount of land and some of the settlers received land from the railroad. Certain acreage was also set aside for schools.

Look in your community for homesteaded sites. Check out your local or state historical societies and historical museums and courthouse records for more information. The National Park Service maintains a website dedicated to the Homestead Act: http://www.nps.gov/home/homestead_act.html. Most areas today have been surveyed and have surveying markers. Check to see where the surveyor marks are (and when they were established) and whether any of the original claim markings remain. Also look for school sites and old railroad beds. If old houses or barns are still standing, see how they were built.

Sometimes you will find family cemeteries or old town or church cemeteries that will help you to identify early settlement sites. Try to construct family trees from the markers. Read the epitaphs. See how old people were when they died. In what era did they live (colonial times, Civil War times, the Great Depression, etc.)? What was the environment like—timber-covered, plowed fields, etc.?

INCOME-PRODUCING ACTIVITIES

The pioneers turned to the environment for their food and clothing and also for business enterprises such as selling and buying natural products from furs to crops. This was part of their daily life and survival. Study the environment both for remains of agricultural practices and for clues to pioneer activities. Can you find old logging roads and abandoned railroad beds? Perhaps they are used for hiking trails today. You can find old railroad sites through the Rails to Trails Conservancy whose mission is—"to enrich America's communities and countryside by creating a nationwide network of public trails from former rail lines and connecting corridors." Were the rivers used for transportation of goods and products? Are there remains of old sawmills or iron furnaces with attendant charcoal pits? What about mills that used waterwheels or sandpits and quarries? What agricultural practices were used? Perhaps a visit to a museum that has old farm implements would be interesting.

ARCHEOLOGICAL "DIGS"

Often an archeological dig reveals the remains of cultures of Native Americans who first lived on this continent—their homes, tools, etc. There are also more recent remains, such as foundations/basements of early homesteads, old cabins, etc.

Archeology departments of universities sometimes offer opportunities for persons interested in early cultures to work on digs for specified periods of time. Check with local and state historical societies and university archeology departments. You can also check the Internet for specific opportunities. People should understand that this is usually hot and tedious work requiring much patience and physical stamina. However, the discoveries can tell important stories and provide real insight into early cultures.

 ## Books on Historical-Cultural Activities

See master publicatons list for cities of Publishers.

Ambrose, Stephen. (1997). *Undaunted Courage: Meriwether Lewis, Thomas Jefferson and the Opening of the American West.* Simon & Schuster.

DeVoto, Bernard. (1997). *The Journals of Lewis and Clark.* Mariner Books.

Earle, Alice Morse. (1993). *Home Life in Colonial Days.* Berkshire House.

Greenwood, Barbara, and Heather Collins. (1998). *A Pioneer Sampler: The Daily Life of a Pioneer Family in 1840.* Houghton Mifflin.

Hawke, David F. (1989). *Everyday Life in Early America.* Perennial.

Hurt, R. Douglas. (2002). *The Indian Frontier, 1763-1846.* University of New Mexico Press.

King, David. (1997). *Pioneer Days: Discover the Past with Fun Projects, Games, Activities, and Recipes.* (American Kids History Series). Wiley.

Internet Sites on Historical-Cultural Activities

Suggested search words: pioneer life/frontier life/colonial life/living history/homestead act/archeology

Association for Living History, Farm and Agricultural Museums: http://www.alhfam.org/

Colonial Williamsburg: http://www.history.org/history/

Discovering Lewis and Clark: http://www.lewis-clark.org/

Homestead Act: http://www.nps.gov/home/homestead_act.html Homestead National Monument of America

Old West Living History Foundation: http://www.oldwest.org/ Cultural heritage of the American West.

National Park Service Archeology and Ethnography Program: http://www.cr.nps.gov/aad/

Reenactor.net: http://www.reenactor.net/ Information about historical reenacting around the world

JUDY BROOKHISER, GREAT SMOKY MOUNTAINS NATIONAL PARK.

ADVENTURE-OUTING SPORTS

Americans pride themselves on their ability to successfully meet the forces of nature at work in the natural environment. The activities and focus of the Bicentennial Celebration of the United States in 1976 and the Lewis and Clark bicentennial 2003-2006 help remind us of the spirit and trials of the colonists and explorers as they pioneered in the early years of our country. We identify with the characteristics of the pioneers and explorers and are challenged by activities that test our abilities in outdoor living skills.

CHALLENGING ACTIVITY

Adventure activities are exciting and challenging experiences, such as rock climbing or cave exploring, that can contribute to increased understanding of self and enhance self-confidence, and self-esteem. Group adventure activities can do much to encourage feelings of unity, empathy, trust, and compassion and the willingness of individuals' working together to solve problems and perform physical tasks. Adventure activities often contain a certain amount of spontaneous unpredictability that facilitates group members' learning about and from each other. The wary are encouraged by others in the group; the reckless are warned of the dangers involved; and all are bound by a common goal of group success.

Adventure activities and sports may appear to be dangerous and involve a high risk factor. The use of the term *risk activities* or *risk recreation* is really a disservice to the very exciting and valuable adventure activities, for *risk* infers *not safe*, whereas the safety record is exceptional. The term *risk* really refers to risk of one's mental toughness and physical skills—two important components in the development of character in individuals. (See Risk Management Section in Chapter 1.) To deny children and youth the important benefits that can be attained through adventure activities is to deny them extraordinary opportunities for personal growth and development.

These guidelines should be followed:

1. Use only qualified leadership.

2. Use proper equipment that is in good condition and appropriate to the size of the individual.

3. Begin with simple challenges until skills are developed that enable safe participation in more difficult endeavors—progression is key.

4. Individuals should be in good physical health (not ill or temporarily injured), but this does not imply that persons with disabilities cannot be avid participants.

5. Never take shortcuts with safety, or unnecessary risks; where needed, use spotters and safety equipment.

HEALTHY LIFESTYLE

Adventure activities and sports also contribute to healthy lifestyles through the benefits of exercise received while engaging in activities. Physical fitness of children, as well as adults, is as important today as at any other time in our history. Not only is exercise a key factor in weight control and the prevention of heart disease and other conditions, but it is also important in stress management, the feeling of well-being, and general mental and physical invigoration. In addition to cardiovascular functions and endurance, fitness includes strength, flexibility, balance, and coordination. Further, adventure activities and sports can contribute significantly to motor development, kinesthetic and spatial awareness, and visual perception. Efficiency of movement and use of force are often key elements in adventure activities. While the foregoing points out what adventure activities and sports are good *for*, not to be overlooked is the good *in* these vigorous outdoor pursuits. With the physically demanding and emotionally challenging pursuits comes a joy of effort and well-being, an exhilaration of experience (often called *peak experiences*), and the gratification of personal achievement and enhancement of self-image and self-esteem.

CHELEY COLORADO CAMPS, CHELEY, CO.

The type of activities/sports selected; the nature of body movement required, and the intensity, duration, and frequency of participation determine the contribution to physical development and fitness. Rope courses and some initiative tasks are particularly good for development of balance, flexibility, coordination, kinesthetic and spatial awareness, visual perception, and general motor development. Hunting and fishing may require and develop physical endurance and conditioning if they include hikes into the woods or along streams in search of game. Field archery also requires walking, visual perception, and strength in the arms and upper body. All require coordination and balance. Canoeing and river running require good physical condition and strength—particularly when portaging—as well as endurance, efficiency of movement, and use of force. Backpacking, too, requires strength, endurance, efficiency of movement, and use of force. Rock climbing calls upon a number of physical capabilities, as does orienteering, including spatial and kinesthetic awareness. Bicycling, hiking, and cross-country skiing and snowshoeing are excellent activities for developing the cardiovascular system and endurance.

When engaging in activity/sport for physical conditioning and weight control, start slow, build up muscles and endurance, and progress systematically. People with special health concerns (such as obesity or heart disease) and older folks should consult their physician before engaging in exercise programs. Even those children, youth, and adults in generally good health should understand the principles of exercise and conditioning. In every community there are exercise/fitness specialists who can describe these principles. Physical education teachers are an excellent resource, as are the YMCA and fitness and wellness centers

FITNESS

Periodically the U.S. Surgeon General issues reports and recommendations on fitness. The recommended amount of daily exercise has been continually updated as a result of scientific studies. According to the President's Council on Physical Fitness and Sports Fact Sheet on Physical Activity and Health: "Adults 18 and older need 30 minutes of physical activity on five or more days a week to be healthy; children and teens need 60 minutes of activity a day for their health." (http://fitness.gov/physical_activity_ fact_sheet.html).

Obesity in America has risen to epidemic proportions. Of course, childhood obesity is a devastating occurrence. It is important that lifelong activities and habits be formed. For weight control, the intensity and duration of activity/sport also determines the number of calories expended in relation to the weight of the individual exercising. Charts of calories are readily available in fitness books and on the Internet (enter keywords *calories and exercise*). For your convenience, here is a limited chart of approximate calories expended per hour of participation for some of the sports included in this chapter and other activities for comparison. Note the difference in calorie expenditure by intensity (speed) of activity and body weight.

Body Weight (in pounds)						
Activity	Speed	99	125	152	178	196
Bicycling	5.5 mph	198	252	306	354	390
	13.0 mph	426	534	648	762	840
	2.5 mph	114	138	180	216	234
Canoeing (flat water)	2.5 mph	276	354	426	498	552
Hiking (40 lb pack)	3.0 m,ph	276	354	426	498	552
Mountain Climbing		390	504	606	714	762
Cross-Country Skiing	5.0 mph	462	588	708	834	912
Snowshoeing	2.5 mph	246	312	378	444	486
Walking	2.0 mph	138	274	210	252	276
	4.5 mph	264	330	402	468	516
Running (11 min mile)	5.5 mph	426	540	648	762	1,068
(7 min mile)	9.0 mph	612	786	942	1,134	1,212

Loss of one pound of body fat requires an expenditure of 3,500 calories; however, exercise not only reduces body fat, but, perhaps more important, strengthens the cardiovascular system, tones-up muscles, and improves general body efficiency and motor skills. To actually reduce weight, a reduction in calories through diet control is usually necessary; however, diet alone does not produce a sound body—exercise is essential. While exercise can be obtained through indoor activities and using exercise machines, it is much more pleasurable to exercise in the invigorating outdoors. Another important aspect, not to be overlooked, is when you feel good and have the physical ability to optimally engage in a sport or outdoor activity, you achieve much greater enjoyment in participation and sometimes reach *peak experiences.*

NATURE-ORIENTED ADVENTURE/CHALLENGE.

When engaging in adventure/challenge activities in the outdoors, it is important to be aware of the environment and comfortable with the environment, not only to enjoy the experience, but also to be safe. The Association for Experiential Education

(AEE), whose mission is to develop and promote experiential education, has developed standards in adventure programming for risk management, safety, and sound practice. This is a voluntary standards program that can lead to accreditation of individual programs. The standards cover ethical concerns; risk management plans; staff qualifications; transportation and technical skills for land, air, and water; plus environmental, emergency and cultural skills.

COMMUNITY-BASED PROGRAMS

The purpose of this chapter is to point out various activities that might be included in community programs and to provide selected references to use in development of such a program. Detailed instructions in the technique of each sport are not included. The reference sections include excellent how-to books as well as other resources on technique. The AEE standards also provide excellent leadership recommendations.

It is important that community programs offer activities that not only provide basic instruction for the novice, but continue to challenge participants as their skills develop and their experience grows. In other words, there should be a sequence of activity that continue to challenge and maintain participant interest while promoting a safe progression of skill development and challenge. Whenever an outing sport uses the natural environment, sound and ethical environmental practices should be followed. (See Chapter 4: Outdoor Living Skills under Environmentally Responsible Use of the Outdoors.)

SECTION A

INITIATIVE/CHALLENGE ACTIVITIES

Initiative activities are fun, cooperative, challenging games in which groups have a specific problem to solve usually revolving around a story designed to elicit creative solutions. This type of challenge activity, frequently called *initiative tasks, team building exercises,* or *adventure learning* has its roots in military training during WWII when it was often a life or death circumstance to get groups of men to become cohesive groups in very short periods of time. In the early days, these activities were called *action socialization experiences.* Today these activities are used with groups starting with children and ranging to groups of corporate executives. Most of these programs have some or all of the following goals:

- To build group cohesiveness that lead to successful outcomes of tasks
- To build trust, respect, rapport, and empathy among group members
- To elicit creativity, flexibility, and different ways of doing things
- To increase effective communication among group members

- To appreciate individual differences and strengths
- To become accustomed to uncertainty and change
- To find new ways of problem solving and working together in a group

For these activities to be effective there must be a well-planned process that begins with setting goals and objectives and continues through the safe conduct of the activities to the final debriefing. A facilitator, who explains the rules, guides the activity, ensures safety, and leads the debriefing, is key to the degree of success achieved. The facilitator must create a nonthreatening environment often in activities that are frightening to most people. The facilitator must be well trained to establish an atmosphere of physical and emotional safety for participants that includes challenge by choice with each participant having the ultimate right to pass on a particular element. It is also the facilitator's responsibility to maintain dignity and confidentiality for each participant. Debriefing allows participants to review what happened and talk about what was learned, which leads to a richer educational experience.

ROPE COURSES

In the early seventies, there was a sharp increase in rope courses that challenge physical agility, balance, and mental and emotional attitude. The armed forces have long recognized the value of such challenge activities. Outward Bound, the Boy Scouts, and similar groups have capitalized on the potential of rope courses, as have corporations that use rope courses as part of their teamwork training.

There are a number of private and nonprofit companies that build ropes courses, and many offer leadership training programs. (A number of these are listed with the resources at the end of this section.) It is important that qualified persons construct rope courses and that the courses are maintained to standards. Leadership must be properly trained and regularly updated. Most ropes courses are constructed with ropes and logs, utilizing the natural features of the terrain. Documentation is kept on rope use and other safety equipment to ensure that it is replaced long before it becomes unsafe.

High and low ropes courses are quite different. High ropes courses require specialized safety equipment and harnesses for most of the elements and special care must be taken both in construction and use of the various elements. Low ropes courses require less safety equipment and, for the most part, are not extremely difficult to build or use. Brief descriptions of some elements frequently included in low ropes courses follow.

ACTIVITIES

Balance Beams. Logs of the same diameter are tied to trees at progressively higher distances form the ground. Logs should be 8–10 inches in diameter and 15–20 feet long. The first one is placed about 1 foot off the ground, the second about 5 feet, the third about 10 feet, and the fourth 15 to 20 feet. It is strange how easily one can walk on the logs near the ground, but how small the same log looks at 20 feet off the ground. Participants should be spotted on all but the lowest log.

Swinging Log. A log 10–15 inches in diameter and 15–20 feet long is suspended about a foot off the ground by ropes that permit it to swing freely. One end of the log is suspended by a single rope while the other end is suspended by two ropes. The freedom of movement in all directions makes it difficult to cross.

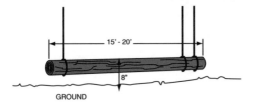

The Wall. There are many ways to construct walls. They can be made of solid boards or a series of logs. The wall should be 8–10 feet wide and 10–12 feet high. If it is made of a series of logs, they should be spaced far enough apart so that participants can pass through the openings. The wall presents many challenges, such as the very simple one of climbing up one side and down the other and the very difficult one of doing that without using hands or arms.

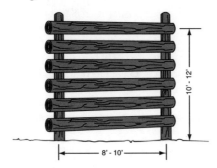

Parallel Ropes. Parallel ropes, tied to trees 15–20 feet apart, should be about 12–18 inches apart and about 5 feet above the ground. These ropes need to be quite taut. There are many different ways of negotiating from one end to the other. Some do it on top—others from below.

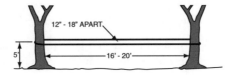

These are just a few ideas for rope elements. Other items frequently included are:

a.   Tarzan swing—a swing attached by a single rope to a branch 30-40 feet above the ground. Can be used to swing across a ravine.

b.   Pegs: 3- or 4-inch diameter poles of different heights placed so that a person can walk from one to the other.

c.   Zip lines—a cable strung across a ravine on an incline; a seat on a pulley is used to cross the ravine.

d.   Rope bridges

e.   Horizontal ladder

f.   Stepping stones

g.   Tree stump walk—cut lengths of logs of various heights and diameter; place in the ground solidly in proximity to each other so children can go from one to another.

TEAM BUILDING

Many groups (youth groups, corporate teams, college orientation counselors, sports teams, etc.) find it valuable to participate in problem-solving situations requiring the completion of a challenging physical task. These initiative tasks may be combined in a series, sometimes called an *Action Socialization Course.* The group is presented a task with specific parameters and then left to themselves, with no instructions and no leader appointed, to solve the task. The entire group must participate, success is only achieved when the entire group completes the task. There is no "right" answer or "one way" to perform the task, and groups should be encouraged to try different, creative approaches.

Following are some examples of initiative tasks. This is not intended to be a complete listing. The reference section includes books dedicated to providing and explaining initiative activities. Your specific environment may provide ideas for additional tasks.

 ACTIVITIES

The Stump. Find a tree stump, preferably 2 or more feet tall, and ask the group to get everyone on the stump at the same time. Ten or more people should be able to get on a stump that has a 12 to 15 inch diameter. As an indoor alternative, a towel can be used that can be folded into a smaller area after each successful completion.

The Wall or Beam. A wall about 9 feet high is constructed of boards. The object is to see if and how each member of the group can get across the wall. The same thing can be done with a beam placed about 8 feet high.

Electric Fence. A wire or string is tied to two posts about 5 feet high. The team is given one pole 8 feet long. The object is to get all members across the "electric" fence without touching the wire and "electrocuting" themselves.

Creating the Monster. A group of 10 people is given the responsibility of banding themselves together so that no more than six feet and five arms touch the ground. This monster must be able to walk 10 feet.

Books on Adventure and Initiative Activities

See master publicatons list for cities of Publishers.

Bower, Nancy. (1998). *Adventure Play: Adventure activities for Preschool and Early Elementary Age Children.* Simon & Schuster. (Project Adventure)

Cain, James Hallie, Jim Cain, and Barry Jolliff. (1998). *Teamwork & Teamplay.* Kendall Hunt:Dubuque, IA.

Cavert, Chris, friends. (1999). *Affordable Portables: A Working Book of Initiative and Problem Solving Elements,* 2nd revision. Wood 'N Barnes Publishing & Distribution.

Darst, Paul W., and George P. Armstrong. (1991). *Outdoor Adventure Activities for School and Recreation Programs.* Waveland Press.

Ellmo, Wendy, and Jill Graser. (1995). *Adapted Adventure Activities: A Rehabilitation Model for Adventure Programming and Group Initiatives.* Kendall/Hunt: Dubuque, IA. (Project Adventure) Written for professionals working in rehabilitation.

Gass, Michael A. (1998). *Administrative Practices of Accredited Adventure Programs,* 2nd edition. Xerox College Pub.

Gass, Michael A. (1993). *Adventure Therapy: Therapeutic Applications of Adventure Programming.* Kendall/Hunt: Dubuque, IA.

Gass, Michael A. (1997). *Book of Metaphors.* Kendall/Hunt: Dubuque, IA. Metaphors are used in adventure programming as change agents. Topics covered include steps for framing experiences, verbal instructions, debriefing, and method for facilitating adventure experiences.

Jones, Alanna. (1999). *Team-Building Activities for Every Group.* Rec Room Publishing.

Jones, Alanna, and Alanna E. Jones. (1998). *104 Activities that Build: Self-Esteem, Teamwork, Communication, Anger Management, Self-Discovery, and Coping Skills.* Rec Room Publishing.

Luckner, John L., and Reldan S. Nalder. (1997). *Processing the Experience: Strategies to Enhance and Generalize Learning.* Kendall/Hunt: Dubuque, IA.

Malone, Jeanette. (1998). Wild Adventures: *A Guidebook of Building Connections with Others and the Earth.* Pearson Custom Pub.

Marcum, Walt. (2004). *Team Building and Group Development: To Inspire Youth Groups.* Abingdon Press. (Audio CD)

Priest, Simon, and Michael Gass. (1997). *Effective Leadership in Adventure Programming.* Human Kinetics.

Rohnke, Karl, and Jim Grout. (1998). *Back Pocket Adventure.* Simon & Schuster Custom Publishing. (Project Adventure) This little pocket book of "propless" activities grew out of one of the author's experiences when his bag of props was stolen just before a presentation and he had to pull activities out of his back pocket.

Rohnke, Karl, Catherine Tait, Catherine, and Jim Wall. (2003), *The Complete Ropes Course Manual,* 3rd edition. Kendall/Hunt: Dubuque, IA.

Rohnke, Karl. (1989). *Cowtails and Cobras II. A Guide to Games, Initiatives, Rope Courses, and Adventure Curriculum.* Kendall/Hunt: Dubuque, IA. (Project Adventure)

Rohnke, Karl. (1996). *Quicksilver: Adventure Games, Initiative Problems, Trust Activities & Guide to Effective Leadership,* reprint edition. Kendall/Hunt: Dubuque, IA.

Rohnke, Karl. (1984). *Silver Bullets. A Guide to Initiative Problems, Adventure Games and Trust Activities.* Kendall Hunt: Dubuque, IA. (Project Adventure)

Rohnke, Karl. (2002). *A Small Book about Large Group Games.* Kendall Hunt: Dubuque, IA. (Project Adventure)

Sikes, Sam, Sikes, Sam W. (1995). *Feeding the Zircon Gorilla: and Other Team Building Activities.* Learning Unlimited Corporation.

Sikes, Sam. (2003). Raptor: and other team building activities. Learning Unlimited Corporation.

Williamson, John E., and Michael Gass. (1993). *Association for Experiential Education Manual of Accreditation Standards for Adventure Programs.* Association for Experiential Education.

 Internet Sites on Adventure Activities/Initiatives

Suggested search words: initiative activities/ropes courses/challenge activities/adventure activities/ropes challenge/adventure education/challenge education/experiential education

Association for Challenge Course Technology: http://www.acctinfo.org/

Association for Experiential Education (AEE): http://www.aee.org/

National Society for Experiential Education (NSEE): http://www.nsee.org/

Outdoor Network. Online portal for outdoor industry professionals: http://www.outdoornetwork.com/

Outdoor Kids' Network. (Texas Parks & Wildlife): http://www.tpwd.state.tx.us/adv/kidspage/kidspage.htm

Ropes Online: http://www.ropesonline.org/ The purpose of Ropes Online is to provide a free source of information to ropes/challenge course owners, facilitators, users, and students"

Wilderness Education Association (WEA). http://www.weainfo.org/ 900 East 7th Street, Bloomington IN, 47405 telephone: 812.855.4095

There are a number of nonprofit and profit organizations that will build or consult on challenge courses. The oldest and best known, which also provides publications and program consultation, is Project Adventure. A few are listed below:

Adventure Network. P.O. 309, Chalfont, PA 18914, http://www.adventure-network.net/index.html

Adventureworks, Inc., 1300 Narrows of the Harpeth Road, Kingston Springs, TN. 37082. http://www.adventureworks.com/

Cradlerock Outdoor Network, P. O. Box 1431, Princeton, N.J. 08542 (609-924-2919). http://www.cradlerock.com/

High 5 Adventure Learning Center: http://www.high5adventure.org Nonprofit organization "dedicated to helping schools and communities use experiential education as an effective tool for improving the way they live, learn and work together." Provides training for all age groups and constructs ropes courses.

Inner Quest Adventures, 1001 Bridgeway #455, Sausalito, CA 94965; http://www.innerquest.com (wilderness adventures.)

Project Adventure. http://www.pa.org/ 701 Cabot Street, Beverly, MA 01915; also office at P.O. Box 2447, Covington, GA 30015.

SECTION B
BICYCLING

Bicycle safety and fun activities have long been a part of most children's experiences. Many of these programs are conducted in conjunction with schools and clubs. Many community recreation agencies have built special tracks or designated specific trails for use by bicycles. Cycling lends itself to activity of all kinds—activities that can lead to many interesting things. Helmets should always be worn by adults and children alike when cycling.

BICYCLE SAFETY.

A safety program is an absolute must in any community. Sometimes a special program is sponsored by schools, law enforcement agencies, civic groups, public recreation departments, or youth agencies. There are many excellent aids available on safety programs, many of which are free. Bicycle maintenance can be an important part of any bicycling program. The ability to repair your own bicycle, as well as keep it in top condition is an important opportunity to learn additional skills and be able to troubleshoot wherever and whenever the need arises. The League of American Bicyclists "promotes bicycling fun, fitness and transportation and works through advocacy and education for a bicycle-friendly America." Resources are available from the league that lend themselves to planning bike fun with your bicycle club, your Scout troop, or your friends.

BICYCLE TRIPPING

Bicycle tripping is an activity that may last for a day or two or extend over a very long distance for a considerable period of time. One great success story is the annual *Great Bicycle Ride Across Iowa*, also known as *Ragbrai*. Sponsored by the Des Moines Register newspaper, it began as a casual ride in 1973 when 114 people completed the entire route and has evolved into the longest, largest, oldest bicycle touring event in the world with annual participation limited to 8,500. It begins when cyclists dip their wheels in the Missouri River and ends with the same ceremony in the Mississippi River. Each year different routes are taken across the state. It is a truly international event that has been emulated across the country and the world. Various clubs, organizations, and summer camps take bicycle trips varying from days and weeks to months in length. Youth Hostels (See Hostelling and Hiking Clubs under Hiking and Backpacking in this chapter) are often excellent, inexpensive lodging options for some trippers, while others prefer to campout. A great deal of specialized equipment for carrying provisions on the bicycle is available from bicycle and outdoor stores. Bicycle trippers must be adept at bicycle maintenance and repair and know bicycle regulations for the areas in which they ride, as well as adhere to strict safety practices for a successful ride.

TYPES OF BICYCLING

Bicycling has increased in popularity with both adults and children. The emergence of mountain bikes, trail bikes, and BMX tracks has spurred much renewed interest. In the 1990s, a new approach to mountain biking emerged called "Freeriding." The International Mountain Bicycling Association defines freeriding as: "a style of mountain biking that celebrates the challenges and spirit of technical riding and downhilling." Freeriding has engendered both enthusiasm and controversy related to risks and environmental issues related to building trails and conducting the sport in the natural environment.

 ## Books on Bicycling

See master publicatons list for cities of Publishers.

Ballantine, Richard. (2001). *Richard's 21st-Century Bicycle Book.* Overlook Press: NY. Includes choosing the right bike, keeping bike in peak condition, latest innovations in cycle design, mountain bikes, commuting by bike, and working in cycling.

Lovett, Richard A. (2000). *The Essential Touring Cyclist: A Complete Guide for the Bicycle Traveler,* 2nd edition. International Marine/Ragged Mountain Press.

IMBA. (2004). Trail Solutions: *IMBA's Guide to Building Sweet Singletrack.* International Mountain Bicycling Association. Presents trail design and maintenance techniques to build environmentally friendly trails for cyclists, hikers, runner, equestrians, etc. Also includes working with government officials, trail groups, and volunteers. Has assessment of what trail users really want and how trails will benefit your community. Includes use of hand tools and trail building & maintenance machines. Available from IMBA site listed under the Internet sites that follow.

Pavelka, Ed (editor). (2000). *New Cyclist's Handbook: Ride with Confidence and Avoid Common Pitfalls.* Rodale. Experienced road cyclists and mountain bikers share knowledge and tips. Includes how to choose the right bike, ride safely with traffic, prevent and treat common ailments, train for a century, fix flats, and perform maintenance.

 ## Internet Sites on Bicycling

Suggested search words: bicycling/ trail bikes/cycling/mountain biking/freeriding

Adventure Cycling Association: http://www.adv-cycling.org/

Bicycle Institute of America. http://www.bikeschool.com/ 401 Williamson Way, PO Box 128, Ashland, OR 97520

Cyber Cycling: Internet Bicycling Hub: http://www.cyclery.com/ bicycling related information, resources & services

GORP Biking page: http://gorp.com/gorp/activity/biking.htm

Icebike: http://users.rcn.com/icebike/Default.htm Site dedicated to winter cyclists, who brave ice and snow and cycle for transportation, recreation or competition in winter.

International Mountain Bicycling Association: http://www.imba.com/ "Creates, enhances and preserves trail opportunities for mountain bikers worldwide."

League of American Bicyclists: http://www.bikeleague.org/index.cfm 1612 K Street NW, Suite 800 Washington, DC 20006-2850.

Mountain Biking: http://mtb.live.com/ "The Internet mountain bike park."

National Bicycle League, BMX site. http://209.248.103.75/nbl/

Ragbrai: http://www.ragbrai.org. Site for the annual Great Bicycle Ride Across Iowa.

USA Cycling: http://www.usacycling.org/ Includes mountain, road, track, cyclo-cross, BMX, and collegiate. "USA Cycling is a family of organizations that promote and govern different disciplines of the sport, and that work as one to build the sport of bicycle racing, assist with athlete development and sustain international competitive excellence."

State laws concerning bicycles: http://www.massbike.org/bikelaw/

SECTION C
CANOEING, KAYAKING, AND RIVER RUNNING

Since the beginning of human existence, it would seem canoeing and kayaking have been engaged in for transportation, fishing and hunting, and pleasure. The light and maneuverable bark and frame crafts of Native Americans soon became the roots of a favorite recreational activity. Canoeing and kayaking on lakes or ponds and other sheltered and calm water has been, and is, an activity enjoyed by tens of thousands each season. Indeed, canoes and kayaks are likely to be found in virtually any body of water throughout this country. Canoeing and kayaking are not only popular in the North Woods wilderness but also on downtown lakes and ponds in many urban areas.

CERTIFICATION

Although many people enjoy canoeing and kayaking without ever having had instruction, the American Canoe Association (ACA), organized camps, and other youth-serving agencies have long offered instruction in the basics of canoeing and kayaking. For instructors already holding certification, the American Canoe Association offers an Adaptive Paddling program designed to teach ACA certified Instructors how to include paddlers of all abilities into their programs. There is little doubt that the skill gained in organized courses adds to the enjoyment and the safety of paddlers.

LEADERSHIP

All organized canoe and kayak outings should be led by individuals who are knowledgeable and skilled as canoeists, who know about potential hazards with groups of novices. All members of the group should wear properly fitting Coast Guard approved, personal flotation devices (PFDs—lifejackets). The American Canoe Association reports that the overwhelming number of serious accidents in paddle sports occurred when PFDs were not worn. Whatever the overall intent of the outing, there should be an orientation to and instruction in basic paddling skills and safety practices. The leader should be both a canoeist and a knowledgeable lifesaver. These precautions may seem to some to be too cautious, but in the few instances when an accident occurs, these simple precautions help ensure that it is only a minor incident and not a tragedy.

WHITEWATER

Canoeing and kayaking are not always confined to sheltered and calm waters. The adventuresome will seek out more exciting challenges, like whitewater rivers, for the thrill of running rapids and sea kayaking which has grown dramatically in participation. River running, whether done in a canoe, kayak, or raft, is a popular sport. Unfortunately, it has also increased the number of fatalities on rivers across the country. The dangers inherent in river running are such that *instruction and qualified leadership are musts!* In spite of the potential hazards of river running, more and more people are attracted to the rivers each year. In some cases, river use is so intense that quotas are established by governing agencies.

Class I	**Easy**—Waves small; passages clear; no serious obstacles
Class II	**Medium**—Rapids of moderate difficulty with passages clear. Most open canoeists should never tackle anything tougher than Class II.
Class III	**Difficult**—Rapids are longer and rougher than class II. Waves numerous, high, irregular; rocks; eddies; rapids with passages clear though narrow, requiring expertise in maneuver; scouting usually needed. Requires good operator and boating equipment.
Class IV	**Very Difficult**—Rapids are generally longer, steeper and more heavily obstructed than class III rapids. Waves powerful, irregular; dangerous rock; boiling eddies; passages difficult to scout; scouting mandatory first time; powerful and precise maneuvering required. Demands expert boatman and excellent boat and outfit.
Class V	**Extremely Difficult**—Exceedingly difficult, long and violent rapids, following each other almost without interruption; riverbed extremely obstructed; big drops; violent current; very steep gradient; close study essential, but often difficult. Requires best man, boat, and outfit suited to the situation. All possible precautions must be taken.
Class VI	**Unrunnable!!!**

RIVER CLASSIFICATION SYSTEM

Rivers are classified according to the International Scale of River Difficulty. This scale, based on the difficulty of the river, provides important information when selecting places to paddle. In river running: start at Class I and work your way up; always be in a group that includes more experienced people than yourself; be familiar with the river; and always wear a lifejacket (PFD).

INSTRUCTION AND TRAINING

For canoeing, kayaking, and rafting, competent instruction and leadership are offered through various whitewater clubs and a few commercial schools and outfitters across the country. Look for groups that have instructors certified by the American Canoe Association. There are numerous rafting outfitters with very good safety records; however, select your outfitter with care. One river guide refers to a private one-or-two raft as being a "suicide raft" or a "kamikaze raft." A very high percentage of the fatalities on rivers involve novices in their own or rented boats who did not wear lifejackets, and who were not familiar with the river. Also, the difficulty of a river may change dramatically with an increase or decrease in the amount of water in the river that fluctuates with the seasons or rainfall. Remember it does not have to be raining at your exact location to experience dramatically escalating water volume from up river. Again, check with local canoe and kayaking clubs for resources and expertise.

RIVER TOURING

River touring is an exciting and challenging activity, but there is no room for ignorance of potential hazards and safety precautions. Ignorance on the river can end in tragedy. There are several organizations dedicated to the enjoyment and promotion of canoeing and river touring that can be found under the Internet sites that follow. Safety codes, technical tips, instruction, and general information are available from most of these groups.

Books on Canoeing, Kayaking and River Running

See master publicatons list for cities of Publishers.

Addison, Graeme. (2001). *Whitewater Rafting.* Stackpole Books: Mechanicsburg, PA.

American Canoe Association. (1996). *Introduction to Paddling: Canoeing Basics for Lakes and Rivers.* American Canoe Association, Springfield, VA.
American Canoe Association encourages people to take their courses. This booklet emphasizes the course goals of safety, enjoyment, and skills.

Angier, Bradford, and Taylor Zack. (1973). *Introduction to Canoeing*. Stackpole Books: Mechanicsburg, PA. (out of print/limited availability)

Bennett, Jeff. (1996). *The Complete Whitewater Rafter*. International Marine/Ragged Mountain Press.

Ford, Kent. Solo Playboating: *The Workbook*. canoe@performancevideo.com, Durango, CO. Pocket personal trainer for whitewater canoe skills.

Glaros, Lou, and Charlie Wilson. (1994). *Freestyle Canoeing: Contemporary Paddling Technique*. Menasha Ridge Press, Birmingham, AL. Freestyle canoeing is based on the quiet, paddling techniques of Native American that produced no ripples.

Gordon, I. Herbert, and Jim Thaxton. (2001). *Complete Book of Canoeing*, 3rd edition. Globe Pequot Press.

Jacobson, Cliff. (1999). *Canoeing*, 2nd edition. Globe Pequot. Small book includes choosing canoe, selecting accessories, portaging, basic paddling strokes, whitewater, currents and how to rescue from capsize.

Jacobson, Cliff. (1999). *Solo Canoeing*, 2nd edition. Globe Pequot. Small book includes choosing right solo canoe, customizing solo canoe for peak performance, braces & ferry strokes, pack & portage, and maintenance and repair.

Mason, Bill. (2002), revised and updated by Paul Mason. *Path of the Paddle: An Illustrated Guide to the Art of Canoeing* Firefly Books: Buffalo, NY. Techniques are illustrated by photographs. Includes techniques from beginning to advanced.

McNair, Robert. (1985). *Basic River Canoeing*. American Camp Association: Martinsville, Ind. (out of print/limited availability)

NRPA. (1995). *Boating Fundamentals*. National Recreation & Parks Association. Published under Aquatic Resources Trust Fund administered by the U.S. Coast Guard. Covers safety and risk management.

Ovington, Ray (1984). *Canoeing Basics for Beginners*. Stackpole Books: Mechanicsburg, PA.

Ray, Slim. (1992). *Canoe Handbook: Techniques for Mastering the Sport of Canoeing*. Stackpole Books: Mechanicsburg, PA. Introduces basic maneuvers for all types of water from quiet lakes to whitewater.

Roberts, Harry. (2000), revised and edited by Steve Salins. *Canoe Paddling: Basic Essentials*. Globe Pequot Press.

Walbridge, Charles, Sundmacher, Wayne. (1995). *Whitewater Rescue Manual: New Techniques for Canoeists, Kayakers, and Rafters*. Ragged Mountain Press: Camden, ME. How to avoid accidents and then how to deal with them when they happen.

Internet Sites for Canoe/Kayak and River Running Organizations

Suggested search words: canoe/whitewater/whitewater rafting/paddling

American Canoe Association: http://www.acanet.org/welcome.htm America's premier canoe, kayak and rafting organization (according to them)

American Rivers. http://www.amrivers.org/ National non-profit conservation organization, dedicated to protecting and restoring healthy natural rivers and the variety of life they sustain for people, fish, and wildlife

American Whitewater: http://www.americanwhitewater.org/ Mission is to conserve and restore America's whitewater resources.

Canoeing for Kids. http://www.canoeingforkids.net/ Canoeing for Kids is a volunteer, non- profit organization serving as both a fund raiser and free recreational outlet for disadvantaged children. Canoeing for Kids' primary function is to provide free canoeing, kayaking, rafting, camping and fishing trips for underprivileged children.

River Discovery. http://www.riverdiscovery.org/ Motto: "Connecting people to America's great rivers and fostering education and appreciation of these natural treasures.

United States Canoe Association: http://www.uscanoe.com/ Non-profit, educational group whose purpose is to encourage the growth of recreational and competitive paddling.

CANOE/KAYAK MAGAZINES

American Whitewater Journal. Periodical of the American Whitewater Association, Nick Lipkowski, office manager, 1424 Fenwick Lane, Silver Spring, MD 20910. http://www.americanwhitewater.org/journal/

Paddler Magazine Online. Periodical of the American Canoe Association. 7432 Alban Station Blvd. Suite B-232 Springfield, VA 22150. http://www.paddlermagazine.com/

Canoe & Kayak. Paddle Sports publication. http://www.canoekayak.com/

SECTION D
CASTING AND FISHING

Of recreation there is none
So free as fishing is, alone;
All other pastimes do not less
Than mind and body, both possess:

My hand alone my work can do;

So I can fish and study too.

—IZAAK WALTON, THE COMPLEAT ANGLER—THE ANGLER'S SONG

Yes, fishing is an American freedom available to all, but most children have parents who never learned the art of angling and have no experience with the sport. The American Sportfishing's Future Fisherman Foundation has several programs that offer "...a variety of fishing and boating programs, equipment and services to community groups and schools across the country." Their purpose is "...to help people of all ages have safe and enjoyable fishing experiences that foster conservation ethics." There is a place for angling and casting in the community nature-oriented program. Some recreation departments sponsor casting clubs and sponsor other fishing activities.

INSTRUCTIONAL PROGRAMS AND RESOURCES

Instruction in the art of casting should include the technique of the various types of casting (fly, bait, spin-cast, spin), how to handle the rod and reel in landing a fish, and an evaluation of various types of tackle. You may wish to use certified Federation of Fly Fishers casting instructors. Instruction in fishing techniques should include the identification of fish, their habitat and feeding habits, types of bait and lures to use according to species, and how to take fish off the hook, including catch and release.

Beginning anglers will appreciate information on what weather conditions are best for a good catch and also weather danger signs when using a small craft. Regulations such as license requirements, bait restrictions, open and closed seasons, catch limits, size limits, and types of equipment that can be used should also be presented. Discussions on conservation and sportsmanship, including their relationship to regulations, the economic aspects of conservation, responsibilities and courtesies to landowners, and the problem of stream pollution are very important in any program on fishing. There are many helpful videos available on most of these subjects. Local county conservation officers, state conservation commissions, and state fish and wildlife personnel can provide many helpful resources.

There have been efforts by the fishing industry, as well as fish and wildlife agencies to promote fishing, especially among children and women. For example, in the early years of 2000 the Recreational Boating & Fishing and the Future Fisherman Foundation partnered with the American Association for Leisure and Recreation and the National Association of School Physical Education to provide Fishing and Boating Education Grants. The purpose of this initiative was to make new and/or improved fishing and boating opportunities available to schools and communities.

COMPETITIVE CASTING ACTIVITIES

There are many fly casting games that are used just for fun, as well as for more formal competitions. The American Casting Association is the coordinating organization for competitive tournament casting in the United States. By entering the search words *casting games* or *fly casting games* in an Internet search, you will find descriptions of many games.

Tournament dry-casting is developed around the same principles important in fishing, including accuracy in delivery of the lure, distance, selection of tackle, etc. Tournaments have many individual events that focus on accuracy and distance or both. Actually the only equipment needed besides the participant's tackle is a set of targets, since most games consist of hitting a specific target at a given distance with designated tackle. Targets can be made from bicycle tires, plywood discs, oil drum lids, floating aluminum targets, or similar objects. The American Casting Association website includes rules and regulations for all events (http://www.americancastingassoc.org/RulesAndRegs/RulesAndRegs.html) and gives suggestions for club organization and technique improvement as well.

Special Activities

- Crafts such as fly tying
- Field trips to hatcheries, fisheries, and aquariums
- Aquatic life activities, such as studying the plant life in the water, water life photography, water life collections, aquariums, etc.
- Earthworm raising
- Minnow propagation

(For additional references see Chapter 6. Section 11: Water, Streams, and Ponds.)

 ## Books on Casting and Fishing

See master publicatons list for cities of Publishers.

Blades, William F. (1980). *Fishing Flies and Fly Tying*. Stackpole Books: Mechanicsburg, PA. (out of print/limited availability)

Hoover, Herbert. (1963). *Fishing for Fun and to Wash Your Soul*. Random House. A classic by the former president. A little book of good cheer.

Leeson, Ted, Schollmeyer, Jim. (1998). *The Fly Tier's Benchside Reference*. Frank Amato Publications.

Lord, Macauley, Dick Talleur, and Dave Whitlock. (2002). *The L.L. Bean Ultimate Book of Fly Fishing*. The Lyons Press.

Walton, Izaak. (1953). *The Complete Angler*, tricentennial edition. Stackpole Books: Mechanicsburg, PA. A classic. To be read by every fishing enthusiast. Also available from: IndyPublish.com, 2003.

Zim, Herbert S., George S. Fichter, and Phil Francis. (1987). *Fishing* revised edition. (Golden Guides), Golden Books Publishing Company.

Internet Sites on Casting and Fishing

Suggested search words: fishing/casting/fly fishing/angling

American Casting Association. http://www.americancastingassoc.org/ 1773 Lance End Lane, Fenton, MO 83026. Coordinating organization for the sport of competitive tournament casting whose objective is "to educate all interested individuals and groups in angling and castings as a recreational activity."

American Sport Fishing Association. http://www.asafishing.org/asa/

Izaak Walton League of America: http://www.iwla.org/

Flyfishingclub.com: http://www.flyfishingclub.com/guest_tour/index.htm

Federation of Fly Fishers: http://www.fedflyfishers.org/ FFF P.O. Box 1595 Bozeman, MT 59771. Has a certification program for instructors.

Trout Unlimited: http://www.tu.org/index.asp

U.S. Fish & Wildlife Service. http://fishing.fws.gov/ Includes activities for kids and locations of fishing sites on government lands.

SECTION E

FIELD ARCHERY

Although archery is almost as old as humanity and has a fascinating history, it began as an organized sport in the United States in 1828 largely for the elite. However, through the years it has increased in popularity and enjoyed incredible growth since World War II.

JUDY BROOKHISER, CENTRAL PARK, MURRAY, KY

TYPES OF ARCHERY

There are basically two types of archery—target archery and field archery. Although target archery is by far the oldest form, it is not the most popular. Some people feel it has too many rules and regulations, too much organization, and demands too much perfection from exactly the same position each time with very little physical movement and no vigorous exercise. Some consider target archery a contest, similar to rifle matches; while field archery is a game likened to golf in which foursomes play a course involving varying distances and types of shots.

Although both field archery and target archery have a common source, they are different in many ways. Field archery is based on hunting and can serve as practice or a substitute for hunting. As a substitute for hunting, field archery has been organized into different types of rounds and has standards for field courses or ranges.

FIELD ARCHERY TOURNAMENTS

Since 1939, the National Field Archery Association (NFAA) has sponsored national field archery tournaments. The NFAA includes many styles of archery, including freestyle, freestyle limited, barebow, bowhunter (competitive, freestyle, freestyle limited), and traditional. Competitions are held in the following categories: cub, youth, young adult, adult, senior, and professional.

Some people think that field archery means going into a field and merely shooting at various clumps, stumps, flowers, and whatever is sticking up, but this is called "roving archery." The basic NFAA course in field archery has 28 targets laid preferably on a scenic, wooded, hilly area or 14, targets that are shot twice to make a round. Four arrows are shot at each target, for a total of 112 arrows per round. Shooting positions vary; some of the shooting positions allow shooting all four arrows from one marked stake; others have stakes at four different positions as the target is approached or in a fan position. The distances vary according to the round. The standard NFAA field round has distances that vary from 20 feet to 240 feet. There are four different sized target faces, the more distant the target, the larger the size. The longest distance, for archers under 14 years is 50 yards; under 12 years it is 30 yards. Targets are round with black and white concentric circles. Inside the circle scores 5 points and outside 2 points, making a total possible 20 points for each target, and a perfect round equals 560 points. Other types of field rounds include the hunter round, similar to the field round except that targets are all black face with a white dot. The animal round has two dimensional targets with an animal printed on a sheet of paper that is usually pasted to cardboard.

A trail system connects the shooting position and target and then leads to the next shooting position. Frequently one shoots across ravines or a valley; travel through a course may require considerable physical stamina. All positions are located for safety so that they can all be shot at the same time without endangering other shooters. The butt backstops or the banks that the targets set into provide good protection. The National Field Archery Association has established recommendations for courses. Although there has been a continuing emphasis on conservation and environmentally appropriate construction of trails, it should be noted that courses may not be nature-oriented. The butt backstops (straw bales) should not be merely set up at specified distances, but the natural environment should be respected, minimizing constructed elements and avoiding disturbance of plants and animal habitats. Sound nature trail construction should be incorporated into field archery courses. (See Chapter 8, Section E: Nature Trails.)

Field archery also differs from target archery in the number of arrows shot (4 in field archery and 6 in target archery) for each end, which is the number of arrows shot at one time at a target.

STARTING A CLUB

Field archery is suitable for both men and women and also for children. If you do not already have a field archery club in your area, you may want to start one as part of your local nature-oriented program. Be sure to call upon local archers to help; they are usually more than willing to be of assistance. If you do not have any local field archers, contact the National Field Archery Association for the nearest club and also the nearest field archery instructor. In addition to establishing a club, the public recreation department may help by providing an area and laying out a field course. This may be desirable even when the club is not sponsored by the department. Other public recreation and community agencies also may want to cooperate with and support club activities.

WINTER ACTIVITIES

Often outdoor activity declines in wintertime, but this is no reason to stop archery! Many archers shoot in the winter and there are other activities related to archery that can be conducted indoors. Quite a few indoor shooting areas are located around the country. Workshops for making equipment, especially bows and arrows can be offered. The enthusiast will also enjoy good archery books. Helpful information on technique, course layout, the various tournament rounds, etc., can be found in the following resources.

 Books on Field Archery

See master publicatons list for cities of Publishers.

Athletic Institute. (1988). *Archery: A Sport for Everyone.* Sterling Publishing Co.: NY. (out of print/limited availability)

Hamlett-Wood, Michael. (2002). *Field Archery: A Complete Guide.* Robert Hale Ltd., Includes fundamentals of sport such as various techniques of shooting; organizing an archery ground; different types of targets, repairing equipment; setting up the wide variety of bows used; and the rules of the regulating organizations.

Hill, Howard. (2000). *Hunting the Hard Way.* The Derrydale Press. Howard Hill devoted a lifetime to the promotion of archery until his death in 1975. He brings to life images of the mystique of archery, oneness with nature, and the adventure of the great outdoors.

James, M.R., G. Fred Asbell, Dave Holt, and Dwight Schuh. (1997). *Bowhunting Equipment & Skills.* Creative Publishing International: Minnetonka, MN.

Pope, Saxton. (2000). *Hunting with the Bow and Arrow.* Sylvan Toxophilite Classics.

Robb, Bob. (1999). *The Field & Stream Bowhunting Handbook.* The Lyons Press.

Schuh, Dwight. (1991). *Fundamentals of Bowhunting.* Stackpole Books: Mechanicsburg, PA.

Spotted Eagle, Douglas. (1988). *Making Bows and Arrows...the Old Way.* Eagle's View Publishing.

Thompson, J. Maurice. (1928). *The Witchery of Archery.* Pinehurst edition, The Archers Company: Pinehurst, N.C. (A classic.)

Internet Sites on Field Archery

Suggested search words: archery/field archery/bows and arrows/bowhunting

International Field Archery Association. http://www.archery-ifaa.com/

National Field Archery Association: http://www.nfaa-archery.org/ NFAA Headquarters 31407 Outer I-10, Redlands, California 92373

SECTION F

FIREARMS SAFETY AND HUNTING

The firearms safety and hunting program can be divided into four major categories of activities: (1) the instructional program, (2) knowledge useful in hunting, (3) clubs and competitive activities, and (4) special activities related to hunting.

INSTRUCTIONAL PROGRAM

The primary function of the instructional program should be, of course, to teach safe practices and techniques and to promote safety. Most states through their fish and game agencies (Department of Natural Resources, Fish and Game Departments, etc.) have hunter safety programs that are, for the most part, voluntary, but are required in some states before youth can obtain hunting licenses. State department personnel and state conservation officers usually are trained and willing to assist in such programs, as are local gun clubs.

The National Rifle Association (NRA) has many firearms safety programs including the Eddie Eagle GunSafe(r) Program that teaches children from preschool to third grade the following four steps to take if they find a gun: (1) stop, (2) don't touch, (3) leave the area, and (4) tell an adult. The NRA's fundamental rules for safe gun handling are: (1) always keep the gun pointed in a safe direction, (2) always keep your finger off the trigger until ready to shoot, and (3) always keep the gun unloaded until ready to shoot.

Since 1985, the NRA has held the Youth Hunter Education Challenge (YHEC). It is their "graduate studies" program in outdoor skills and safety training for young hunters and is open only to youth who have completed hunter safety training at state or provincial level. Among other things the program includes rifle, bow, and muzzle-loader shooting at life-sized targets, wildlife identification, and use of map and compass. The NRA also sponsors youth sports shooting camps.

Instruction in shooting should include knowledge of the various weapons, proper maintenance and storage, as well as proper shooting technique. Again the NRA has extensive materials and resources including rules for storing guns. An instructional program using air rifles can be particularly effective with young boys and girls.

In addition to regular firearms and hunting instructional programs, especially youngsters, airguns can be both fun and educational. Daisy Outdoor Products has offered shooting safety programs for over 40 years. Daisy will assist any qualifying organization, church, or civic group in establishing and conducting a shooting education program of their own. The company will provide knowledge and advice along with assembled complete Shooting Education Kits that include airguns, ammunition, target backstops, shooting range plans, and training manuals. Daisy's 10 gun safety rules are:

1. Always keep the muzzle pointed in a safe direction.
2. Treat every gun as if it were loaded.
3. Only load or cock a gun when you are shooting.
4. Check your target and beyond your target.
5. Anyone shooting or near a shooter should wear shooting glasses.
6. Never climb or jump with a gun.
7. Avoid ricochet.
8. Keep the muzzle clear (never obstruct).
9. Guns not in use should always be unloaded.
10. Respect other people's property.

KNOWLEDGE USEFUL IN HUNTING

The following knowledge areas should be included in hunting education:

*   Rules and regulations, including seasons, limits, protective regulations, purchasing, carrying and mailing weapons, licenses

- Clothing and equipment for hunting
- Instruction in shooting and stalking/tracking game
- Preservation and cleaning of hides
- Effect of climate, light, and wind on hunting
- Sportsmanship and conservation
- Outdoor survival/living skills

CLUBS AND COMPETITIVE ACTIVITIES

Clubs are organized by various organizations and agencies, such as police departments, sportsmen's clubs, military units, public recreation departments, etc. They may be organized either under local autonomy or in affiliation with the National Rifle Association or the Daisy Outdoor Products program.

Competitive activities may be sponsored by organized clubs or by hunting-related businesses. Such shooting programs include conventional target rifle matches and leagues: shotgun, sporting rifle, and pistol competition; and air rifle and pellet gun. The National Rifle Association has a series of ratings, with badges, for various levels of achievement. The clubs or sponsoring agencies may also have information sessions for parents who contemplate getting their child a firearm. There also may be instructional or information sessions for parents to provide advice when considering purchasing a gun for a young person. Skeet and trap shooting are also popular, but they are most frequently sponsored by sportsmen's clubs.

SPECIAL ACTIVITIES RELATED TO HUNTING

Dog training, taxidermy, crafts (stock making; plaster casts, making turkey calls, etc.), gun collecting, field trips to museums to see gun collections, and trips to game preserves, wildlife refuges, and gunsmiths are all interesting to those who love hunting and want to learn the proper use and care of guns.

Books on Firearms Safety and Hunting

See master publicatons list for cities of Publishers.

Davies, Ken. (1992). *The Better Shot: Step-by-Step Shotgun Technique with Holland and Holland.* Quiller Press.

Donnall Jr., Thomas E. (1981). *To All Things a Season: Twelve Months Afield with Fly Rod, Shotgun and Longbow.* Wilderness Adventures Press.

Internet Sites on Firearms Safety & Hunting

Search words: hunting/firearms/guns/shooting sports/hunting safety

National Rifle Association, Education and Training Programs:
http://www.nrahq.org/ Waples Mill Road, Fairfax, VA 22030. Firearms
safety program, organizing clubs, club activities, training, and competition materials.

National Shooting Sports Foundation: http://www.nssf.org/ Flintlock Ridge
Office Center, 11 Mile Hill Road, Newtown, CT 06470-2359. Hunting
and Shooting Sportsmanship; Shooting, Fun for Everyone; How You and
Your Friends Can Start a Gun Club.

Daisy Outdoor Products: http://www.daisy.com/ Daisy Outdoor Products,
P.O. Box 220, Rogers, Arkansas 72757-0220. (800) 643-3458.
Instructional program on air rifles for youth, organizing clubs, and club
activities.

Remington Arms Company, Inc.: http://www.remington.com/ 870
Remington Drive, P.O. Box 700, Madison, NC 27025. 800-243-9700.
Leaflets and pamphlets.

Sporting Arms and Ammunition Manufactures' Institute:
http://www.saami.org/ 11 West 42nd St., 13th floor, New York, NY
10036, 212-642-4900. They publish industry standards, coordinate technical data, and promote safe and responsible firearms use.

Winchester Rifles & Shotguns, Division of U.S. Repeating Arms:
http://www.winchester-guns.com/homepage/index.asp 344 Winchester
Avenue, New Haven, CT 06511. Gun Charts.

SECTION G

HIKING AND BACKPACKING

The National Survey on Recreation and the Environment 2000
(http://www.srs.fs.usda.gov/trends/Nsre/nsre2.html) reported that walking for pleasure remains the most frequently engaged in outdoor recreation pursuit—but a walk
is not necessarily a hike. Too frequently a walk is a saunter or stroll and this is not a
hike in the sense used as part of the adventure-outing sports aspect of nature-
oriented program. When hiking, the person moves with spirit and some consistency
and degree of pace. Usually a destination, a purpose, or covering a certain distance is
involved.

The art of hiking has been lost for most people as we are a "population on
wheels." Yet, some of the finest places of beauty and serenity can be reached only on
foot and the thrill and exhilaration of adventuring against the elements can only be

experienced by walking. Hikes also may be organized for the purpose of getting to a local area such as a farm, fish hatchery, rock quarry, lake, or museum. A hike can also be a special activity in itself, such as a hike through the woods lasting a few hours or a hike on a trail lasting several days. Hiking can be done any place, any time! It is something people of all ages can engage in with a great deal of satisfaction in every season of the year.

Here are a few pointers and a couple of resources to help you in your planning:

1. A Hike Should be Planned. Anticipation is half the fun of the activity—looking forward to going, planning, and anticipating the adventure. Do not deny participants this pleasure by planning it all yourself. Every hike taken as a group should involve the group in the organization and operation of the hike. Discuss such things as:

- Where to hike to? What is the objective of the hike? Are there activities en route?

- How long a hike? Keep in mind the experience of the group and the length of time available.

- When to hike? Date, time of day?

- What will be suitable clothing to wear; what equipment will be needed, if any; what food will be taken, if any?

- Are permissions needed, such as fire-building permits, permission to go on property, parent/guardian permissions?

- Review good hiking manners and techniques, and safety precautions to be taken.

- Shall we go rain or shine? Warm or cold?

2. The Hiking Program Should Have Variety and Progression. Nobody, without prior conditioning, can enjoy a 50-mile hike! The program should provide for progressive experiences for the participants to gain skill, stamina, and endurance. Hikes should be short and on fairly easy terrain at first so that a good pace can be kept, and when the end is reached, the group still would like to do a little more. Gradually the length and difficulty of terrain should increase. In such progressions, the hikers can learn what they need to know to be safe and comfortable, such as what clothing to wear for specific conditions; how to change pace and plan rest intervals for effective use of energy; what types of equipment and foods are best; and how to plan times and routes. This is also the time to break in new hiking shoes or boots.

While the length of the hike and type of terrain do provide for hiking variety, variety should be part of the objectives of the hike. There are map and compass hikes (see in this chapter Section H: Navigating in the Outdoors), evening hikes, nature hikes to points of natural interest, winter hikes, water hikes where a stream or brook is followed, historical and community hikes that visit a specific place of interest in the community, rain hikes, etc. Hiking can be done also on established cross-country trails provided by hostels, Rails-to-Trails Conservancy, or other groups; in parks and forests; etc.

3. Proper Hiking Techniques Add to the Enjoyment. Take care of your feet. Hikers are no better than their feet! Get your feet in condition by daily walks and progressively longer conditioning hikes. Toenails should be trimmed straight across to prevent corners from cutting into the skin. Shoes should be well broken in. They should fit properly with ample room for the toes and snugly in the arch and heel, providing support and preventing friction.

Socks should *fit well* (they should be snug, but not too tight to be constricting) and have no holes where they will irritate the skin. If your feet get cold easily, use wool socks, which have the best insulating ability, but still wicks sweat away from the feet effectively. Choose soft wool with finer fibers over regular wool. If your feet tend to sweat, a synthetic sock may be better. They are faster at wicking away sweat. Powder helps keep the feet dry, thus adding to comfort. Immediately attend to a spot tender from rubbing. If the skin has not broken, place athletic tape over tender areas; if it has already blistered, wash thoroughly and cover with clean bandage and with athletic tape. Put on clean socks and change footwear if possible.

4. Comfortable Clothing Is Essential. Wear comfortable clothing. Like many other things, clothing has gone high tech. There are many synthetic materials specifically developed for keeping warm or cool and dry. However, you still can get along well with regular clothing if you select the right items. Remember John Muir hiked from Louisville to Florida with a sackful of stale bread and tea in 1867 and no high-tech equipment. For open-county hiking in warm weather, short-sleeved shirts and shorts are suitable; but for cross-country hiking in the woods and in areas with tall grasses or brush, a long-sleeved shirt and long pants are best. Wearing apparel should have a hard finish so that burrs and other natural objects will not easily stick to the fabric. Many people recommend a hat of some type, particularly if hiking in the sun or rain. If the weather is apt to get cool, take a sweater. If worn under the shirt, it will provide more warmth because the air spaces of the loose weave serve as an insulator. For very cold weather, do not hesitate to wear long underwear. Also, in cool weather, several layers of lighter clothing are warmer than one or two heavy pieces of clothing because of the air-space insulation. This also provides the option of shedding layers if you get too hot. If there is any chance of rain at all, take a poncho or raincoat. Don't forget *mittens* if it is cold; they are warmer than gloves. Pants and shirts *must not* restrict movement, which is tiring and can cause rubbing and skin irritation.

5. Carry Only Equipment that Is Absolutely Necessary. When hiking, your *hands should be free.* Carry some things in your pockets, but do not make them bulge or have pointed objects that will make you uncomfortable when hiking. Carrying a small backpack is preferable if your load is not too large. If you are going on a longer trip, you should have a good backpack with an external or internal frame.

Some standard equipment for your hike: matches in waterproof container or matches waterproofed with fingernail polish or wax; roll of athletic tape; knife; handkerchief; toilet paper; first-aid kit; water purification tablets or canteen/plastic bottles of water (if water is unavailable along the way); insect repellent (if insects are likely to be a problem); flashlight (if hike lasts past dusk). Other specialized equipment needed, such as cooking equipment, map and compass, GPS receiver, etc., depend on the nature of the hike.

6. An Army Travels on its Stomach and So Does the Hiker. Don't forget the *food!* Of course, the amount and type depends upon the length and objective of your hike. Sometimes you will want a cold meal prepared beforehand and at other times a hot one, or a cold meal with a warm drink. Here are some tips for good trail meals. Wrap each food item separately. Pack heavy things in the bottom of the sack. Avoid salty, very sweet, easily smashed, and messy foods. Often it is better to take "fixings" for sandwiches and beverages than to prepare beforehand. Sandwiches, especially, will not then be soggy or misshapen. If sandwiches are made before starting, butter the inside of both slices of bread to keep bread from becoming soggy. Foods that quench the thirst such as raw vegetables (carrots, celery) and apples are excellent.

A trail lunch or snack high in food value and quick energy (sometimes called "birdseed") can be made by mixing sugar-coated cereal, M&M's, unsalted peanuts, and raisins. For a group of six or seven, mix about 4 oz. of cereal, one-6 oz. package of candy, 8 oz. of Spanish peanuts, six 1-½ oz. packages of raisins. Mix and carry in a plastic bag and eat by the handful. Other food suggestions are in the sources cited.

7. Learn to Walk Correctly. Keep your head up and look ahead 12 to 20 feet down the path. When possible, use your eyes to look down, not your head. Keep your spine straight and avoid "sway back" in the lower back. Swing your arms naturally. Keeping your arms extended for long periods of time may lead to tingling and numbness. To avoid this, swing your arms in a bent position some of the time. This position does burn more calories, so for endurance, hikes use this method sparingly. For especially steep slopes, a sideway position tends to give better foot placement and provides more support and balance. A rhythmic and steady pace should be established.

8. Set an Appropriate Pace. While speed is governed by the slowest hiker, how fast you can go will be determined by terrain. A mile can be covered on a flat surface in 12 to 15 minutes at a steady, even pace. If you are climbing steep terrain, this will be reduced considerably. A 2 to 3 minute rest stop every half hour works better than long rest stops less frequently; however longer rest stops of 10 to 15 minutes should be allowed for approximately each two hours of hiking. It is best to use your natural stride; trying to alter your stride may be harmful to your back. Hip flexibility is what governs speed and quicker steps are more efficient than trying to unnaturally lengthen your stride.

The longest-legged hikers should *not* be placed in front of the group for they will "run away" at too fast a pace. Likewise, if the group is strung out (preferably, keep together with leaders both in front and in back of the group), too frequently those in front rest until the stragglers have caught up, then start out again—and the ones who really needed the rest didn't get any!

9. Hikers Should Observe Good Outdoor Manners and Environmental Practices.
Good outdoor manners mean courtesy on the road or trail. When hiking on a road,

keep as far left as possible, facing oncoming traffic. Bright orange vests should be worn, with reflecting strips at night. It is best, however, *not* to follow roads wherever possible. Get permission ahead of time to cross private property; respect the right of ownership. Watch your fires; do not let them get too large or out of control, practice good conservation principles; do *not* pick flowers or other growing things. Do not litter along the way—pack it in, pack it out! One should be conscious of the impact of hiking on the environment. Look at how deep the trails are worn; how switch-backs and shortcuts can cause deep erosion. Check to see if roots of trees are uncovered or there are gullies caused by rushing water. Observe the trail edges particularly. If you do go off the trail, beware of trampling fragile ecosystems. The Leave No Trace Center for Outdoor Ethics provides information on good outdoor practices. http://www.lnt.org/ (See introductory material in Chapter 4 for Environmentally Responsible Use of the Outdoors.)

JUDY BROOKHISER, GREAT SMOKY MOUNTAINS NATIONAL PARK, TN

HOSTELLING AND HIKING CLUBS

Although many people form their own outing clubs, a good number prefer to organize under a national organization. Hostelling International-USA serves groups throughout the country through 34 local councils. A network of hostels throughout the world provides economical lodging in locations from big cities to some of the most remote locations.

The American Volksmarch Association sponsors clubs in all 50 states. A Volksmarch is a noncompetitive 6-mile (10 kilometer) walk along a prescribed trail designed to encourage physical fitness, promote camaraderie, and enjoy nature. It is not a test of speed or endurance. Each participant is encouraged to walk at a pace that is comfortable and enjoyable. Volksmarch is a German word that means "a people's walk." Local clubs host walks chosen for natural beauty, scenic interest, historical value, and safety. The trails are well marked or maps are provided. Trails may be in cities, towns, parks, forests, or anywhere there is a pleasant or interesting area to walk.

BACKPACKING

Backpacking is one of the most popular adventure sports. Essentially it is a hike where equipment and supplies are carried in a pack on your back. As with hikes, backpacking can be done locally or in backcountry areas. It can be short in duration such as an 8 to 10-mile loop hike or it can last for weeks. The pointers for hikes apply to backpacking. Backpacking also involves selecting the right backpack for the intended purpose, selecting the best things to pack to meet your needs without excessive weight, packing everything you need for your hike so that the load is balanced correctly, and wearing the backpack so that you can hike most efficiently. There are excellent resources at the end of this section that will provide the details on all of this information. Outdoor equipment stores can also be extremely helpful when planning for a trip. They are often staffed by experienced backpackers.

 ## Books on Hiking and Backpacking

See master publicatons list for cities of Publishers.

Conners, Tim, and Christine Conners. (2000). *Lipsmackin' Backpackin': Lightweight, Trail-Tested Recipes for Backcountry Trips.* Falcon Publishing Company.

Curtis, Rick. (1998). *The Backpacker's Field Manual: A Comprehensive Guide to Mastering Backcountry Skills,* Three Rivers Press. A carry-along field guide covering trip planning, equipment, cooking, nutrition, first aid, navigation, wilderness travel, safety and weather.

Fletcher, Colin and Chip Rawlins. (2002). *The New Complete Walker IV,* Alfred A. Knopf: NY. Once called the "Hiker's Bible," the first edition was one of the earliest popular backpacking books. Contains all the basic information and lots of resources and details. An added bonus is the author's philosophy of the out of doors and hiking. At nearly 850 pages, not a carry-along book.

Hampton, Bruce, and David Cole. (1995), *Soft Paths,* revised edition. Stackpole Books: Mechanicsburg, PA. National Outdoor Leadership School (NOLS) publication and used by Leave-No-Trace organization.

Harvey, Mark. (1999). *The National Outdoor Leadership School's Wilderness Guide.* Fireside, NY. In addition to all the basics about equipment, skills and camping techniques, it includes a considerable amount about group dynamics and human behavior in the outdoors.

Hart, John. (1998). *Walking Softly in the Wilderness: The Sierra Club Guide to Backpacking,* 3rd edition. Sierra Club Books: San Francisco.

Jardine, Ray. (1999). Beyond Backpacking: Guide to Lightweight Hiking, 3rd edition. Adventure Lore.

Kestenbaum, Ryel. (2001). *The Ultralight Backpacker: The Complete Guide to Simplicity and Comfort on the Trail.* International Marine/Ragged Mountain Press.

Lanza, Michael. (2003). *Winter Hiking & Camping: Managing Cold for Comfort and Safety.* Mountaineers Books: Seattle, WA. Includes techniques for winter backcountry travel, hiking, snowshoeing, and easy ski touring; navigation in ice and snow, gear, camping comfortably; keeping clothes and gear dry; and winter cooking techniques.

Manning, Harvey. (1986). *Backpacking One Step at a Time,* 4th edition. Random House: NY.

Randall, Glen. (1999). *The Outward Bound Backpacker's Handbook.* Lyons Press. Includes chapters on basic equipment—boots, tents, packs, clothing, stoves; cooking, safety and emergency procedures, winter camping, camping with children, and low impact practices. Small enough to carry along.

Townsend, Chris. (1997). *The Backpacker's Handbook,* 2nd edition. International Marine/Ragged Mountain Press. Heavier book, not necessarily for carrying along. Includes complete range of information from preparing, planning and executing trips with low impact. Also includes a chapter on backpacking abroad.

VanLear, Denise. (1982). *The Best about Backpacking.* Sierra Club, Random House Trade Paperbacks.

Internet Sites on Backpacking/Hiking

Suggested search words: backpacking/backcountry/hiking/hostels/hostelling.

American Hiking Society: http://www.americanhiking.org/

American Volksmark Association: http://www.ava.org/

Appalachian Trail Conference: http://www.appalachiantrail.org/

Backpacker Magazine: http://www.backpacker.com/ (9 issues a year). 33 East Minor St., Emmaus, PA 18098; (610) 967-8296

Hiking & Walking Homepage: http://www.webwalking.com/hiking.html

Hostelling International USA: , http://www.hiayh.org/ . 8401 Colesville Road, Suite 600, Silver Spring, MD 20910, 301-495-1240

Hostels.com: http://www.hostels.com/

Lightweight Backpacker: http://www.backpacking.net/

National Outdoor Leadership School (NOLS): http://www.nols.edu/

Rails-to-Trails Conservancy. http://www.railtrails.org/. Includes a trail finder.

Thebackpacker.com: http://www.thebackpacker.com/

Wildernet: Guide to Outdoor Recreation. http://www.wildernet.com/

SECTION H
NAVIGATING IN THE OUTDOORS

Most everyone who enjoys going cross-country in the outdoors likes to use different navigation techniques for traversing the countryside. Whether it be a map and sighted landmarks, a compass, or a global positioning system (GPS), there are a variety of methods from which to choose. To prepare for such navigation, there are many simple training games for the beginner, and as skills are developed, even the most experienced outdoors person can find continuing challenges.

Many activities can be carried on not only with the combined map and compass but also with map and compass separately. Although GPS systems can be used alone, they are most effectively used in the wilderness with maps. These activities are suitable for young boys and girls as well as older youth whether they are in camp, on the playground, or part of a club or troop program. There are many instructional materials available. (See resources at the end of this section.)

MAPS

Although most everyone has used a road map to find destinations, and many backwoods sports enthusiasts have used maps while hunting and fishing, not as many people are familiar with the sport of orienteering, long popular in certain parts of Europe. Orienteering is a form of land navigation that uses a map and compass. It can be enjoyed as a walk in the woods or as a competition. There are competitions for all ages and degrees of fitness and skill. The object of the sport of orienteering is to find the fastest route through a wooded area, checking in at control points in a set order. The courses may be as long as 6 miles (10 km). It is designed for rugged, adventurous persons and demands accuracy, intelligence, and stamina.

Three basic types of maps and map-reading skills can be used in activities related to orienteering: (1) learning to read and to use the common road map (for younger beginners), (2) making and using a sketch map, and (3) using topographical maps to travel through an undeveloped area on a hike or scavenger hunt. Topographical maps are divided into specific quadrangles and are available from many outdoor supply stores and can be downloaded from the Internet. At the U.S. Geological Service website, you can find maps through an interactive search process. Maps can also be obtained from a number of commercial websites and from many outdoor supply stores. (See Internet sites at the end of this section.)

COMPASS

The compass is an invention that doesn't often receive the credit it deserves for revolutionizing exploration by sea, resulting in expediting the discovery of continents. The Chinese were the first to invent a compass in the 200s B.C.; when fortunetellers used lodestones (a mineral made of iron oxide that aligned itself in a north-south direction) to make fortune Telling boards.

The orienteering compass is designed for easy use by youngsters and for convenience in direction finding with topographic maps. The compass housing revolves on a transparent base plate that acts as both a protractor and direction finder. It, like other compasses, comes in different models—air-filled, induction-dampened, and liquid-filled. However, the inexpensive air-filled Silva Compass has proved to be completely satisfactory for beginners in orienteering. It also will take many hard knocks.

Check the resources at the end of this section for instructions on how to use the compass, as well as games and other activities. Map and compass games are included in Chapter 3, Section A: Map and Compass Games. In addition, the compass treasure hunt and the compass trail to a cookout or other site are excellent activities. In both of these activities, one group of participants (or the leaders) lay a compass trail to the treasure or site by taking a series of degree readings and distances between items and the remainder of the group tries to follow the trail, using the directions supplied, to the proper location. This makes a treasure hunt much more fun and the cookout will seem much more like being out in the woods.

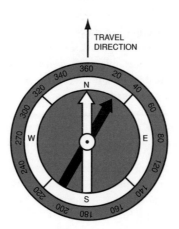

MAP AND COMPASS COMBINED (ORIENTEERING)

Four types of orienteering activities are provided for using map and compass together. They are: (1) the orienteering hike, (2) project orienteering, (3) orienteering races, and (4) wilderness orienteering.

ACTIVITIES

The Orienteering Hike. The orienteering hike involves traveling cross-country using a map and compass. Choose your starting point on the map either where you are or where you can easily get to; then, select one or more points to which you want to hike. Now, using your map, determine the route you would like to take, get your distances and compass reading. And don't forget to plan the return route unless you plan to have someone pick you up at the other end.

The orienteering hike can be done in pairs or in small groups. It is better to have small numbers such as 2 to 3 people with at least one compass for each two participants. As always use appropriate progression according to skill levels. Beginners will have an easy course and as their skills improve move up to continually challenging hikes. The length of the hike also can be adjusted to the skill levels and may range from an hour to all day.

Project Orienteering. In project orienteering, a prelaid route is used with stations designated en route. As each station is reached, there are directions to do a "project," hence the name project orienteering. The project may be as simple as collecting 10 different leaves, or it may be to boil water, chop wood, or decipher a Morse code. A judge is usually at each station to score the quality of the project done. Route and stations are indicated on the map by the participant as part of the total project.

Orienteering Races. Orienteering as a sport involves racing through a predetermined course. This sport has been popular in Europe for some time. Rules, directions for course setup, and videos are available from books and websites. (See resources at the end of this section.) In an orienteering race, participants run, walk, ski, or mountain bike to a series of points shown on the map. They must choose routes, on and off trail, that will enable them to find all points and get back to the finish line in the shortest possible time. Points on the course are marked with orange and white flags and punches are available so that they can prove they have been at each control marker. Each control marker is located on a distinct feature such as the top of a knoll or a stream junction. The person, who completes the course in the shortest amount of time having checked into each control point, wins the race.

Wilderness Orienteering Ambitious outdoors enthusiasts will eventually use orienteering skills for traveling in unknown wilderness areas as they explore, camp, hunt, and fish. Such adventures must not be undertaken by beginners in orienteering, although the principles of going from map to field are the same as in known territory. They must also have adequate camping skills.

There are also some activities related to orienteering that are both fun and educational and may prove useful in outdoor adventures and camping. These activities are measurements—measure heights, depths, distances, and volume. In orienteering you will have learned your own pace and you may wish to know other personal measurements, too. Some measurements you might like to take without use of traditional measuring instruments are depth of water by soundings, deflection caused by water, locating a spot on a lake for fishing, distance across a river, height of cliffs and trees, age of trees, number of board feet in trees, estimating an acre, or determining a half-mile. Methods of estimating these measurements are available in books and on websites listed at the end of this section.

GLOBAL POSITIONING SYSTEM (GPS)

Although the Global Positioning System (GPS) has been around for some time, it was only in the late 1990s that it became available to the general public when GPS receivers became small enough to carry on a hike and affordable to the average citizen. It can be found as a stand-alone device or in cars, watches, and packaged with a multitude of other electronic devices. GPS was developed by the U.S. Defense Department (DOD) and is a system of over 20 satellites orbiting 12,000 miles above the earth. It has been the government policy to make the system available to all users without charge. In the beginning, the DOD, to protect against perceived enemies, degraded the accuracy of the signal limiting maximum location accuracy available to the general public to approximately 300 feet. After May 1, 2000, when the DOD stopped degrading the signal, the accuracy improved to approximately 50 feet. This is when the use of these devices increased dramatically.

The GPS receiver is a sensitive microwave radio receiver combined with a computer. They are very fast and have a high degree of accuracy. When it is turned on and you have an adequate view of the sky, the receiver will display your location in latitude and longitude and you can find that location on your map. Many receivers have extra features that also display things like sunrise and sunset data, moon phases, and sun azimuth/elevation.

Here Are Some of the Things the GPS Receiver Can Tell You.

- Your exact location to within 50 feet (depending on the quality of your receiver)
- The direction and distance to your next destination. By entering the coordinates of your destination, the receiver can tell you the distance and the compass bearing to travel to your next destination.
- Calculate direction and rate of travel and provide estimated time of arrival
- GPA systems can track and log actual route, limited only by the amount of memory in the receiver. This track logging can also allow backtracking. Over 100 waypoints (landmarks) can be stored in most receivers and most devices can be connected to computers to download data.

What GPS Can Do that the Compass Cannot Do. You can take a bearing with a compass only if you can see landmarks and take sightings on them. A GPS receiver can tell you your exact location without any landmarks and provide bearings to travel to any coordinates that you enter. This is particularly useful in "white out" conditions or in landscapes where there are no landmarks.

BRYCE HUNT, GIRL SCOUTS OF LIMBERLOST COUNCIL, FORT WAYNE, IN

Using GPS with the Compass. At current levels of technology available for civilian use, GPS system use must be accompanied by the use of map and compass for effective navigation in the backcountry. As with most technology, GPS receivers have gotten smaller, more compact, and often more powerful. Much of the weight is in the batteries. The receiver is unaffected by clouds, snowstorms, darkness, or other low visibility circumstances. However, they must have a clear view of the sky and that could be a problem in some forested or mountainous locations. On rare occasions, the receiver may not be able to locate a satellite signal. The receiver operates on batteries that must be charged. Because the receiver needs to be on for only a few minutes each hour, a receiver with a four-hour battery life could last four days in the backcountry. The receiver is an intricate device that can fail or be broken. GPS must be used with map and compass to plot location. Some receivers have moving maps, but currently, the level of detail is not sufficient to provide information without a map. It is not as accurate as advanced altimeters that can determine altitude within 30 feet.

For trail hiking, it is not practical within the limits of current technology to keep the receiver on and track the route as traveling. The variability of the path will cause the receiver to lose its lock. Therefore, it is best to stop and take readings at rest points and cross check with the map and compass. To avoid obstacles when hiking with the map and compass, the hiker must select a series of landmarks in a roughly three-sided square around the place to be avoided. The GPS receiver tells you the direction and distance to your next landmark regardless of how far you have strayed off the path. Route reversal features make backtracking easy. GPS navigation is particularly useful in desert landscape where there are few or no landmarks for the hiker with a compass alone.

Like all technology, GPS systems are fast evolving. GPS systems in the backcountry at the beginning of the 21st century must be used with map and compass. These systems have improved the capability of cross-country exploration, relocating favorite remote spots, plotting trails for hiking and bicycling, and many other activities.

Resources for Navigating in the Outdoors

See master publicatons list for cities of Publishers.

Burns, Bob, Mike Burns, and Paul Hughes. (1999). *Wilderness Navigation: Finding Your Way Using Map, Compass, Altimeter, & GPS.* Mountaineers Books. Good basic book with enough detail on tools of navigation to get started.

Disley, John. (1979). *Orienteering.* Stackpole: Mechanicsburg, PA.

Grubbs, Bruce. (1999). Using GPS: GPS Simplified for Outdoor Adventures. Falcon: Helena, MT. Small, carry-along guide book.

Jacobson, Cliff. (1999). *Map and Compass: Basic Essentials,* 2nd edition. Globe Pequot: Guilford, CT. A carry-along guide with basic information with up-to-date information about the changes in agencies related to navigation, maps, etc.

Kals, W.S. (1983). *Land Navigation Handbook.* Sierra Club Books: San Francisco. Excellent carry-along guide book.

Kjellström, Björn. (1994). *Be Expert with Map and Compass.* John Wiley & Sons. A classic author in this field; has published five editions of this book since 1955.

Legbert, Robert and Joseph King. (2003). *The GPA Handbook: A Guide for the Outdoors.* Burford Books: Short Hills, NJ. Guide to selection and use of GPS receivers. Includes information on how GPS works, choosing and using equipment, linking to laptops, cell phones and PDAs, coordinating with maps, software options, etc.

Letham, Lawrence. (2001). *GPA Made Easy: Using Global Positioning Systems in the Outdoors,* 3rd edition. Mountaineer Books: Seattle, WA. Clear language and illustrations aimed at general users. Includes practical examples and use with maps in rough terrain. For beginners to advanced users.

Peters, Jack. (2003). *GPS Navigation Guide: Your Complete Resource for Outback Navigation.* GPA Navigator Magazine.com: Eugene, OR. Covers using GPS with map, compass, computer and radio tracking. Includes a Topo Companion(tm) map ruler.

Randall, Glenn. (1998). *The Outward Bound Map & Compass Handbook,* revised edition. Lyons Press. Includes using GPS receivers. Another good carry-along guidebook.

Ratliff, Donald E. (1993). *Map, Compass, and Campfire.* Binfords and Mort, Publishers: Portland, OR.

Silva, Inc., now a division of Johnson Outdoors, Inc., has a service unit Orienteering Services, USA, P. O. Box 1604, Binghamton, N.Y. 13902 (800-345-7622). It has many instructional materials, including reference textbooks, teaching outlines, instructional pamphlets, workbooks; videos; training aids and kits; meet accessories, map and compass games; and orienteering area layout and course markers. Will aid in workshops and clinics. Johnson has expanded and includes canoe companies (Old Town is one), boat motor companies, diving supply companies, Eureka tents, Camp Trails, and Silva.

 ## Internet Sites on Navigating in the Outdoors

Suggested search words: orienteering/map and compass/backcountry navigation/topographic maps

U.S. Orienteering Federation: http://www.us.orienteering.org/

The Fascinating World of Maps & Mapping: http://oddens.geog.uu.nl/index.html

International Orienteering Federation: http://www.orienteering.org/

Kjetil Kjernsmo's illustrated guide on how to use the compass. http://www.learn-orienteering.org/old/ A tutorial intended for individuals and non-profit organizations, and may be printed out and used free of charge as long as his name is on it.

MapLink. Map supplier. http://www.maplink.com/

Maptech. Supplies computer software for maps, handheld GPS systems. http://maptech.com/

Maps & Geography (a National Geographic site): http://www.nationalgeographic.com/resources/ngo/maps/

Online Orienteering. http://www.online-orienteering.net/

O-zine, the International Orienteering Federation electronic newsletter: http://www.orienteering.org/headline.htm

Silva Compass. (video).By Map and Compass. Orienteering Services (See Silva. Excellent instructional color film (27 min.) giving basic fundamentals of map and compass use. Suitable for showing to youngsters as well as adults. http://www.silvacompass.com/

US Geological Survey. http://geography.usgs.gov/ Find and purchase maps.

SECTION I
ROCK CLIMBING

Mountain climbing has been a challenging activity for all who go to or live in the mountains. The grandeur of the peaks dares people to ascend. Most mountain peaks can be reached through routes that will test a person's physical condition, stamina, and the will to conquer, but are relatively safe and not too difficult. There always is that rock, though, or that sheer face of the peak, that dares that skills be tested. It dares the adventurer to try to climb it, to take the risk involved, both in conquering a challenging task and testing courage, for it is difficult for a person to admit defeat in the face of danger.

CHELEY COLORADO CAMPS, CHELEY, CO.

However, to have fun one does not have to scale high and rugged peaks. The techniques of rock climbing can be learned on small cliffs, indoor rock walls, and even structures that present a wall to be negotiated up and down with ropes; then, short weekend trips can be taken to mountains of modest height. Rock climbing is another outing sport that grew rapidly in the early 1970s and gained a large following as is demonstrated by the number of stores that specialize in handling the necessary equipment.

SAFETY

While rock climbing and descending appear frightening to the novice or observer, they really can be quite safe if done properly. The best procedure for beginners is to go in small groups with a trained leader. A person seriously interested in climbing extensively should attend a course that provides accreditation upon having attained certain levels of performance.

EQUIPMENT

Technological advances have made significant improvements to rock climbing equipment, clothing, shoes, and various supplies. Recommendations concerning ropes, slings, pitons, and wedges can be obtained from the books at the end of this section and from reliable stores. Seasoned rock climbers take pride in and care of their equipment. They depend on their ropes to save their lives and so do not lend them to others indiscriminately.

Before people interested in rock climbing purchase equipment, it is advisable to go climbing with experienced people where they will be introduced to a variety of ropes and other climbing equipment. Then they can purchase what best suits their own needs and interests.

Books on Rock Climbing

See master publicatons list for cities of Publishers.

Creasey, Malcomb. (2001). *Complete Guide to Rock Climbing* (Practical Guide). Lorenz Books.

Cox, Stephen and Kris Fulsaas (editors) and Hanson, Kurt (editor). (2003). *Mountaineering: The Freedom of the Hills,* 7th edition. Mountaineers Books. First published in 1960 and often considered the classic mountaineering text.

Horst, Eric J. (2002). *Training for Climbing: The Definitive Guide to Improving Your Climbing Performance,* 2nd edition. Falcon Publishing Company.

Mendenhall, Ruth and John Mendenhall. (1983). *The Challenge of Rock and Mountain Climbing,* 3rd edition. Stackpole Books, Mechanicsburg, PA.

Raleigh, Duane. (2003). *Knots & Ropes for Climbers.* Stackpole Books: Mechanicsburg, PA.

Twight, Mark F. and James Martin. (1999). *Extreme Alpinism: Climbing Light, Fast & High.* Mountaineers Books.

Internet Sites on Rock Climbing

Suggested search words: mountaineering/climbing/rock climbing

American Alpine Club: http://www.americanalpineclub.org/ The American Alpine Club was founded in 1902 and is the leading national organization in the United States devoted to mountaineering, climbing, and the multitude of issues facing climbers.

American Mountain Guide Association: http://www.amga.com/ A nonprofit organization that seeks to represent the interests of American mountain guides by providing support, education, and standards.

American Safe Climbing Association: http://www.safeclimbing.org/index.htm Their mission is to replace deteriorating anchors on classic climbs in the U.S. and educate climbers and the public about climbing safety.

Climbing magazine online: http://www.climbing.com/

Mountain Zone.com: http://www.mountainzone.com/

SECTION J
CROSS-COUNTRY SKIING AND SNOWSHOEING

CROSS-COUNTRY SKIING

Skiing has grown to an increasingly popular activity both downhill (Alpine) and cross country (Nordic). Downhill skiing can involve a considerable investment in time to master the skills, equipment, traveling to ski sites, and purchasing lift tickets. On the other hand, cross-country skiing and snowshoeing have very short learning curves and can take you to places deep in the woods and wilderness where you can enjoy nature and serenity. The equipment is not as elaborate or as expensive. Many people live within walking distance of areas that are suitable for cross-country skiing and snowshoeing. Further, cross-country skiing includes a wide range of participation levels from casual recreation to racing and Olympic competition. It is an excellent special event for a club group.

It is one of the healthiest activities available, and using every major muscle group, it is an excellent aerobic activity that is nonjarring and easy on the joints. Cross-country skiing is one of the most efficient aerobic activities available. The Professional Ski Instructors of America certifies instructors in three levels for both track and down-hill Nordic skiing.

SNOWSHOEING

Although there is overlap, most snowshoes fall into one of three categories: mountaineering, recreational, or sport. Mountaineering snowshoes, also called backcountry or backpacking snowshoes, are for use in demanding terrains including ice and steep slopes where durability, maneuverability, and good traction are necessary. Recreational snowshoes, also called walking or hiking snowshoes, are scaled-down models of mountaineering shoes. Sports snowshoes, also called running, racing, or cross-training shoes, are designed for moving as quickly as possible across the snow and ice.

Many adventure activity sport shops rent cross-country skis with shoes and snowshoes at reasonable rates and will conduct clinics for beginners to learn elementary techniques and care of equipment. Attendance at such a clinic is highly recommended.

Cross-country skiing and snowshoeing provide an exciting outdoor activity, good physical exercise, and a unique method of travel that can take you to many places otherwise not accessible. Cross-country skiing and snowshoeing combine beautifully with outings, picnics, and trips.

Books on Cross-Country Skiing and Snowshoeing

See master publicatons list for cities of Publishers.

Brown, Nat, and Natalie Brown-Gutnik. (1999). *The Complete Guide to Cross-Country Ski Preparation.* Mountaineers Books.

Cazeneuve, Brian. (1995). *Cross-Country Skiing: A Complete Guide.* W.W. Norton & Company.

Griffin, Steven A. (1998). *Snowshoeing.* Stackpole. Includes how-to techniques and practical information on care and repair of equipment, also information on competitive snowshoeing.

Moynier, John. (2001). *Basic Essentials: Cross-Country Skiing.* Adobe e-book, downloadable 4538K. Globe Pequot Press.

Older, Jules. (1998). *Cross-Country Skiing for Everyone.* Stackpole Books.

Prater, Gene, Felkey, Dave, Felkey (2002). *Snowshoeing: From Novice to Master,* 5th edition. (Outdoor Expert). Mountaineer Books. Described as "classic how-to manual" with information on equipment and all types of terrain and snow conditions.

Petersen, Paul, Lovett, Richard A (1999). *The Essential Cross-Country Skier.* International Marine/Ragged Mountain Press.

Zwosta, Marianne. (1997). *The Essential Snowshoer:* A Step-by-Step Guide, McGraw-Hill.

(See also Chapter 8, Section B: Winter Activities.)

Internet Sites on Cross-Country Skiing and Snowshoeing

Suggested search words: cross-country skiing/backcountry skiing/Nordic skiing/snowshoeing/wilderness travel

American Cross-Country Skiers: http://www.xcskiworld.com/ Founded in 1998, the AXCS serves U.S. Master (age 25 and older) cross country skiers with a wide range of education, promotion and communication programs.

Cross Country Ski Areas Association: http://www.xcski.org/ (cross country and snowshoeing information.

Cross Country Skier. http://www.crosscountryskier.com/ The journal of Nordic skiing.

The Winter Backpacker (covers snowshoeing): http://www.backpacking.net/winter.html (Part of the Lightweight Backpacker site)

Trailsource Cross-Country Skiing. http://www.trailsource.com/ skiing/index.asp Find cross country skiing locations.

Cross-Country Skiing Online. http://www.cross-countryski.com/ Has lists of clubs in U.S. and Canada

S E C T I O N   K

SPELUNKING (CAVE EXPLORING)

Few adventure activities challenge a person's emotional and mental fortitude as does cave exploration. Crawling through complete darkness, extremely small crawl spaces, and cold water are enough to make all but the hardiest turn back. The sport of spelunking, however, is the type of activity that is so challenging and interesting that once people try it, most want to do it again. The National Speleological Society, a membership organization founded for the purpose of "advancing the study, conservation, exploration, and knowledge of caves," has more than 12,000 members in 200 grottos (groups of cavers) across the country. An excellent way to begin individually or with a group is to contact the grotto nearest you. These groups have extensive knowledge and experience and emphasize environmentally sound practices, plus they know the caves in your area.

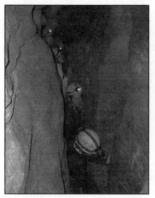

KELLY ROGERS, MURRAY STATE UNIVERSITY
FACULTY, MURRY, KY

LOCATING CAVES

The better caves for amateur spelunkers are found in limestone areas that have been unlocked by the glaciers. Some of the more frequently visited areas are western Iowa, southern Indiana, Kentucky, and Missouri. The geological story of the formation of caves, caverns, and interesting designs is a fascinating study of its own.

CAVE SAFETY

Caving can be a very dangerous sport and every year people get lost, are trapped by rising water, or are injured in an accident. Most of these misfortunes, however, are not the fault of the sport itself, but of carelessness on the part of the participants and leaders. Caving can be a safe, pleasant experience if you follow a few common sense rules. Here are some suggestions:

1. Go with experienced cavers until you become proficient in skill and judgment regarding cave environments.

2. Go in small groups—never alone—and go with an experienced leader and "tail." The minimum number recommended is four so that if injury does occur, one can stay with the injured and two go for help.

3. Have proper equipment—coveralls are highly recommended, hard hats, knee pads, three sources of light, canteen.

4. Novices should go only into small and uncomplicated caves.

5. Always tell someone where you are going and when you expect to return.

Because of the even temperatures in caves, there is no need to worry about outside temperature variations. There is no need to be concerned about rain, but because many caves have water flowing through them, they can be subject to flooding. The best way to obtain up-to-date information concerning conditions in the interior is to talk with people who have just come out of the cave or people you meet in a cave. So, if you are the type of person who thrills with the challenge of attempting to negotiate your body through a crawl space barely large enough to get through, with rocks scraping at the top as well as bottom in complete darkness, and two or three inches of cold water sending shivers up your spine, then you have available to you some of the most beautiful and mystifying sights and you will be justly rewarded.

Books on Spelunking (Caving)

See master publicatons list for cities of Publishers.

Aulenbach, Nancy. (2001). *Exploring Caves: Journeys into the Earth*. National Geographic.

McClurg, David R. (1998). *Adventure of Caving: A Beginner's Guide for Exploring Caves Softly and Safely.* D&J Press: Carlsbad, NM. For first-time cavers to experienced cavers. Information ranging from finding a club or experience group to rappelling and prusiking techniques.

Rea, Tom. (1992). *Caving Basics*. National Speleological Society. Covers what beginners need to know about exploring caves safely and responsibly. Includes some information on cave sciences—biology, geology, and archeology.

Taylor, Michael Ray. (2001). *Caves: Exploring Hidden Realms*. National Geographic.

Internet Sites on Spelunking/Caving

Suggested search words: caving/speleological/karsts

    Cave laws by state: http://www.metgrotto.com/resources/cavelaws.php

    National Cave Rescue Commission: http://www.caves.org/io/ncrc/ Serves as the National Speleological Society representative on issues of cave rescue, training, and operations. A volunteer group that trains and tracks cave rescue resources throughout the U.S.

    National Caves Association: http://cavern.com/ A nonprofit organization of publicly and privately owned caves and caverns developed for public visitation. Natural resource conservation is stressed, as well as visitor relations. Includes a member caves directory.

    National Speleological Society: http://www.caves.org/ 2813 Cave Avenue, Huntsville, AL 35810: A membership organization founded for the purpose of "advancing the study, conservation, exploration, and knowledge of caves."

    U.S. Geological Survey Library. http://library.usgs.gov/index.html The USGS began its library in 1879. It is now the largest library for earth sciences in the world. It includes four libraries that are open to the public. The catalog can be found on the Internet site and items can be requested on interlibrary loan through local libraries.

GENERAL RESOURCES

Selected resources have been provided following certain sections; however, the following list includes general nature resources. These resources have ideas and projects relating to all of the sections in this chapter.

Copies of most all of the books cited have been reviewed, as have all of the Internet sites recommended. Brief annotations are provided for some of the resources.

Some references that are older and out of print have been purposely included when they provide excellent information. Frequently these resources can be found in public/school libraries or on the Internet. County extension agents frequently have a variety of helpful resources including pamphlets, software, and booklets.

The resources and information available on the Internet is ever expanding. A few sites have been suggested and although we have tried to select sites from well-established organizations or agencies (public, private, and governmental) that are likely to remain over time, there are always changes. We have provided suggestions for search words that we have used with some success when looking for information about specific topics

Lists of ever-evolving, new materials can be found in periodicals and publication catalogs. Nature centers, conventions and workshops, and bookstores are also good places to check out the latest resources.

General Adventure Books

Frank, Laurie. (2001). *The Caring Classroom: Using adventure to Create Community in the Classroom and Beyond.* GOAL Consulting: Madison, WI. (Project Adventure) Includes detailed adaptations for children with disabilities.

Graham, John. (1997). *Outdoor Leadership: Technique, Common Sense, and Self-Confidence.* The Mountaineers: Seattle, WA. Focus on improving leadership skills in outdoors. Includes a chapter on women in leadership.

Ogilvie, Ken. (1993). *Leading and Managing Groups in the Outdoors.* National Association for Outdoor Education: United Kingdom. Focuses entirely on leadership skills.

Marshall, Ian. (2003). *Peak Experiences.* University of Virginia Press. Following Maslow's hierarchy of needs, covers physiological needs, safety needs, esteem needs, and self-actualization.

Panicucci, Jane. (2002). *Adventure Curriculum for Physical Education: Middle School.* Project. Adventure: Beverly, MA. Includes lesson plans.

Panicucci, Jane. (2003). *Adventure Curriculum for Physical Education: High School.* Project. Adventure: Beverly, MA. Includes lesson plans.

Priest, Simon, and Michael Gass. (1997). *Effective Leadership in Adventure Programming.* Human Kinetics: Champaign, IL. Covers philosophy, history, individual behavior and group dynamics, practical and organizational skills, instructional methods, facilitation, various leadership skills, and professional ethics

Internet Sites on General Adventure

Suggested search words: adventure sports/challenge sports/peak experiences

Adventure Sports Online: http://www.adventuresports.com/

Leave No Trace: http://www.lnt.org/

National Oceanic & Atmospheric Administration (NOA) weather forecasts: http://www.noaa.gov/

Outside Magazine online: http://outsidemag.com/index.html

Recreation.gov: http://www.recreation.gov/index.cfm

Tread Lightly: http://www.treadlightly.org/index.mv

United States Adventure Racing Association: http://www.usara.com/
Adventure racing can include shredding through tight single-track on a mountain bike or orienteering and hiking through a dense forest. Adventure racers may find themselves ripping down rapids in a canoe and then rappelling off a 100 foot rock face. The races can last a few hours or

several days and often cover 100 miles or more!

The Weather Channel: http://www.weather.com/ (look under activities or recreation for national parks and skiing areas)

Wildernet: http://www.wildernet.com/

  Internet Sites for Related Government Agencies

Excellent info and educational areas for all of these:

Bureau of Land Management: http://www.blm.gov/nhp/index.htm

National Park Service: http://www.nps.gov/

US Forest Service: http://www.fs.fed.us/

US Fish & Wildlife Service: http://www.fws.gov/

U.S. Geological Survey: http://www.usgs.gov/

PROGRAM THEMES

This chapter focuses on program "themes" with the integration of many types of nature-oriented activities directed toward a specific environment or setting. The themes are as follows: (1) nighttime activities, (2) winter activities, (3) campfire programs, (4) native americans, and (5) trail and related activities

SECTION A

NIGHTTIME ACTIVITIES

Nighttime is one of the most fascinating program themes and encompasses many aspects of nature. Too frequently nature-oriented night activities are not only neglected, but often omitted entirely, yet some of the finest hobbies and most captivating outdoor adventures take place at night. Take night walks, have stargazing parties, or visit an observatory during any season, especially in the winter.

This section covers the following topics: creatures of the night, sounds of the night, phototropism, lights in the night, celestial bodies, and campfires

CREATURES OF THE NIGHT

Many creatures hunt, eat, mate, and raise families during the night. Your evening is their morning! Who are the animal prowlers out at night in search of food? How do they see at night? What are the habitats of nocturnal animals? Have you observed a beaver noisily building its home at night? What about the habits of owls and bats?

SOUNDS OF THE NIGHT

Listen! Can you tell who's up? Many people are frightened of the night because of the eerie night sounds, sounds that are eerie because they are unknown. A part of your program could involve identifying the various sounds and then learning something about night creatures' activities and where they might be found. Take "sensory walks"—cover your flashlight with red cellophane so animals are not scared off by the light—or sit quietly (Seton Watching, see Chapter 6, Animal section) in different habitats such as alongside a pond or stream or in a meadowlike area (park/golf course). There are audio reproductions of night sounds that you can use to get ready to identify sounds on your night adventures. (See Resources.)

PHOTOTROPISM

Who's this at my window or light bulb? Light draws many insects—they cannot help themselves. (Moths to the flame.) This "pull" of the light is called *phototropism*. However, some insects are negatively phototropic; they skitter away from the light. What is a bug bulb and why doesn't it draw insects? The world of insects is indeed a fascinating one! (Also see Chapter 6: Section C, Insects.)

LIGHTS IN THE NIGHT

What makes a firefly light up in the night? What effects do city lights have on viewing the stars and planets at night?

CELESTIAL BODIES

What is a falling meteor or shooting star—what causes them to travel across the sky? Have you seen the Northern Lights (Aurora Borealis)? Why are they more brilliant at certain times of the year? What happens when there is an eclipse of the moon? Have you seen the moons of Jupiter, the rings of Saturn, or the craters of the moon? Through space exploration we have received phenomenal pictures from the surface of Mars, among the rings of Saturn, and out into the galaxies. Can you imagine these images as you look into the night sky?

Why are constellations different in the various seasons of the year? What is the Evening Star, and what is the Milky Way? Viewing and discussing these phenomena and objects are fascinating activities for your nighttime, nature-oriented program. (See Chapter 6: Section F, Astronomy.)

PLANTS THAT BLOOM AT NIGHT

Did you know that some plants bloom at night and close during the day? Which ones are they? Besides the absence of light, note the temperature change, as well as the change in moisture. What makes dew form on plants? (See Chapter 6: Section D, Plants.)

FELLOWSHIP AROUND THE CAMPFIRE

Whether you camp out all night or just have an evening campfire and then return home, the fellowship of the campfire can be a highlight in your nature-oriented program. Singing, storytelling, sharing experiences, and stargazing can all be included in the campfire program.

 Books on Nighttime Activities

See master publicatons list for cities of Publishers.

Brown, Vinson. (1982). *Reading the Outdoors at Night.* Stackpole Books: Mechanicsburg, PA. 1982. (out of print/limited availability)

Caduto, Michael J., and Joseph Bruchac (1994). *Keepers of the Night: Native American Stories and Nocturnal Activities for Children.* Fulcrum Publishing, 1994.

Hickman, Pamela. (1999). T*he Night Book: Exploring Nature after Dark with Activities, Experiments, and Information.* Kids Can Press:

Holt, La. (2003). *Stikky Night Skies* (Learn 6 constellations, 4 stars, a planet, a galaxy, and how to navigate at night- in one hour, guaranteed). Four Walls Eight Windows:

Jeunesse, Gallimard. (1998). *Night Creatures* (First Discovery Books). Cartwheel Books: (ages 4-8)

Lawlor, Elizabeth P. (1995). *Discover Nature at Sundown: Things to Know and Things to Do.* Stackpole:

Internet Sites on Nighttime Activities

Suggested search words: nature night/nighttime/nighttime activities

Nature by Night: http://www.inquiry.net/outdoor/night/nature.htm

Discover Nature at Night with Your Child. Florida Fish & Wildlife Conservation Commission site:
http://www.floridaconservation.org/viewing/withyourchild/night.htm

Naturalists Notes: Night Lights of the Forest:
http://wildwnc.org/natnotes/lights.html (wildwnc.org nature center website)

SECTION B
WINTER ACTIVITIES

Winter brings opportunity for additional program themes—whether you live in a snowy or cold environment or travel to these places. Do you take advantage of such opportunities, or do you close up your "outdoor shop" when winter comes and move almost entirely to indoor programs? If you stay indoors, you're missing the opportunity of a lifetime! Winter is a wonderful time to be outdoors and the nature-oriented program should take advantage of the stimulating possibilities.

Winter program activities include, but are not limited to: (1) snow and ice sports, (2) winter/snow camping, (3) snow games, (4) tracking, (5) snow sculpture and painting, (6) winter carnivals, (7) nature in winter, and (8) nature crafts and photography.

SNOW AND ICE SPORTS

Do not forget the many fine winter sports. (See Chapter 7.) Plan active cross-country skiing, skating, sledding, or tobogganing outings. Although sleighs are not as common as when they were used for transportation two generations ago, sleigh riding or equipping a hay wagon with runners and using it as a sleigh can be great fun, especially on a moonlit night. Hiking in the snow, ending with a picnic or barbecue—yes, even in winter—can be highlights among social activities when it's cold outside. End the evening with an enchanting winter campfire.

WINTER/SNOW CAMPING

Both day and resident camping can be done on weekends and during holidays, as well as trip camping. "Camp-ins," especially for the enjoyment of winter sports, frequently are held in resident camp facilities by families who camp together in the summer.

SNOW GAMES

Following are some games that can be played in the snow.

ACTIVITIES

Snow Angels. Most children like to make patterns in the snow. One of the most popular is snow angels. Lie down in the snow, preferably on a slope, with arms straight out. Now move arms toward the head to make angel wings and legs out to make the robe. Get up carefully and you will have an angel in the snow.

Fox and Geese. An old-time favorite. Tramp off in the snow a *large* circle in sort of "follow the leader" fashion, then make two paths across the center dividing the circle into four parts. If many play, the circle should be extra large and two concentric circles can be used with six cross paths. Tramp a "home" in the center about three feet in diameter. Players must remain in the paths to avoid tramping down all the snow. One person is "it"—the fox. The fox chases the others who are "geese." When the fox tags a goose, the goose becomes the fox and chases someone else. Players cannot be tagged when standing at "home." To speed up the game when larger numbers are playing, more foxes may be used.

Snow Snake. This is an old Native American game that called for highly skilled players and special "snakes" (sticks). Today children play a variation. They can make their own snakes by taking a branch 3 to 4 feet long, 1½ to 2 inches thick, peeling it, and then whittling it down to about 1 inch thick with an egg-shaped ball on one end for the snake's tail and some type of snake's head at the other end. An even stretch of snow is packed down well with a slight groove in which the snakes will travel. Hold the snake at the head end, with the ball end resting in the groove in the snow. With the forefinger on the end and the thumb and other fingers on either side of the stick, the player propels the snake down the groove in somewhat of a bowling motion. The snake that goes the farthest wins.

Many outdoor games can be modified for snow play—hide and seek, dodge ball, snow football, bombardment, capture the flag, or snowman target.

Winter Tracking. Tracks tell a story. Tracks lead to adventure. Tracking in the snow is a winter hobby many enjoy. Tracking involves not only following footprints, but also examining animal scat (waste) to see what animals are eating in the winter. (See Chapter 2: Nature Games.)

Snow Sculpture and Painting. Who hasn't made a snowman—but have you tried your hand at making other creatures? Snow sculpture is an old art that can be done on any day when the snow packs well. Simple packing of snow is the commonest type of snow sculpture by youngsters, but older youths and adults take great delight and pride in other methods of sculpturing—hacking and carving on a block of snow ice, working with snow slush using armatures to stabilize, etc. Snow sculpture house decorations and competitions are an important part of winter carnivals. Sculptures can be painted on a day when the snow has settled but is not too crusty.

Winter Carnivals and Celebrations. Around the winter holidays, special activities such as natural bird feeder Christmas trees and other activities related to Hanukah and Kwanza can use natural settings for meaningful celebrations. In summer you have the Fourth of July, in fall Halloween—what about winter? Why not have a gala winter carnival with a king and queen, snow sculpture, contests of all kinds, or the ice and snow sports?

Nature in Winter. We often think of the summer sky and stargazing, but actually the winter star show often is more brilliant than the summer one. The winter positions of constellations provide an interesting study in comparison to summer positions. (See Chapter 6: Section F, Astronomy.)

Nature Crafts and Photography. Crafts are not omitted in winter—have you made winter decorations and bouquets from natural materials you have collected in the winter woods and fields? Because most plants are dormant, there usually is not the danger of harming the environment that may be associated with collecting living plants. (See Chapter 2: Nature Games) The study of snowflakes is a fascinating endeavor. Of the billions of snowflakes, no two are alike. Their only similarity is the six-sided pattern shared by all. In summer, everyone seems to have a camera, but winter photography offers new challenges and opportunities. Black and white photography can produce stunning results in winter settings. (See Chapter 6: Section I, Nature Photography.)

CHELEY COLORADO CAMPS, CHELEY, CO.

 Books on Winter Activities

See master publicatons list for cities of Publishers.

    Albert, Toni. (1998). *A Kid's Winter EcoJournal: With Nature Activities for Exploring the Season.* Trickle Creek Books, Mechanicsburg, PA. Provides writing pages where kids can keep a journal or write expressively. Includes short stories about nature and is chock-full of activities for kids in winter.

Drabik, Harry. (1985). *The Spirit of Winter Camping.* Nodin Press: Minneapolis.

Gorman, Stephen. (1991). *AMC Guide to Winter Camping: Wilderness Travel & Adventure in the Cold-Weather Months.* Appalachian Mountain Club. Used by some outdoor education classes. Covers essentials for staying warm and safe in cold weather. Includes information on backcountry skiing and snowshoeing.

Heinrich, Bernd. (2003). *Winter World: The Ingenuity of Animal Survival.* Ecco, 2003.

Lanza, Michael, and Brad Adler. (2003). *Winter Hiking & Camping: Managing Cold for Comfort & Safety (Backpacker).* Mountaineers Books.

Lawlor, Elizabeth P. (1998). *Discover Nature in Winter: Things to Know and Things to Do* (Discover Nature, No. 6). Stackpole Books.

Quinn, John R. (1976). *The Winter Woods.* Devin-Adair Publishing

Stokes, Donald W. (1979). *Stokes Guide to Nature in Winter.* Little, Brown and Co., Boston.

Teale, Edwin W.(1981). *Wandering through Winter: A Naturalist's Record of a 20,000-Mile Journey through the American Winter.* Dodd, Mead, & Co.: NY. (out of print/limited availability)

 Internet Sites on Winter Activities

Suggested search words: nature winter/winter outdoor activities/winter camping

Outdoor Action Guide to Winter Camping:
   http://www.princeton.edu/~oa/winter/wintcamp.shtml

Animals in Winter, Connecticut Audubon Society:
   http://www.ctaudubon.org/Nature/animals.htm

Winter Camping Manual:
   http://wnyliving.net/outdoors/winter_camping_manual.htm

Winter Camping, University of Alberta, Canada:
   http://www.ee.ualberta.ca/~schmaus/winter.html

SECTION C

CAMPFIRE PROGRAMS

The campfire program can be one of the most meaningful program themes in a nature-oriented program. While there are the traditions of the summer resident camp campfire, with all of its special meanings built up over the years, there are other outdoor settings in which the campfire program can play a significant role, including parks and other public recreation areas, playgrounds, day camps, public campgrounds, the short-term outing or weekend campout, and small group social functions.

The first part of this section describes the settings and the role of the campfire in programming. However, regardless of the setting, there are some basic principles of campfire planning that apply across all settings including: (1) the physical arrangements of the site and circle, (2) construction of the fire, including methods of lighting the fire, and (3) the campfire program.

SETTINGS FOR CAMPFIRE PROGRAMS

There are many suitable settings for campfire programs including campfires in parks and other public recreation areas; campfires on playgrounds; small group campfires; campfires in resident camps; campfires in day camps; and campfires in campgrounds/family camping to name a few.

Campfires in Parks and Other Public Recreation Areas

Many people have attended an evening campfire in a national park. These evening campfires are found in family camp areas not only in national parks, but also in other public recreation areas at the federal, state, and local levels. Sometimes they are referred to as "interpretive campfires," because their function is to interpret the local natural or historic features as well as to entertain and are often conducted by interpretive services professionals.

The usual pattern of the program is a brief welcome to the campground, 10 to 15 minutes of singing the "old favorites," a few announcements of upcoming activities in the area, and the remaining time spent in a talk or illustrated lecture about the history of the locale and its people. The ending is precise so that everyone knows the program is completed and ends with "Good night folks. We hope you have enjoyed the evening and tomorrow . . . ," or something similar. People particularly enjoy singing along with an enthusiastic song leader and this should be an integral part of the program. Having a guitar available can greatly enhance this part of the program. Sometimes a few audience members like to remain to watch the glowing campfire embers.

The campfire circle design is somewhat different from the summer camp campfire circle. Usually there is a half or three-quarter circle with the fire in the opening and the speaker beside the fire. If slides or video are shown, the audience may turn and face the opposite direction for viewing, or a shield may be placed so as to screen out the light of the fire. When the audience becomes very large, a portable loudspeaker system is usually used. While many of the campfire sites have log seats in tiers, there appears to be a trend toward the more formalized outdoor-theater type seating because of the large crowds attending evening programs.

Campfires on the Playground

Sometimes the campfire program is used as a special evening event on the playground. The fire draws attention to the location of the activity and provides a general setting for the program. The program is usually entertainment either by a performing outside group or by the children from the playground. Frequently an evening activity may close with toasting marshmallows or with other refreshments that do not require "cooking."

For a very effective campfire program on a playground, the planners can make use of the fire as a program medium, building around the mystique and inspiration of the fire. The playground children can be encouraged to do special creative programming with emphasis upon their own participation rather than performance for parents and friends. An inspirational closing with poetry and singing and watching the embers of the fire can top off a very successful evening.

Often the site of the fire is a problem on hard-surface playgrounds. The fire itself, in such cases, may need to be portable, such as on a wheelbarrow or top of a steel drum. If possible, the site should be in a secluded wooded area of the playground. Always check local fire regulations before starting an open fire in any location.

For additional help in planning the program and preparing the fire, see the part on programming under this section.

The Small Group Campfire

The usual concept of the campfire program is that of a large group, or the opposite extreme, the family or a few close friends lingering around the fire. However, one of the finest experiences is that of the small group campfire—a Scout troop or a patrol, a club, a cabin group in a camp, etc. These campfires are informal and spontaneous. The program is one of sharing—sharing in a song, poetry, and stories; sharing of oneself. It is in this type of atmosphere that individuals can become better acquainted and feel a part of the group. It is useful at the beginning of some experience and it is also very meaningful as an ending to an experience where a group has been together for some time.

Campfires in the Resident Camp Setting. The work *campfires* causes most people think of the camp campfire that is full of symbolism and tradition, whether for fun or inspiration. It is usually held in a secluded spot reserved exclusively for campfires. Participation of the campers in the program is an integral aspect, rather than the group's being entertained by outsiders. Singing plays a dominant role.

Principles of Planning the Campfire

Wherever the campfire is set, the basic principles are the same. This part provides suggestions relating to: 1) the physical arrangement of the site and circle, (2) the structure of the fire, including methods of lighting the fire, and (3) the campfire program.

Physical Arrangement of Site and Circle. While a campfire may be placed anywhere a fire may be laid, usually it is held outdoors. The indoor fireplace loses much of the romanticism of the night with its sounds and lights. However, if natural logs are used, an indoor experience around the fireplace can be an inspirational and enjoyable experience for small groups.

In selecting a site, consider that is:

1. Should be near enough to the central area to be practical, but remote enough to give some seclusion. Usually the site is reserved only for campfires.

2. Should be well drained and free from insect pests. May be necessary to spray for mosquitoes prior to the campfire.

3. Is desirable to have a natural amphitheater (sloping ground), particularly for large groups. See the later section on council ring layout. The site should provide sufficient space overhead to prevent fire hazards and be able to be cleared underneath to prevent fire creeping.

4. Should be accessed by a winding trail to give a more secluded feeling in approaching the site. However, selection of the site for other reasons is more important—you can carry firewood! The path should be well constructed so participants will not be likely to stumble in the dark. It should be narrow, although may be wide enough for two.

5. Should take prevailing winds into consideration with placement of the fire so that the participant will not have to contend with smoke most of the time. Natural windbreakers also are desirable.

6. Should also be accessible to persons with limited mobility.

The Campfire Circle. There are quite a few varieties of "campfire circles"-an informal ring of logs around a fire, excavated fire circle, Native American Hogan style, on rafts in the water, etc. The following suggestions, though, will be concerned only with the ordinary, common type of campfire circle.

1. The diameter of the circle itself should be no greater than 24 to 30 feet. To have a larger circle destroys intimacy and group feeling. To provide for more seating, add a second or third row of seats. Some authorities say that there should be no more than three rows. This, of course, limits the size of the group that can be accommodated. The additional rows should be raised in tiers.

2. The "circle" may be more elliptical than circular in shape. The seats are ¼ to ¾ the distance around—not completely around, for if there is any performance, part of the audience cannot see what is going on. It is usually better to have semipermanent, sturdy, off-the-ground seats. These may be logs 5 to 6 feet long and 1 foot wide that are staked in, planks

across log pieces, logs cut flat on top and set in the ground, or other seating material.

3. For better programming, there should be only one entrance—behind the fire. Performances should take place between the fire and the audience. If there is a campfire leader or council chief, that person should be seated opposite the entrance. (See diagram.)

4. At all times, the campfire circle should be kept clear of litter.

BUILDING THE FIRE

The focal point of the campfire circle is the fire itself. The success of the program can depend on the success of the fire—does it light quickly, burn brightly, and last long enough? Many a fine program has been marred because the fire was a failure.

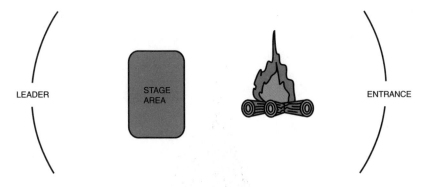

CAMPFIRE FOCAL POINTS

The purpose of the fire is light, not heat. The ideal fire is not a big bonfire that can be a fire hazard and drive people away from the fire because of the heat. The fire should be built so that it burns on an outside structure, is self-feeding, and will last 1 to 1½ hours with a minimum of tending. If should be built in a fire pit—an area cleared so that there is no danger of spreading. If there is difficulty in making a cleared area, the fire might be built upon a platform. The fire pit usually is encircled or lined by nonporous rocks or logs of sufficient size.

There are three commonly used campfire lays: the log cabin fire, the top-lighted fire, and the teepee fire.

Log Cabin Fire. The fire lay rests on two large logs that allows lighting from the bottom. The space between the logs as the lay is built up should be filled with smaller pieces of wood to get a quicker, brighter start on the fire. The ideal log cabin fire has larger logs on the outside frame that catch fire and burn brightly for the remainder of the campfire.

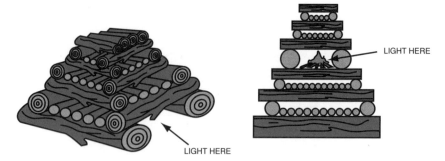

LIGHT HERE

LIGHT HERE

Top-lighted Fire. This is an adaptation of the log cabin fire with the fire lay (the small teepee of kindling and tinder) placed on the fifth or sixth layer. Several layers are built above this. The fire thus burns at the top first with the coals falling down and igniting the lower platforms. Except for the place of lighting, this is constructed similarly to the log cabin fire.

The Teepee Fire. The wood is stacked on end with logs resting together at the top like a teepee. The fire is lighted at the bottom. This style is not as neat looking as the first two, since the logs sometimes fall down at odd angles as they burn.

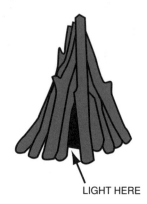

LIGHT HERE

After building the fire, it is important to pick up all the chips and debris as a safety measure. Neatness greatly adds to the whole effect. Also, *no* debris should be put on the fire. A well-laid fire may be ruined by adding bark, leaves, and chips that cut off the draft. The starting tinder and kindling should be twigs, not leaves or paper.

Someone should be designated as the Keeper of the Fire, and if the fire needs replenishing with fuel, the keeper should quietly and quickly add it. A woodpile of logs of proper size and length should be easily accessible, preferably out of view.

To build and light the fire is only half the job. It is important that the Keeper(s) of the Fire remain after the program to properly extinguish the fire.

LIGHTING THE FIRE

WARNING

Extreme caution should be exercised when using the forms of fire lighting so no accident will occur. Always check local fire regulations and have experienced adult supervision.

Lighting the fire is usually a part of the opening ceremony of the campfire. In such a fire-lighting procedure, it is important that the fire lighting be done in a very short time; that an alternate method be ready in case of failure of the planned method; that if a new method is to be used, it has been practiced ahead of time; and that there be sufficient tinder and kindling. Some different methods of lighting fires for special occasions:

1. Fireball of blazing stone ("fire from heaven"). Run a thin guide wire from the center of the campfire to a nearby treetop. Saturate the kindling and campfire wood with alcohol or kerosene. Attach a stone which is covered with cotton saturated with alcohol to a spool threaded on the guide wire in such a way that it will slide down the wire lighting the fire in a flash.

2. Use of chemicals. Safety precautions are extremely important in use of chemicals, which should be handled only by adults.

    *   Magic quick fire. Mix 2 tablespoons of potassium chlorate crystals with 2 tablespoons of granulated sugar. Rig up the campfire so that, by pulling a wire, a 1 1/2 oz. bottle of concentrated sulfuric acid will pour onto the first mixture which will the ignite and start the campfire. An easy way to rig up the acid is to suspend a small bottle like a test tube between two small stakes so that, when tipped, it will dump into the chlorate and sugar. A short distance in front of the bottle, bring the string over the fork of the stick and out to the edge of the fire circle so it can be pulled at the proper time. Build this rig first and then lay the campfire around it.

    *   Magic delayed-reaction fire. Place one teaspoon potassium permanganate in a cone-shaped paper cup. Set paper cup into fire lay, leaving space at backside so that someone may reach in with an eyedropper. When it's about time for the fire to be started, someone should go to the fire lay as if checking it and have an eyedropper of glycerin in hand, but shielded from sight. Drop eight drops of glycerin into the paper cup. In about two minutes, fire bursts into flame igniting the fire lay. A trip device can be set up so that the glycerin is dumped into the paper cup by use of a device similar to that in the quick magic fire. However, one must test the viscosity of glycerin to

be sure that eight drops will flow into the potassium permanganate. This is the safest of the magic fires.

3.   Have a torchbearer bring the light for the fire into the fire ring.

4.   The flaming arrow is the same as #1 above, except that an arrow is attached by two spools to the wire and the tip ignited (sparkler or ball of lightweight material like cotton saturated with alcohol), then fired down into the fire lay.

5.   A pipe can be laid underground from the fire lay to a point outside the circle or to the leader's chair. A long fuse may then be used to ignite the fire.

6.   The fire snake is made from 3/4" rope, 3' long, wrapped with some dark absorbent cloth that has been lightly dipped in paraffin (old candle wax). Attach the snake by three spools which are threaded on a strong, thin black wire about 3" from the ground. This wire goes from the snake's place of hiding near the edge of the circle to a stake in the fire. Be sure it is protected and covered as participants enter the circle. At the proper time, someone lights the snake and a person on the opposite side pulls it into the fire lay by means of thin black wire attached to its nose. When the snake reaches the fire lay, it of course lights the fire.

Colored flames also can be used for special effects by adding chemicals to the campfire directly or in magazine logs. Here is how to make the logs:

ACTIVITY

Make Blue Vitriol Magazine Logs
4 lbs. blue vitriol (copper sulphate powder, not crystals)
2 lbs. coarse salt
2½ gal. water

Put the above formula into a 5-gallon, flat-bottomed crockery or earthenware jar. The solution is highly corrosive, so glass or earthenware must be used. Stir slowly with a long-handled wooden spoon, paddle, or stick.

The logs are best made of slick paper magazines rather than newsprint. Roll each magazine as tightly as possible and tie firmly with several turns of strong cord at each end. The larger magazine should be tied in the center as well. Immerse each log endwise into the solution until the jar is filled. Let stand four to six days. At the end of each 12-hour period, turn the logs so that the solution will penetrate evenly. At the end of the period, take the logs out of the jar and set up on papers to dry. Any solution left should be stored in large-mouthed glass jars. *Never* pour solution into drains.

Place these dried logs into a low-burning fire or embers of a fire to get best results. These logs will burn blue, green, and purple. Other chemicals may be used in the logs to produce different colored flames. Drugstores that handle prescriptions can obtain chemicals for you or may have them on hand. These chemicals also can be used to soak pinecones, which, when dry, can be added to a fire to give it color.

Chemical	*Color*
Potassium chloride	Lavender
Common salt	Yellow
Potassium nitrate	Purple
Strontium nitrate	Crimson
Copper ammonium sulfate	Light blue
Calcium chloride	Red
Barium nitrate	Green

The campfire is many things. It is:
A circle of friendship
A proof of leadership
A place of tradition, history, story
A stage for drama
An arena for fun, games, contests
A focus for music, song
A court for recognition, ceremony, honor
A shrine for memories
A symbol of the soul of the camp.

—LA RUE A. THURSTON, THECOMPLETE BOOK OF CAMPFIRE PROGRAMS

CAMP VOYAGEUR, ELY, MN

THE PROGRAM

A good campfire program does not just happen. It, like other good programs, takes planning in considerable detail ahead of time. First, planning should be done *with* the group that is participating. It is not entertainment planned and executed by someone else. Second, there must be an alternate program in case of rain when the campfire cannot be held at the site anticipated.

Everyone should have a role and participate fully. There should be a total group involvement. Stories and poems certainly are acceptable, but there should be no speeches as such. It is helpful to have a theme to tie things together and to make planning easier. The program should not be just a hodgepodge of activities. Initially the mood should be set, and at the end the participants should be "brought back down" if they have been having an exciting time so that they will not run wild upon leaving the campfire area. Forty-five minutes to one hour is usually long enough for a campfire.

Content

Generally speaking, campfires can be classified into three primary types by program content—inspirational, ceremonial or ritualistic, and in addition, "fun," although some of each are in every campfire. While the specific content emphasis differs, the sequence of activity is the same for all.

1. Opening-entry into campfire circle (relatively short); lighting of the fire; activity to give a feeling of unity, friendship
2. Buildup of activity, reaching a climax (main body of program)
3. Quieting period and closing (relatively short)

The closing may use music (taps, musical prayer, goodnight song), friendship circle, organization pledge or benediction said in unison (frequently a short poem or Native American sign language), symbolic ritual, or silence.

Some of the activities often found in the main body of the program include:

*   Native American ceremonies, legends and lore (See Section D: Native American Life.)
*   Contests and challenges
*   Dramatics and stunts
*   Songs
*   Storytelling and poetry

 **Books on Campfire Programs**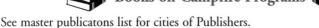

See master publicatons list for cities of Publishers.

Drake, Jane, and Ann Love. (1998). *The Kids Campfire Book*. Kids Can Press, Ltd.: Tonawanda, NY. Covers collecting wood & building campfire, some cooking, songs and lots of campfire activities.

Hanson, Bob (editor), and Bill Roemmich (editor). (2000). *Stories for the Campfire*. American Camp Association: Martinsville, IN.

Pearse, Jack. (1996). *Campfire Programs*. Camp Tawingo Publications, R.R. #1, Huntsville. Ontario, Canada POA 1KO.

Pearse, Jack, Jane McCutcheon, and John Jorgenson. (1988). *More Campfire Programs*. Camp Tawingo Publications: R.R. #1, Huntsville, Ontario, Canada POA 1KO.

 Internet Sites on Campfire Programs

Suggested search words: campfire programs/campfire songs/campfire/skits and stunts/ice breakers

The American Camp Association: http://www.acacamps.org/

The MacScouter, Scouting Resources Online Songs for Scouts & Scouters. Maintained by a scout. Large selection of songs. http://www.macscouter.com/Songs/

SECTION D

NATIVE AMERICAN LIFE

Native Americans, and the way they lived before the coming of the Europeans, have been an inspiration to many people. Their extensive knowledge about the outdoors and the resourcefulness with which they used indigenous materials to serve their everyday living needs are truly arts to be envied. Native Americans, their skills, and their way of life (customs) have served as an appropriate theme for many camping and recreation programs.

When activities that focused on Native Americans are used in a program, *every effort should be made to make these activities as authentic as possible.* A great deal of injustice and injury have been done to Native Americans when leaders have suggested, "Let's play cowboy and Indians." In these situations children tend to imitate the stereotypical Native American, thought of as bloodthirsty savages with weird, nonsensical dances and chants.

Actually, Native Americans had a very wholesome and unique outlook toward the outdoors. They considered themselves part of every living thing they observed. They did not see themselves as rulers of nature or masters with all living things subject to their whims and desires. Rather they believed they were related to the living creatures they encountered. This feeling of kinship with the animal world led them to develop an attitude of respect and love for all forms of life.

Native Americans did not kill game for the sake of killing or just for the sport involved, as did many of the European settlers. They did not kill more than they needed for food and clothing. There was no room for ruthless slaughter in their approach to the natural environment. It is no wonder that they had difficulty in understanding the ways of the settlers and that they rose up in protest when they saw unnecessary and wasteful attacks on the buffalo and other forms of wildlife.

With this orientation to the outdoors, it was natural for Native Americans to look for and find beauty in all the natural world. They did not recognize as ugly those aspects of nature that seem to impress the white people as being so. The Native Americans' philosophy concerning the entire outdoor surroundings and all of nature was good and beautiful. Nothing natural could be ugly—if it was ugly, it was so because people had made it so.

The Native Americans gave expression to their philosophy and feelings through games, crafts, living skills, ceremonials, dances, stories, and legends. Each of these areas offers a wealth of material for use in nature-oriented programs.

Games. Most of the Native American children's games were based upon the life situations in which adult Native Americans found themselves. These were games in which the children would imitate or attempt to portray social customs, ceremonies, hunting, warfare, or the skills involved in homemaking. There were no toyshops from which to purchase ready-made toys, so frequently they would turn to the materials found in the outdoors (branches, logs, stones, bones, and shells) from which they would make their toys. Many of the games in which the boys participated were based on man-to-man combat and included running, throwing, and wrestling.

Crafts. Crafts for Native Americans were completely utilitarian and functional rather than recreational. They revolved around the making of utensils and equipment for kitchen use, costumes and ornaments for ceremonials, and hunting equipment. Native American crafts can be used in craft programs as well as in preparation for evening campfire and ceremonial programs.

CHELEY COLORADO CAMPS, CHELEY, CO.

Outdoor Living Skills. Native Americans developed a high degree of skill in the areas related to outdoor living. Their abilities to find their way, to hunt animals, and to use native materials to provide comfort for their families were amazing. People can be challenged to develop some of their powers of observation and to gain greater knowledge of the outdoors through studying and participating in projects that demonstrate the Native Americans' way of life. Native American life can be simulated through building shelters, going on hunts, and looking for edible plant life. Actual authentic practices should be used.

Ceremonials and Dances. Ceremonials played a very important part in the lives of Native Americans. In these celebrations and ceremonies, they were able to give expression to their inner feelings through dances, colorful costumes, and makeup.

Many of the ceremonies Native Americans observed were connected with the changing of seasons. These were related to seasonal activities, such as celebrating the planting of crops in the spring. The pilgrims adapted the ceremony of giving thanks at harvest time that later became our Thanksgiving. Other ceremonies had to do with hunting and warfare or were related to religious practices of driving out evil spirits.

The Native American's dance was composed of intricate but meaningful steps and figures designed for specific purposes. Learning Native American dances will give your participants a better understanding of the Native American cultures as well as help develop dancing skills.

Stories and Legends. Tribal traditions were handed down from parent to child through the telling of stories. Most of these were legends and myths describing the creation of the world and natural events such as storms. Some described the experiences of brave warriors and medicine men. Others told how animals got their distinctive features.

 Books on Native American Life

See master publicatons list for cities of Publishers.

Adam, Winky. (1997). *North American Indian Activity Book.* Dover Publications.

Bruchac, Joseph. (2000). *Pushing Up the Sky: Seven Native American Plays for Children.* Dial Books for Young Readers.

Caduto, Michael J., and Joseph Bruchac. (1999). *Keepers of the Earth: Native American Stories and Environmental Activities for Children.* Fulcrum, Inc.: Golden, CO.

—(1990). *Keepers of the Earth Teachers Guide.* Fulcrum, Inc.: Golden, CO.

—(1997). *Keepers of Life: Discovering Plants through Native American Stories and Earth Activities for Children.* Fulcrum, Inc.: Golden, CO.

—(1997). *Keepers of the Animals: Native American Stories and Wildlife Activities for Children.* Fulcrum, Inc.: Golden, CO.

—(1992). *Keepers of the Animals Teacher's Guide.* Fulcrum, Inc.: Golden, CO.

Carlson, Laurie. (1994). *More than Moccasins: A Kid's Activity Guide to Traditional North American Indian Life*. Chicago Review Press:

DeAngulo, Jaime. (1984). *Indian Tales*. Hill & Wang Publications.

Keeper, Berry. (2000). *The Old Ones Told Me, American Indian Stories for Children*. Binford & Mort Publishing.

MacFarlan, Allan A. (1982). *Exploring the Outdoors with Indian Secrets: Skills for Observing and Matching Wits with Nature*. Stackpole Books: Mechanicsburg, PA.

—(1985). *Handbook of American Indian Games*. Dover Publications: Mineola, NY.

—(1961). *Living Like Indians*. Association Press: NY. (out of print/limited availability)

Mason, Bernard S. (1946). *The Book of Indian Crafts and Costumes*. Books on Demand, UMI, Ann Arbor, MI. (out of print/limited availability)

Miller, Jay. (1997). *American Indian Games: A True Book*. Children's Book Press.

Norbeck, Oscar E. (1974). *Book of Authentic Indian Life Crafts*. Galloway, Corvallis, OR. (out of print/limited availability)

Soeder, Pamela, Pam Creasy, and Yosta Boots. (2000). *Discover American Indian Ways: A Carnegie Activity Book*. Roberts Rinehart Publications.

Van Laan, Nancy. (1995). *In a Circle Long Ago: A Treasury of Native Lore from North America*. Knopf.

Internet Sites on Native American Life

Suggested search words: Native Americans/Indians/Indian crafts/Indian stories

First Nations Histories. Compact histories, 50 encyclopedia-like histories of Native American people: http://www.tolatsga.org/Compacts.html

Native Americans and the Environment. Non-profit project relating to Native Americans and the environment: http://www.cnie.org/NAE/

NativeWeb. Resources for indigenous cultures around the world. Has extensive information and links to many resources. A good starting place. http://www.nativeweb.org/

SECTION E
TRAIL AND RELATED ACTIVITIES

Thomas Huxley has said that for many people a walk through the woods is like a tour through an art gallery with all of the pictures turned toward the wall. People look, but do not see; hear, but do not perceive; move in the outdoors, but are oblivious to it.

NATURE TRAILS

Walking and hiking on nature trails are the most popular outdoor activities. All trails are nature trails; however, they may be roughly classified into three types: (1) the nonguided trail, (2) the guided walk over a trail, and (3) the self-guiding trail.

A *nonguided trail* has an established route that is marked, particularly at turns. It has a known destination. Frequently these are paths to places of special interest located at a distance easily covered on foot. Or they may be longer trails over terrain noted for its beauty and ecological patterns. Two nationally known nonguided trails extending over many miles are the Appalachian Trail in the East and the Pacific Crest Trail in the West. Both are marked and have shelters en route for overnight stops; however, most trails are not of this length. One-half mile to two miles is a more common length for trails most people enjoy.

The *guided walk*, as distinguished from the field trip which is considered later, is the second type of trail activity conducted by a naturalist or informed guide. The trail taken may be short and require only one-half hour for walking, or it may take a whole day. The guide stops at appropriate places to explain features of interest, seeking to stimulate the participants to further activity in the out-of-doors. Guided walks are most effective when a seasonal approach is used with a series of walks related to the season: for instance, walks in the spring to look for birds or wildflowers. Optimum group size is 10 to 12 persons, although more often have to be accommodated.

A leader is not always available, thus it may be advisable to have some type of explanation regarding the natural area through which the trail is laid. In such situations a *self-guiding trail* is established. Self-guiding trails have signs, trailside displays, or hand printed leaflets with information about specific locations on the trail. These trails are most frequently ½ to ¾ mile in length, almost never longer, and take about 45 minutes.

Most trails, regardless of type, are located where people naturally congregate for outdoor activity—parks, picnic area, nature centers, playgrounds, and camps. When trails begin off the roadside, there must be a parking area and well-marked notices about where the trail begins. Where a trail begins is called the *trailhead*.

Wherever the trailhead begins, the entrance must be easily accessible and obvious. Few people will hunt for a trail, but they are often curious enough to follow one they happen to come across. Frequently, at the entrance, there may be a trailside museum or kiosk, luring people onto the trail by describing its features. Also, a bulletin board may be used which displays a map of the area, information about the surroundings, or notices of other activities offered in the vicinity.

Nature trails should be established only when there is a worthy natural or cultural feature. Features will vary; a trail may be constructed to show things of generalized or specialized interest. General trails might include various types of vegetation, while a specialized trail might include a glacial deposit. People like to call a trail by name—names create a feeling of familiarity—and to make use of the special or general feature of the trail in the name helps to identify it.

Purposes of Nature Trails

The purposes vary with the type of trail. The nonguided trail caters to the hiker—to the person who enjoys vigorous activity on foot, bicycle, or horseback. The person who likes the outdoors needs little stimulation to "take to the trails," although he does need information about available trails that have been constructed for public use, particularly in areas where he is not accustomed to hiking. As indicated, the guided walk is an effort to interpret the outdoors to the general public, with the hope of stimulating interest in more outdoor activities. It is often used also for educational information, especially with youth organizations and schools. The self-guiding trail, which is short, seeks to induce persons only mildly interested or even disinterested in nature to "try" a little bit of nature and perhaps thereby become more involved. The self-guiding trail may also be used for self-testing. Where there is no naturalist or guide on duty or nearby, the labels provide information about the trail. Inspiration may also result from the manner of labeling and the scenic beauty of a self-guiding trail.

Service Learning and Community Service

The foregoing purposes of trails relate primarily to the trail user. The program theme "trails" also includes an excellent opportunity for *service learning* and *community service* activities that interpret nature to others. While a trail project can be undertaken by an individual, it is much more enjoyable and rewarding to join in these nature-oriented projects with a group or with one of the many community organizations, such as a city or county park department, a nature center that serves as the "trail head," a school and its environmental education program, or a camp with a system of trails through different ecosystems.

A trail that is already laid may be selected to maintain or enhance it, or a group can construct an entirely new trail. The group can make an interpretive, self-guiding trail, with labels, develop a guide booklet, make the trail accessible for persons with disabilities, or develop a wayside exhibit or kiosk, or the group may want to lead a nature walk for anyone from preschoolers to seniors. Suggestions for the various projects follow. The focus of a service project is to help others to better enjoy nature by learning about it and developing desirable environmental ethics.

Keep in mind that the purpose of the trail project is to stimulate curiosity, not satisfy it; to put people into a receptive frame of mind for further interpretation and information. Information, as such, is not interpretation; interpretation is revelation based on information. Interpretation of what is being displayed or described must be related to something within the personality or experience of the participant.

There are many guiding principles regarding interpretation, but those of longest standing are the six from Freeman Tilden's *Interpreting Our Heritage:*

1. Any interpretation that does not somehow relate what is being displayed or described to something within the personality or experience of the visitor will be sterile.

2. Information, as such, is not INTERPRETATION. Interpretation is revelation based upon information. But they are entirely different things. However, all interpretation includes information.

3. Interpretation is an art, which combines many arts, whether the materials presented are scientific, historical or architectural. Any art is in some degree teachable.

4. The chief aim of INTERPRETATION is not instruction, but provocation.

5. Interpretation should aim to present a whole rather than a part, and must address itself to the whole man rather than any phase.

6. Interpretation addressed to children (say, up to the age of twelve) should not be a dilution of the presentation to adults, but should follow a fundamentally different approach. To be at its best it will require a separate program.

MARK TANTRUM, SAN JOSE, CA

Constructing and Protecting Trails

Other values of trails, particularly important as they become an activity in camp, on the playground, or at the nature center, lie in their construction. Persons who participate in the construction of trails gain direct contact with the outdoors. They learn what information must be acquired in order to lay a trail. Construction itself incorporates principles of pioneering, handicraft, elementary engineering, and an awareness of the natural environment (essential to selecting the specific path of the trail). Responsibility for maintenance of the trail, both physical maintenance and keeping information current, is essential.

Some Basic Principles

1.   Make the trail narrow, necessitating single-file walking; otherwise, the wilderness quality of the surroundings may be destroyed. However, consider making portions accessible to persons with limited mobility; retain the wilderness character as much as possible.

2.   The trail should be natural and winding, but the turns and twists should be for a purpose—taking the user past a special feature. Sharp corners invite shortcutting; avoid them. Do not tear up, destroy, or fake—use what is there! Trails should go through several types of areas, unless it is a special-feature trail.

3.   Avoid steep grades and extremely low areas that may lead to erosion and seasonal wet spots. To go up a hill, use zigzag paths. Steps of logs may be used if necessary.

4.   To mark a trail for construction, walk through the area with a ball of twine, unwinding as you go. The path of twine should indicate where footpath is to be kept. Walk over the area several times to be sure you have spotted the most interesting features. Do not have long distances in open sunlight.

5.   Once a trail is established, keep it up-to-date! Periodically go over the signs, changing them, if necessary, as the seasons and developments in the area change. Also, keep the trail maintained and beautiful. Remove any evidences of vandalism *immediately* as well as any other damage from natural elements, or litter and mutilation resulting from human inconsideration.

6.   Short trails definitely should not connect two main points so that they become heavily traveled thoroughfares.

7.   Self-guiding trails, particularly, and trails used for guided walks normally should be constructed as a loop with exit and entrance at the same point—but be sure the entrance is well-marked and the exit obscure so people do not start wrong. Sometimes a figure-eight trail is constructed so that people may take either the shorter or longer trail, depending on the time they have available and their interest. Although the entrance should be obvious, the rest of the trail should be secluded from other activities.

8. Minimize natural hazards; eradicate poison ivy, remove stinging nettle, etc. However, you may keep small patches of poison ivy under control so persons can learn to identify it.

9. Benches and other rest spots and facilities might be appropriately placed along the trail or in the immediate vicinity.

10. When it's necessary to build bridges and railings, they should be sturdy, permanent, and of native material.

11. Always think about ways to make trails more accessible to persons with disabilities. Oftentimes disabilities are narrowly defined as mobility impairments. Think about other conditions that affect eyesight, hearing, and cognitive impairments.

Self-Guiding Trails/Labels

The following are tips for labels and displays on self-guiding trails:

- Markers should be attached to stakes in a manner to suggest permanency and in keeping with the woods. They should not be attached to trees.

- Markers should be placed near enough to each other so that the next one can be seen clearly. About 20 feet is a good distance. The first label generally explains the purpose of the trail. It may actually not be a label at all, but a trailside museum at the entrance.

- Repetition of common names several times along the trail may reinforce learning.

- Markers should be of a variety of types to add interest to the trail. Color, too, may be used, e.g., green for botanical markings, brown for geological, and red for zoological.

- Wording should be short and catchy with no attempt at the scientific approach of Latin identification, but the *labels must be scientifically accurate.* Wording must also be simple.

Here are some more pointers on wording:

- Give something more than just the name: Staghorn sumac: the red top of sumac was used by the Native Americans to make "lemonade."

- Include something to help the reader remember the information: Happy are cicadas' lives for they all have voiceless wives.

- If applicable, use informality or humor for emphasis: Just touch me to learn Why I'm called "touch-me-not."

- Labels may indicate evidence of ecology: In 1945, cultivation of this open field was stopped. Seeds dropped by birds or blown in by wind have changed it into a thicket. Now, different kinds of wildlife have come to use the new good, cover, and nesting sites.

- Labels may mention economic values: Red cedar is often known as the lead-pencil tree for it is the favorite wood for making the common pencil. Cedar chests are made from this tree also.

- Labels may include inspirational material:

I am the heart of your hearth on the cold winter nights, the friendly shade screening you from the summer sun, and my fruits are refreshing draughts quenching your thirst as you journey on.

I am the beam that holds your house, the board of your table, the bed on which you lie, and the timber that builds your boat.

I am the handle of your hoe, the door of your homestead, the wood of your cradle, and the shell of your coffin.

I am the bread of kindness and the flower of beauty.

Yee who pass by, listen to my prayer; harm me not.

     —PORTUGUESE PRAYER OF THE WOODS

Linen tag markers may be used but sparingly and for temporary, seasonal labels only. India-ink lettering or computer generated type sprayed with clear plastic will withstand many rains.

A sheltered label is protected from rain.

A turnover label gives a question and an answer.

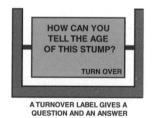

A TURNOVER LABEL GIVES A
QUESTION AND AN ANSWER

An object, such as a glacial boulder, flower bed, etc., may be pointed out by "aiming" such a sign at the object.

A string attached to a sign, like this, makes it possible to single out a specific thing such as an individual flower among many in a large bed.

An interesting variation to the pointer type sign is a 1-inch hole drilled in a post to focus on a more distant object, such as a high nest. Or mount a 1-foot length of 3/4-inch pipe and similarly focus it on an object.

This sign, made by rolling the top and bottom edges of sheet metal (aluminum or galvanized iron) is very handy for frequently changed messages, such as sequential information about the rapid development of a flower bed.

An insect cage, made of a roll of cellulose acetate with sewed-on muslin ends, makes it possible to observe insects at work in the natural surroundings of their food plant. A temporary sign above can be changed often to follow the rapid development of the insects' life cycle.

A triangular block, made of three pieces of plywood fitted to triangular boards and rotated on a dowel, provides another action marker and permits three-part messages for more important natural phenomena. When messages need to be long, it is best to break them up into two or three parts.

This type of wooden sign, painted first, can be lettered with India ink by preparing the surface with Fuller's earth to prevent the ink from running

Labels may correct superstitions and misinformation.

- A snake feels like dry linoleum—is not slimy.
- A snake's forked tongue is a feeler—is not a stinger.
- A snake has no eyelids, but over 100 pairs of ribs.

Timeliness is important—labels should reflect the current season:

- This is jack-in-the-pulpit. Can you find Jack? (Spring when plant is in flower)
- Here is the red-robed congregation that jack-in-the-pulpit preached to last spring. (Fall when plant is in fruit)

Remember that the coming of winter does not necessitate closing the nature trail. Winter plants and animal tracks in the snow are two of many attractions of this season.

Labels may mention conservation values, calling attention to fire prevention, erosion, etc.:

- Nature provides a soft, lush carpet in the forest. But it is more flammable than your living room rug. Don't set it on fire!
- You wouldn't build a fire on your living room carpet. Outdoors you also need to use the proper fireplace. Save the rug!*

Labels may play upon an association:

- American hornbeam is as tough as the muscular branches suggest.

Labels may suggest an activity:

- Silence! You may hear a red-eyed vireo singing nearby.

Words may be supplemented or supplanted with pictures; e.g., hand-drawn or cutout pictures pasted on the label and spar varnished or sprayed with clear plastic to withstand the weather.

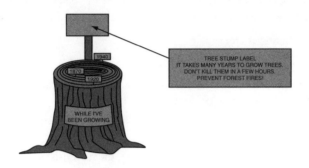

Labels may provide questions -and -answers:

Is this tree named for a dog?

Early pioneers cut dogs, or skewers, from this tree: hence, the name DOGWOOD.

Labels may enhance remembering by using an adage:

Five needles to the cluster;

Five letters to the name: W-H-I-T-E pine.

The Printed Guide

Another form of self-guiding trail information is the printed leaflet that describes the natural feature of the trail. Usually locations along the way are numbered to correspond to the descriptions in the booklet. The booklets are found at the beginning of the trail in a sheltered box, and another box for returning the booklets is located at the end of the trail. A person who would like to keep the booklet, deposits a nominal amount, frequently 10 cents or 25 cents.

Some advantages of a self-guiding trail having booklets and numbered locations are:

- Along the nature trail people like to do things. Therefore markers that require some activity are very good. In this type, a question is shown on the outside panel and the hiker lifts the hinged panel to learn the answer. The message may be changed by tacking on paraffin-dipped or plastic-sprayed cards for questions and answers.

- There are no signs and displays to protect from normal weather damage or damage from vandalism.
- The trail has a neater appearance when no signs or displays are in disrepair.
- For a nominal fee the user has a booklet to take along.
- The booklet can provide information in greater detail than a trail sign and may give supplemental information about activities and the area.

But some disadvantages are:

- Some people who wander on the trail do not bother to pick up a booklet.
- Many people do not want to stop to read at given locations, much preferring the brief, visual, obvious signs en route.
- A few people forget to return the booklets or deposit their fee at the end of the trail.
- The booklet is not as flexible in keeping the materials on the trail up-to-date. Once printed, that's it until they're all used up; although it is possible to have seasonal booklets available.

Wayside Exhibits

Trailside "museums" or kiosks are self-explanatory exhibits that tell a story of the natural history of the immediate environment. They are distinguished primarily from junior museums and naturemobiles in that they deal with a single object or specific region. Persons may read or view the exhibit and relate its information directly by observing the natural phenomena which it describes. Frequently a trailside "museum" is alongside the entrance to a nature trail or at a wide rest point along the way. Such "museums;" however, should not be restricted to trail use but also should be placed on picnic sites and campgrounds, roadside lookouts, and scenic observation points.

Field Trips

The term "field trip" has various meanings. To some it means leading a group out to a definite location for the specific purpose of obtaining information about that natural area, of observing a specific natural phenomenon, or of gathering natural specimens. However, to others the term "field trip" is used in place of a nature walk or nature hike as related to the guided-trail experiences because they feel the term is more acceptable to the public. The discussion in this section is focused upon the first meaning; however, many of the same procedures are indeed applicable to the latter since both involve leadership of a group seeking interpretation of the natural environment.

Techniques

Following are techniques for successful field trips:

- Every field trip should have a purpose and a plan. The group should not only know the purpose at the time of departure but should have taken part in the planning for the field trip.

- The length of the field trip depends upon the purpose and the nature of the group. A rock-collecting field trip with the "Rock Hounds Club" might be an all-day adventure, while a field trip to collect native materials with the youngsters on a playground might involve only an hour. Some experienced leaders feel that a 45-minute trip is a desirable length for children.

- Practice of outdoor good manners is of extreme importance. The example of the leader is undoubtedly the best teacher. The leader should also insist upon good manners by the entire group—using disposal receptacles for litter, leaving flowers for others to enjoy rather than picking them, using fire prevention procedures when smoking, etc.

- A field trip is *not* a lecture. The leader talks *with* the group, *not at them.* There should be a feeling within the group that they are free to ask questions and the leader must have no qualms about saying, "I do not know, perhaps we can look that up together."

- Stops on a field trip should be meaningful—stops should be made to observe something. Rest stops on field trips are unnecessary as each person rests when stopping to observe. On extended field trips, provision should be made for the physical comfort of the individuals.

BRADFORD WOODS OUTDOOR CENTER, MARTINSVILLE, IN

- The group should be kept together and be small enough for all to hear what the leader is discussing and to participate in the observations and gathering of information and materials. This means that is desirable for groups to be no larger than 15 to 20 persons.

- The leader should have planned for the field trip not only by knowing the specific purposes but also by having made an advance trip to the area to know what to expect and how to make maximum use of the time available.

- An effort should be made to have a "buildup" (anticipation for the field trip through group planning and other motivating devices.) There also should be followup with the information obtained or the specimens collected. Why go if you are not going to use what you acquired? It may be desirable to plan a series of field trips in order to accomplish the group's goal.

- While a field trip is taken for a specific purpose, the leader and group should be flexible enough to take advantage of unusual natural situations which present themselves.

- Prepare the group adequately for the field trip by supplying plans for starting time and return time; suitable footwear, raincoats, and other garments; lunch; etc. Also, prepare the group through the use of background materials so that they may have the proper foundation to gain maximum benefit from the experience.

- Evaluate the field trip so that future trips may be improved.

Mobile Facilities and Presentations

An interpretive nature program must go to the people, as well as have the people come to a nature center. For this reason, mobile facilities are of particular value.

Naturemobile. A naturemobile is usually a large, enclosed trailer equipped with exhibits and displays interpreting local natural history. It is designed primarily for educational use in the schools and youth groups, but it serves also as an important factor in stimulating interest in other community nature-oriented activities, particularly those of the nature center, if there is one. The naturemobile, as the name implies, travels to the people in schools, in camps, on playgrounds, and at other locations. Each location may have the naturemobile for a given length of time and then it moves on.

Starwagons. A starwagon may be an "observatory-on-wheels" with a telescope and charts, or may also include a planetarium projector. An interpreter, of course, accompanies the starwagon. For further description of the Milwaukee Starwagon, see section on Astronomy in Chapter 6, Projects and Hobbies.

Animal Loan Service. Many children are not able to obtain and care for an animal permanently—they may not have adequate space or the parents may not permit it; yet a child can gain valuable experience in caring for a live pet for a short period of time. Some zoos, nature centers, and children's museums have animals which may be loaned for a week or so at a time. Care instructions, of course, are important. Sometimes loans are also made to schools.

Audio-Visual Loan Service. Portable exhibits and displays should be available for loan on a short-term basis to schools, clubs, camps, and special events. They can stimulate considerable interest, as well as serve an important interpretive role.

In today's technological society, many audio-visual alternatives are available. Both computer-generated and long-standing technology including motion pictures, filmstrips, 35mm slides, etc. should also be made available to groups interested in nature interpretive programs. See the next section for further details.

Audio-Visual Presentations

To promote enjoyment of the outdoors, as well as to develop a wholesome attitude toward the natural environment, adequate communication between the interpreter and the public is essential; therefore, audio-visual presentations are integral to an effective interpretive program. An interpretive program should use the mass media for communication (television, radio, newspapers, and magazines), exhibits and displays, literature (e.g., nature-trail guides, newsletters), and personal appearance programs (lecture, campfires, slide presentations).

Although as interpretive devices, audio-visual materials are important, it must be emphasized that they are interpretive—interpretive of the "real thing," the natural environment to which they relate. They should not be so pretentious that they, in themselves, become the showpiece. Their purpose should be to stimulate curiosity about the outdoors and to lead the viewer to firsthand experiences with the real thing. Factual information is communicated, but the primary purpose and focus of these audio-visual materials should be to reveal meanings and relationships. Original objects are often a part of the displayed materials.

There are many types of audio-visual materials; already mentioned in the preceding sections are trail labels, naturemobiles, and trailside displays. Additional important materials are both indoor and outdoor exhibits and displays, including dioramas, relief maps, models, automatic and action displays, and live exhibits. Bulletin boards, posters, brochures and pamphlet, videos, 16mm films, slides, cassettes, and recordings are also a part of audio-visual materials used for interpretive purposes.

Video recording and computers can be valuable program tools. Technical advances not only have made low cost equipment of convenient size available but also have simplified operation of such equipment for the general user. Video recordings and computers can be used effectively to disseminate information that cannot be observed readily, but that makes direct experiences more meaningful. For example, video presentations can show plants and animals in their environment at other than the current season. Also, through time-lapse photography, growth concepts can be dramatically portrayed. Computers are especially

attractive when they are used for involvement of the learner, permitting the learner to find information, to ask questions, and to see alternative responses and situations.

While each of these has its own particular techniques to use for effectiveness, some general principles can be applied to all types of audio-visual interpretive materials.

Principles of Audio-Visual Interpretive Technique

Subject Matter
Significance. There are so many interesting things to tell, it is important that stories most worthy of presentation are selected, especially those that are significant to the immediate area. Because there are so many choices worthy of presentation, you may tend to select too many. Each display, exhibit, and bulletin board should center around one theme, one single idea to get across and focus upon.

Relevance. Select subject matter that can be made relevant or meaningful to the participants or audience.

Content
Simplicity. The manner of presenting content must be influenced by the audience for whom the audio-visual material is being made. The viewer must be able to understand what is being presented. For the most part, viewers are nonprofessionals and the concepts must be presented so that they relate to something within the personality or experience of such a person.

Accuracy. In an effort to simplify presentation and to attract interest, one must not sacrifice accuracy. All materials presented must be scientifically accurate.

Up-to-dateness. While some displays may tend to be semipermanent, most audio-visual materials should change with the seasons and be kept up-to-date, both with the changing outdoor environment and with any new scientific materials. The viewer who returns from time to time should find new and stimulating presentations to further encourage him in firsthand experiences.

Appearance

Neatness. A presentation that is not neat leads not only to disrespect and vandalism but also to the loss of whatever appeal it might have had to stimulate the viewer toward firsthand experiences with the natural environment. The quality of neatness extends not only to the initial preparation but to regular maintenance also.

Placement. In viewing a sequence, it is most normal to go from left to right as this is the way we read in our American culture. So the sequence of exhibits, posters, etc., should move from left to right. Another factor important in placement is that the presentation must have its focus at *eye level.* People just do not tend to look upward unless their attention is attracted by the presentation. Similarly, audience participation presentations should have their action mechanisms appropriate for various ages which might be viewing.

Layout. There are five elements of layout:

1. *Balance.* Informal balance is usually more attractive than formal. The main point of emphasis may be effective slightly off center.

2. *Mass.* Too often the amateur designer of a display tends to want to get too many things in the display or on the board. Solid blocks of material should be broken up with blank space for effect. Long sentences and captions will not be read and remembered. Keep captions brief, specific, and interesting. Captions with pictures tend to be much more appealing than captions alone. Symbolic diagrams can be used effectively to get an idea across.

3. *Texture.* Having variety of texture for surfaces and lines add immeasurably to the appeal of the presentation. For surfaces, use such materials as cloth, corrugated cardboard, screening, foil, newsprint, etc. For lines, use yarn, ribbon, rubber bands, wire, pipe cleaners, etc.

4. *Color.* The greater the contrast between lettering and background, the more easily and quickly the lettering can be read. Contrasting intensities should be used. Children usually notice colors more than adults and prefer brighter colors and combinations of intense colors. Older children and adults prefer more sophisticated color combinations. Unless you are deliberately emphasizing one thing, never have a color appear only once. Repeat it somewhere in the design or lettering. This directs the eye to different parts and relationships.

5. *Lettering.* Lettering is a most essential element of the presentation, for it points up the meaning. Kepp lettering simple. Let one style dominate. Not more than three sizes of letters should be used in any one presentation.

Uppercase letters are forceful and attract attention easily but can be difficult to read because all the letters are the same height; therefore, use them for short words and simple phrases that need special emphasis.

In formation of letters, heavy, even strokes are easier to read than light strokes. Also, spacing is extremely important. There should be sufficient space between letters. If condensing is necessary, use a narrower letter rather than make an important word smaller, and condense space between letters, not between words.

The computer, while mentioned as an instructional tool, also is a very valuable graphics aid, both for lettering and illustrations. The principles of lettering remain, but the ease of lettering and illustrating with a computer should mean regular use of a computer. There is much software to facilitate such use.

Mechanical Devices. There is a trend toward audience participation, the use of action in displays and exhibits. Mechanical devices must be carefully set up where they can be serviced regularly and conveniently. There is nothing more annoying to a viewer than an "out-of-order" sign.

Whereas one often thinks of lights going on or buzzers ringing for audience participation, the use of the computer provides a different dimension of involvement, one that allows a user to pursue in more depth a particular questioning or quality of information. The user has many more options, options that can take only a very brief time or which can be more extended, thus providing a more individualized experience.

Lighting. Even lighting is generally desirable on a display or other presentation; however, spotlights or shadow effects may point up something special that is being portrayed.

SECTION F
CLASSIC NATURE-ORIENTED AUTHORS AND READINGS

Interpretive programs often use quotes, stories, and biographies of important nature-oriented author-environmentalists. Following is a list of authors who wrote about nature-oriented topics. Most all were pioneers and champions of the environmental movement who made significant contributions at critical times. This list is by no means complete and not all of each author's books are listed, but they all should be familiar to persons dedicated to the highest possible quality of nature-oriented experience. In addition to their own works, excellent biographies have been written about most of the people on this list. These biographies can also be outstanding sources of information and inspiration.

Audubon, John James.. (1785-1851). As most people know, Audubon was famous for painting and describing birds. Birds of America became the standards against which all 20th and 21st century bird artists are measured.

Burroughs, Edward. (1837-1921). An immensely popular nature writer of his time, Burroughs wrote about nature in several periodicals, sometimes under pseudonyms. He published 23 volumes of essays extolling nature and encouraging people to experience the natural world. Several books have been written that include his essays. One of the best is Our Friend John Burroughs written by Clara Barrus and published in 1914 by Houghton Mifflin.

Carson, Rachel. (1907-1964). Scientist, ecologist, and writer, Carson was instrumental in saving whole species of birds from extinction by bringing to public attention the dangers of synthetic, chemical pesticides, especially DDT. She did this with great courage in the face of significant pressures from big chemical companies. Silent Spring. The Sea Around Us.

Douglas, Marjory Stoneman. (1890-1998). Champion of the Everglades. The Everglades River of Grass.

Douglas, William O. (1898-1980). Longest serving Supreme Court Justice (36+ years) who championed environmental causes. Wilderness Bill of Rights. My Wilderness. Muir of the Mountains. Of Men and Mountains

Fabre. Jean-Henri. (1823-1915). Known as the "entomological philosopher" and the "psychologist of the world of insects," Fabre dedicated his life to the study of insects and nature. He wrote eloquently about them. Marvel of the Insect World. Social Life in the Insect World. Field, Forest, and Farm.

Frome, Michael. (1920-)Author, educator, and tireless guardian of natural resources. Proponent of need for national ethics of environmental stewardship. Battle for the Wilderness. Strangers in High Places. Conscience of a Conservationist. Greenspeak.

Frost, Robert. (1874-1885). Leading 20th century American poet, many of Frost's poems gave life and inspiration to simple things in nature. Birches. West-Running Brook. Snow. The Sound of Trees.

Leopold, Aldo. (1887-1948). A forester and naturalist who worked all his life in government and academia, Leopold produced inspirational words for the environmental movement. A Sand County Almanac

Marshall, Robert. (1901-1939). Marshall worked for the forest service and was a tireless advocate for preserving forest lands and promoting outdoor recreation as a necessary inspiration. He was known to hike 50 miles in one day with a pack. With Aldo Leopold and others, he founded the Wilderness Society. The People's Forests.

Muir, John. (1838-1914). Born in Scotland he moved to Wisconsin at age 12 and at age 30 entered the Yosemite Valley in California. He became one of the most well known voices for preservation in the nation as he promoted and fought for environmental causes. He founded the Sierra Club. My First Summer in the Sierra. Our National Parks. The Yosemite.

Nash, Roderick. Leader in the field of environmental history, management and education with a special interest in problems related to wilderness. Wilderness and the American Mind. The Rights of Nature: A History of Environmental Ethics.

Seton, Ernest Thompson. (1860-1946). Artist, writer, naturalist, story teller, philosopher, Seton started the Woodcraft movement that preceded the Boy Scouts. He chaired the founding committee of the Boy Scouts and served as Chief Scout from 1910-1915. How to Play Indian. The Manual of the Woodcraft Indians. The Book of Woodcraft.

Sigurd Olson (1899-1982). Nature writer and conservationist, Olson played an important role in the preservation of national parks, seashores, and wilderness areas. The Singing Wilderness. Listening Point. The Lonely Land. The Singing Wilderness.

Thoreau, Henry David. (1817-1862). One of the earliest prophets of the value of wilderness and ecology. Walden.

Tilden, Freeman. (1883-1980). An accomplished novelist and playwright, Tilden began writing about the National Parks in 1940. His small book, Interpreting Our Heritage, became the seminal work in the interpretation field. The National Parks: What They Mean to You and Me. The State Parks: Their Meaning in American Life

Webb, Kenneth. In the 1960s and 1970s, Webb published several books that captured the spirit and inspiration of organized camping Light from a Thousand Campfires; As Sparks Fly Upwards.

Classic Nature Internet Sites

John James Audubon: http://www.audubon.org/nas/jja.html
John Burroughs: http://www.johnburroughs.org/
Rachel Carson: http://www.rachelcarson.org/
Jean-Henri Fabre: http://www.efabre.net/
Robert Frost: http://www.robertfrost.org/
Ernest Thompson Seton: http://www.etsetoninstitute.org/
Sigurd F. Olson: http://www.uwm.edu/Dept/JMC//Olson/

MASTER PUBLISHERS LIST

Abingdon Press – Nashville, TN – www.abingdonpress.com
Academic Press – London England
Adventurelore Press – Arizona City, AZ – www.adventurelore.com
Aladdin: NY – Simon & Schuster Imprint – New York NY – www.simonsays.com
Almar Press – Binghamton NY
American Camp Association Camping Magazine – Martinsville
   – www.ACAcamps.org
American Forests Magazine – Washington DC – www.americanforests.org
American Press – Boston MA – www.americanboston.com
Amherst Media – Amherst NY – www.amerherstmedia.com
Amphoto Books – New York NY
Appalachian Mountain Club – 4 Joy Street, Boston, MA 02108
   – www.outdoors.org/
Artisan Sales – Thousand Oaks CA
Association for Experiential Education – Boulder, CO – www.aee.org
Association of Nature Center Administrators – Dayton, OH
   – www.outdoors.org
Association Press – New York NY
Audubon Magazine New York, NY – www.audubon.org
Backpacker Magazine Emmaus PA – www.backpacker.com
M. Barrows & Company – New York NY
Berkshire House – Lee MA – www.berkshirehouse.com
Binford & Mort – Portland, OR
Blandford Press – Poole, England
Borgo Press – San Bernardino, CA
Brooklyn Botanical Gardens – Brooklyn, NY – www.bbg.org
Burford Books – Springfield, NJ – www.burfordbooks.com
Carolhoda Books – Minneapolis MN
Cartwheel Books – New York NY
Caxton Printers – Caldwell, ID – www.caxtonprinters.com
Children's Book Press – Chicago IL
Chilton/Haynes – Radnor, PA
Christian Camping International Journal Colorado Springs CO
   – www.cci.gospelhome.net/ccihome
Clarkson Potter – New York NY

Comstock Books – Ithaca, NY
Conservationist Magazine – Albany NY – www.dec.state.ny.us/website/dpae/cons
Council Oaks Books – Tulsa, OK
Country Press – Grangeville, OH
Creative Publishing International – Minnetonka, MN
    – www.creativepublishinginternational.com
Crown Publishers – New York NY – www.creativepublishinginternational.com
D & J Press – Carlsbad NM
Dawn Publications – Nevada City CA – www.dawnpub.com
Derrydale Press – Lanham MD
Devin Adair – Old Greenwich, CT
Dial Books for Young Readers – New York NY
Dodd, Mead, & Co. – New York NY
Dog-eared Publications – Middleton WI – www.dog-eared.com
Dover Publications – New York NY (there is also a Mineola, NY)
    – www.doverpublications.com
Dutton Books – New York NY
Eagle's View Publishing – Liberty UT
EEK Environmental Education for Kids – Wisconsin Department of Natural
    Resources – www.dnr.state.wi.us/org/caer/ce/eek
Ecco – Hopewell NJ
Ecopress – Corvallis OR
Exley Giftbooks – Spencer MA
Falcon Press Publishing Co – Billings MT
Firefly Books – Buffalo NY
Fox Chapel Publishing – East Petersburg PA – www.woodcarvingillustrated.com/
Frank Amato Publications – Portland OR
Fulcrum Press – Golden CO – www.fulcrum-books.com/
Galahad – New York NY
Galloway – Corvallis OR
Gibbs Smith – Layton UT – www.gibbs-smith.com/
Globe Pequot – Guilford CT – www.globepequot.com/globepequot/index.cfm
Golden Books – New York NY – www.randomhouse.com/golden/
Good Apple, Inc – Carthage, IL
Grammercy – New York NY
Gryphon House – Beltsville MD – www.ghbooks.com/
Guild of Master Craftsman Publications, Ltd – Lewes, UK
Harper Collins – New York NY – www.harpercollins.com/
Harvard University Press – Cambridge MA – www.hup.harvard.edu/
Herald Press – Scottdale PA
Hill and Wang – New York NY
Houghton Mifflin – Boston MA – www.hmco.com/indexf.html
Human Kinetics – Champaign IL – www.humankinetics.com
Incentive Publications – Nashville TN

Institute for Earth Education – Greenville WV – www.eartheducation.org/
International Marine/Ragged Mountain Press – Camden ME
International Mountain Bicycling Association – Boulder CO
Indy Publish – IndyPublish.com
Jossey-Bass – San Francisco CA – www.josseybass.com/WileyCDA/
Journal of Experiential Education – Boulder CO – www.aee2.org
Journal of Marine Science –
Kendall/Hunt – Dubuque IA – www.kendallhunt.com/
Kids Can Press – Buffalo NY – www.kidscanpress.com
Klutz Press – Palo Alto CA – klutz.com/
Alford A. Knopf – Westminster MD – www.randomhouse.com/knopf/home.html
Lark Books – Ashville NC – www.larkbooks.com/home/home.asp
Laurence Holt Books – New York NY
Learning Unlimited Corporation – Tulsa OK
Little, Brown – Boston MA – www.twbookmark.com/
Lorenz Books – London England
Lyle Stuart – New York NY
Lyons Press – Guildford DE – www.lyonspress.com/
Mariner Books – Boston MA
McGraw Hill – New York NY – www.mcgraw-hill.com/
Mc Millan Publishing Co. – New York NY
Menasha Ridge Press – Birmingham AL – www.menasharidge.com/
Millbrook Press – Brookfield CT – www.millbrookpress.com/
Miles Kelly Publishing – Essex England
Mountaineers Books – Seattle WA – www.mountaineersbooks.org/
National Geographic – Washington DC – www.nationalgeographic.com
National Georgraphic Magazine – Tampa FL – www.nationalgeorgraphic.com
National Outdoor Leadership School (NOLS) – Lander WY – www.nols.edu
National Parks & Conservation Magazine – Washington DC – www.npca.org
National Recreation & Parks Association – Ashburn VA – www.nrpa.org
National Speleological Society – Huntsville, AL – www.caves.org
National Wildlife Federation – Reston VA – www.nwf.org
Natural History Magazine – New York NY – www.naturalhistorymag.com
Nature Study Guild – Rochester NY – home.att.net/~naturebooks/index.html
New Society Publishing – Gabriola Island BC, Canada – www.newsociety.com
Nodin Press – Minneapolis MN
North Light Books – Cincinnati OH
    – www.artistsnetwork.com/nlbooks/about_nl.html
NorthWood Press – Chanhassen, MN
    – www.americanletters.org/northwoodspress.htm
Outdoor American – Izaak Walton League – Gaithersburg MD – www.iwla.org/oa
Outside Magazine – Santa Fe NM – outside.away.com/index.html
Overlook Press – New York NY – www.overlookpress.com/index.php
Owl Publications – Bayard Canada

Paul H. Brooks – Baltimore MD
Perennial – New York NY
Pearson Custom Publishing – Boston MA
Pinehurst – Pinehurst NC
Quiller Press – London England
Ragged Mountain Press – Camden ME
Ranger Rick Magazine – National Wildlife Federation – www.nwf.org/kids
Random House – New York NY – www.randomhouse.com
Rec Room Publications – Richland, WA
Rinehart Publications – Grand Forks ND
Robert Hale, Ltd. – London England
Roberts Rinehart – Boulder CO – Taylor Trade Publishers
    – www.rlpgtrade.com/Index.shtml
Rodale Books – Emmaus PA – www,rodale.com/
St. Martin's Press – New York NY – www.stmartins.com
Search Press Ltd. – Tumbridge Wells, Kent, England
Shelter Publications – Bolinas CA – shelterpublishing.com
Schiffer – West Chester PA – www.schifferbooks.com/newschiffer
Scholastic – New York NY – www.scholastic.com
Scribner's – New York NY – www.gale.com/scribners/
Sierra Club Books – San Francisco CA – www.sierraclub.org/books
Simon & Schuster – New York NY – www.simonsays.com/
Simon & Schuster Custom Publishing – Needham Heights MA
Stackpole – Mechanicsburg PA
    – www.stackpolebooks.com/cgi-bin/StackpoleBooks.storefront
Sterling Publishing Co. – New York NY – www.sterlingpub.com/home/home.asp
Stevens Publishing – Dallas TX – www.stevenspublishing.com/
Stewart, Tabori & Chang – New York NY
Storey Books – Pownal VT – www.stevenspublishing.com
Sylvan Toxophilite Classics Manufacturer/Publisher
Syracuse University Press – Syracuse NY
Taunton Press – Newton CT – www.taunton.com/
Thames & Hudson – London England
Three Rivers Press – New York NY
Time-Life Books – New York NY – www.timelife.com
Trickle Creek – Mechanicsburg PA
University of British Columbia – Vancouver Canada
University of New Mexico Press – Albuquerque NM – www.unmpress.com/
University of North Carolina Press – Chapel Hill NC
    – www.uncpress.unc.edu/default.htm
University Press of New England – Lebanon NH
    – www.uncpress.unc.edu/default.htm
University of Tennessee – Knoxville TN – www.utpress.org/
University of Texas Press – Austin TX – www.utexas.edu/utpress

University of Virginia Press – Charlottesville VA – www.upress.virginia.edu
W.W. Norton & Co – New York NY – www.wwnorton.com/
Walker Publishing – New York NY – www.walkerbooks.com/
Waterford Press – Chandler AZ – www.waterfordpress.com/
Waterfront – Burlington VT – www.waterfrontbooks.com
Watson-Guptill Publications – New York NY – www.watsonguptill.com
Waveland Press – Prospect Heights IL – www.waveland.com
Wesleyan University Press – Hanover NH – www.wesleyan.edu/wespress
Wilderness Magazine – www.fromthewilderness.com
Wilderness Adventure Press – Fowlerville MI – www.wildernesspress.com
John Wiley & Sons – New York NY – www.wiley.com/WileyCDA
Wiley Text Books – Hoboken NJ
William C. Brown – Dubuque IA
Williamson Publishing (VT) – Charlotte VT
Wood 'N" Barnes Publishing & Distribution – Oklahoma City, OK
Workman Publishing – New York NY – www.workmanweb.com
Xerox College Publications – Lexington MA

INDEX

Rafting, 219-22
Ragbrai, 216
Rails to Trails Conservancy, 203, 232
Recreational Boating and Fishing, 223
Reproductions, nature crafts made from, 53-59
River running, 218-20
Rock climbing, 244-46
Rock quarries, 24
Rocks and minerals, 51-52, 176-79
Rope courses, 210-12
Ropecraft, 106-08

Sand, 52
Sanitation, 114
Saws, 110
Schoolyard Habitats program, 169
Searching and seeking games, 76-79
Seed pods, 50
Seton watching, 156, 157
Seton, Ernest Thompson, 156, 157, 292
Shells, 52
Shelters, 102-03
Sierra Club, 28, 98, 149
Sketching, 59
Snowshoeing, 247-48
Soil Conservation Districts, 29
Soil impaction, 151
Soil pollution, 151
Spelunking, 249-51
Sports and adventure activities, 205-53
Starwagon, 286
Stick cooking, 138-41

Terrariums, 172
Thoreau, Henry David, 96, 292
Tilden, Freeman, 277, 292
Tin can cooking, 141-44
Toolcraft, 108-10
Tracks and tracking, 157
Trails, 275-84
Trees, nature crafts made from, 37-46

Union of Concerned Scientists, 150
United States Bicentennial, 23
United States Defense Department (DOD), 241
United States Forest Service, 22, 29
United States Geological Survey, 29

Van Matre, Steve, 147
Volksmarch, 235

Water pollution, 149-50
Water, streams, and ponds, 24-25, 191-96
Weather and atmosphere, 183-90
Webb, Kenneth, 292
Wetlands, 24-25
Whittling and wood carving, 37-42
Wildlife Conservation Society, 28
Wildlife Preserves, 21
Wind chill, 187-88
Winter activities, 258-61
Woodcraft Indians, 156
Woodlands, 22
World Wildlife Fund, 149
WorldWideLearn (website), 13

YMCA, 30
Youth hostels, 216
Youth Hunter Education Challenge (YHEC), 229

Zoos, 26